AF335286

Harmony and Cacophony in Large-scale Assessments in Education

Comparative and International Education

THE HISPANIC AMERICAS

Series Editors

Carlos Ornelas (*Metropolitan Autonomous University, Mexico*)
Allan Pitman (*University of Western Ontario, Canada*)
Miguel A. Pereyra (*University of Granada, Spain*)

VOLUME 1

The titles published in this series are listed at *brill.com/caieha*

Harmony and Cacophony in Large-scale Assessments in Education

A Mexican Account

By

Israel Moreno Salto

BRILL

LEIDEN | BOSTON

Cover illustration: iStock.com/jamesteohart

All chapters in this book have undergone peer review.

The Library of Congress Cataloging-in-Publication Data is available online at https://catalog.loc.gov

Typeface for the Latin, Greek, and Cyrillic scripts: "Brill". See and download: brill.com/brill-typeface.

ISSN 2949-8791
ISBN 978-90-04-68282-5 (paperback)
ISBN 978-90-04-68283-2 (hardback)
ISBN 978-90-04-68284-9 (e-book)

Contents

PART 3
Expanding Our Understandings of Large-scale Assessments

Foreword

Choreographing the Governing of Education

Susan L. Robertson

Making visible subjects in the landscape, and directing their activities through shaping their mentalities is, as Miller and Rose (1990) point out, an important object of governing. And governing education in Mexico through large scale assessments is at the heart of Israel Moreno Salto's book – *Harmony and Cacophony in Large-scale Assessments in Education*. What's new, you might ask, after more than three decades of work that has graced the pages of books, journals, and blog posts, and rested on the heaving bookshelves of libraries around the world?

Drawing on the seminal work of Foucault and his governmentality lectures, Miller and Rose (1990) were some of the first academics to direct our attention not simply to the institutions of government, but to the way in which governing emerges out of the choreographing of an assemblage of discourses, policy instruments, strategies, and tactics, that regulate the social and economic life of a population. Just as we don't view an orchestral piece through the activities of the conductor, nor ought we view the regulation of citizens through the institutions of government. Hardly surprising, Foucault's contribution to governing has been powerfully taken up by a wide range of researchers seeking to understand how governments in national and subnational settings, state like actors like the European Commission, or multilateral organizations like UNESCO and the OECD, govern contemporary life.

This is particularly so in education, where multilateral institutions, such as the Organization for Economic Cooperation and Development (OECD), The World Bank (WB), and the United Nations Educational, Scientific and Cultural Organization (UNESCO), have taken on an expanded agenda regarding directing national education systems around the globe. Where once the OECD's (now infamous) large-scale assessment, the Program for International Student Assessment (PISA), collected data from its member states, now a suit of assessments takes in other populations from adults to early years learners, it ranges well beyond its member states, and its areas of assessment include not only science, mathematics, and literacy, but also critical thinking, well-being and global competences.

Paralleling the spectacular rise of the OECD over the past three decades has been a program of research, much of it critical of the OECD's instrumental politics, others attentive to the technical limitations of its instruments. Much of this work has been either directly or at least gently influenced by the discourse turn that Foucault's governmentality work encouraged. Grek's (2009) governing by numbers account of the OECD and Europe registers some 15,000 downloads and well over 600 citations.

This is not to suggest that such studies are wrong, or even limited, but they do deflect attention away from historicizing the challenge of governing when the governor has limited juridical powers over a population, or the value of empirical studies of policy enactment rather than policy production to shed light on the governed, and their material practices. To riff off the metaphor in the title of Moreno Salto's book, a musical score might look ordered and symphonic on the page, but what does it sound like when the business of playing gets under way? Whilst for the conductor a cacophony would be a disaster, it nonetheless is a distinct possibility, if a particular set of circumstances were to eventuate. Getting it right takes more than the skill of the conductor; it requires the whole ensemble to come together with their various instruments, notes, and nods that register engaging.

So what might historicizing governing by numbers tell us. One is that this is not a new instrument of government; it became possible through the collection of census data, and was perfected, for example, by the highly centralized French state over several centuries. And indeed, the go to, and well cited work, *The Politics of Large Numbers: A History of Statistical Reasoning* (2002) was written by France's chief statistician, Alain Desrosieres.

Second, that governments in systems (especially Federal) with limited constitutional powers to direct subnational governments have turned to the use of indicators, big data and statistics to govern in the absence of sovereignty. In the late 1950s the United States faced just such a challenge. The Russian's launch of Sputnik galvanized the US Federal government into action, allocating funding to states across the USA to invest in national interest initiatives that included large investments in science (labs, curriculum), languages and technology. But given the Federal government could not demand that the various recipient states be accountable to the Federal government, it was challenged to come up with a set of tools to steer a system of accountability to the Federal level. Its development of a national evaluation center that collected data around sets of indicators set of stage for the OECD, who would learn from and import this model as it established itself. As numbers, statistics oozed objectivity, and with objectivity came trust (Porter, 1995). Legitimacy is then secured in the face of limited or little sovereignty.

Third, in the early years of the OECD indicators and statistics were deployed for the purposes of directing development, mindful of an alternative model under socialism. However, what gave its various programs of large-scale data collection now a new edge was their deployment in representing countries on a vertically organized ordinal scale. Now countries were not simply to learn from the various assessments of others. This learning was shaped by a new V-8 engine; that of competition in a race to the top. This 'vertical vision' (Robertson 2022) not only had the effect of suggesting that everyone on the race had an equal chance of getting ahead, but the direction of travel was clear. Upward, with the ever-present anxiety about a potential loss of height akin to a fall from grace. In this ensemble of governing, Andreas Schleicher takes the podium as conductor extraordinaire. The choreographer of many of the different programs for large scale assessments developed by the OECD, Schleicher is a master choreographer. His various public presentations, slicing data this way and that has enabled him to keep his putative education musicians on their toes. In short, over time, the nature of the instruments for governing using numbers has altered, and so has its modalities of power, to include temporal horizons, comparison, and the use of affect.

But what does governing really look like down in the trenches, or to continue with our musical metaphor, in the orchestra pit? What do those who the OECD says it is providing data for to enable teachers to inform their classroom practices, know about large scale assessments, and how does it shape what they know and do? This is an important empirical question and one that has been neglected in the work on large scale assessments. Answering this question could indeed raise all kinds of questions; is the outlay by governments on rounds of PISA data collection, for example value for money? What kind of moral economy of value and worth is set in motion? Could the money be better spent elsewhere? Is it simply a question of 'lost in translation' – between the bars and lines of data collection, outcomes to practices, and what crucial steps are missing, if indeed a school or system believes that large scale assessments have value? Do large scale assessments end up distorting education systems aims and goals by encouraging quite a narrow focus on specific skills? Might the outcomes present the large-scale assessment industry with an inconvenient truth: that the assessments get limited traction on practices in classrooms and have amplified effects at the level of politics? After more than two decades, large scale assessments clearly have not exhausted the kinds of questions we need more research on, and reflections regarding why it matters.

This book by Israel Moreno Salto takes us on a very important journey that overcomes some of the concerns I outlined above. To begin, it is a corrective to a policy as discourse only analysis. This is a theoretically informed empirical enquiry that uses different methods to get access to different actors in the education policy and practice world in Mexico. Second, by bringing in multiple actors who operate at different scales of the education system in Mexico, we are also able to see and appreciate the complex architecture of education policy and practice at different levels of Mexico. Third, its originality also lies in asking: what happens at the level of policy and practice when multiple large-scale assessments are at play? Do they work with or against each other, especially as their rationalities – human rights versus human capital – differ.

In all, this is an incredibly important book. It is rare in its conception, articulate in its arguments, and has a depth of insight that adds to its virtuosity. And from it we have not only a deep and rich understanding of education in Mexico, but as a rigorous piece of work on large-scale assessments in Mexico, it ought to be on the desks of all policymakers.

References

Desrosieres, A. (2002). *The politics of large numbers: A history of statistical reasoning.* Harvard University Press.

Grek, S. (2009). Governing by numbers: the PISA 'effect' in Europe. *Journal of Education Policy, 24*(1), 23–37.

Miller, P., & Rose, N. (1990). Governing economic life. *Economy and Society, 19*(1), 1–31.

Porter, T. (1995). *Trust in numbers.* Princeton University Press.

Robertson, S. L. (2022). V-charged: Powering up the world-class university as a global actor. *Globalisation, Societies and Education, 20*(4), 423–424.

Figures and Tables

Figures

Tables

PART 1

The Large-scale Assessment Assemblage

Introduction

Problematizing Large-scale Assessment Programs

1 Locating the Problem

The year 1994 is a momentous one for the education sector in Mexico, if these two global initiatives can be read as marking a shift in direction for education policy and planning. First, this Aztec nation joined the rich country's club – the Organization for Economic Co-operation and Development (OECD). Since the early 1960s, the OECD had sought to shape the economic development strategies of post-war Europe, the USA and allied developed economies through horizon scanning, data gathering, planning and lesson learning (Robertson, 2012a). Secondly, the United Nations Educational, Scientific and Cultural Organization (UNESCO) advanced an ambitious project in Mexico City; the Latin American Laboratory for Assessment of the Quality of Education – or LLECE – for its acronym in Spanish. On the one hand, LLECE was to carry out part of UNESCO's mission regarding the development of people and society through education in Latin America. On the other hand, a more instrumental mission was evident in the development of a common culture of policy development based on common regional indicators.

Both initiatives were to eventually involve Mexico in two international large-scale assessments (LSAs) focused on student learning; the Program for International Student Assessment (PISA) at the global scale, and the Regional Comparative and Explanatory Study (ERCE for its acronym in Spanish) at the regional Latin-American scale. Both continue to this day, and have important, though not equally consequential, outcomes for the Mexican education system. Add to this complexity the fact that in 2004 Mexico began developing and implementing its own series of domestic national tests based on the image and technical features of its international homonyms, and the testing landscape in the Mexican education system could be argued to be nothing less than a complex, contradictory, education evaluation ensemble whose ongoing interactions, as well as outcomes, is important to understand. In calling this combination of three distinct cross-scale large-scale assessments an evaluation ensemble, I am drawing from the term "education ensemble" coined by Robertson and Dale (2015a) who use it to refer to the combination of ideas, discourses, actors, technologies, institutions, and practices that give rise to education as a sector, as well as its constitutive events and practices.

The literature in the field of education policy in which education testing and evaluation are part of an education ensemble will be elaborated and explored in more detail in Chapter 3. For the moment, I wish to note that much of this literature seems to take for granted the type of large-scale assessment setting occurring in Mexico. It assumes that fundamentally different evaluation programs with distinct purposes and scopes, and that deliver at different political scales, not only co-exist but can operate, and cooperate, harmoniously in the same context. However, as it will be explored in this book, when LSAs in Mexico are examined both separately and together, not only in relation to their detail but also in terms of the claims that they make, important discrepancies and tensions begin to emerge between them. The question here, of course, is what this means for the Mexican education system more generally, and how those participating in the system make sense of these different tests and what they involve, more specifically.

Since their inception, PISA, ERCE and the National Plan for Learning Assessment (PLANEA for its acronym in Spanish) have overlapped in time, space and in aims with regard to the data they each produce. Although some of these have slightly shifted over the past 20 years as explained in Chapter 4, they essentiality consist of generating data for: (a) aiding policy decisions; (b) aiding education practice improvement; (c) informing public opinion about the state of learning of their education systems; and (d) developing indicator databases for accountability, comparative and research purposes.

Central to LSAs is the presupposition that the evidence they produce would be helpful to all of the above aspirations and agents implicated in their processes. Where did these logics arise from? How are they sustained? What are their effects at distinct scales? And most importantly, in what ways is this problematic? These issues will be discussed in the theoretical (Chapters 2 and 3) and thematic sections (Chapters 5 to 7) of this book. In addition, drawing upon the work of Mortimore (1999), it will be pointed out that LSAs neglect to recognize that the distinct audiences and groups to which their data is directed to, operate differently. Yet, despite this diversity, large-scale tests work by seeing the spaces or territories of governing in ontologically flat ways (Robertson, 2012b), and they intervene and offer solutions that are a one size fits all prescription of how to improve. This double flattening of space and solution, of populations and purpose, are deeply problematic in the education system in that in a structural sense they make inequalities invisible, in turn producing new inequalities.

Large-scale assessment aspirations are contingently active in present-day education practices and policies in Mexico (Chapters 5 to 7). Chapter 7 of this book explores the ways in which LSAs have occupied a central role in the 2013 education reform, mainly employed by reform advocates as central motives for requiring drastic change on the one hand, whilst enacting as essential references for instituting and developing important sections and components of the new national curriculum for compulsory education, on the other. The particularities regarding the ways in which LSA evidence functions in relation to policy decisions is a contested matter. In the case of the initiatives and outcomes explored in this book, these phenomena will be explored and explained drawing on what might be described as sociological thinking tools; in this case those advanced by Robertson (2012a, 2017) and Fourcade (2016) (Chapters 3 and 8).

The ambitions embedded within LSA aims are addressed in this book as particular kinds of governing activities in that they are concerned with coordinating the distribution, production and reproduction of key aspects of education provision and regulation (Dale, 1997; Robertson & Dale, 2013). Leading literatures presented and discussed in Chapter 3 will indicate in what broad ways LSAs seek to coordinate, and govern, distinct aspects of the education sector around the world in recent years. From a conventional standpoint, large-scale assessments are viewed as "tests administered to sizeable numbers of people for such purposes as placement, course credit, graduation, educational admissions, and school accountability" (Bennet, 1998, p. 7). However, as this book will argue, assessment programs operating in Mexico surpass the classic scope advanced by Bennet and others. LSAs have evolved both as assessment and political tools (Chapters 2 and 3). They are assessment tools in that they collect data which is intended to reflect student learning, against which value judgments are developed according to expected competences or outcomes; they are political technologies in that as tools of governing, and thus power, they have acquired allocative authority and in doing so, indicate what is to be valued, and thus of value. In their most original form, these tests were used by the United States government to determine who would occupy authority positions within the military (Popham, 2001a) (Chapter 2). This very specific purpose has now been extended way beyond its original intent, to include a wide range of sectors whose institutions and practices are influenced by data gathering around sets of indicators which in turn are intended to shape education efforts and thus outcomes.

Today, LSAs use their authority to allocate value in subtler ways, two of which will be explored in this book. First, they use their authority to determine what is to be valued by determining which country's policy formulas and practices should be followed or emulated by other nations (OECD, 2016a). Secondly, they use this authority to determine which international organizations and intergovernmental programs should be embraced and emulated (e.g., OECD or SABER). A good example of the latter is identified by Meyer and Benavot (2013), who argue that PISA enables the OECD to "assume a new institutional role as arbiter of global education governance, simultaneously acting as diagnostician, judge and policy advisor to the world's school system" (p. 5). In this respect, PISA has enabled the OECD to claim authority for the OECD to act upon, and exert its influence, well beyond the boundaries of PISA. Bearing in mind that LSAs are political tools, ergo they could be understood as governing technologies as well. It is within this context of an historical framing, and of shifting political dynamics, that the relationships between LSAs and governance will be explored and explained in this book.

The three assessments which operate in Mexico today have been developed and supported by one or more national and/or international organizations. Each of these entities has what we can describe as their own distinct program ontology and purpose. In Chapter 4 I draw upon the seminal work of Pawson and Tilley (1997) on program ontologies – which tries to elucidate the theory of change inherent in the policy intervention to elaborate further on this matter. Briefly for my purposes here, I will argue that the OECD's PISA has a human capital program ontology, whereas OREALC-UNESCO and ERCE lean towards a human rights program ontology. This issue is particularly relevant and is addressed in Chapter 8, where I will argue that it is fundamentally important to discriminate between the program ontologies of different assessment programs for it is here that we are also able to see how they also "work" as governing tools.

Summing up, PISA, ERCE, PLANEA and its predecessors have conducted over 20 assessment rounds in the course of the last 20 years. As this assessment ensemble progresses into its second decade of life, students' results on tests indicate only minor overall variances. This evidence of persistently low achievement levels suggests that we need to take seriously that as a model of improvement there are questions to be asked about why this improvement has not materialized. These are questions that seem obvious, particularly in the case of Mexico, however in viewing much of the research this aspect has been neglected. For those interested in school performance and improvement, this issue is important. What were the educational reasons for why the Mexican education system embraced three LSAs? How did these arrangements come to be? And how do they sit alongside each other as distinct technologies aimed at governing system and student performance? Are they largely symbolic, and if not, what kind of outcomes, intended and unintended, do they have in and on the Mexican education system? So far most published research on this matter has been limited to studying individual issues through the lens of isolated programs (Bazan, Backhoff, & Turullols, 2016; Jimenez-Moreno, 2016; Martinez-Rizo & Silva-Guerrero, 2016). Today many questions emerge regarding the outcomes of these assessment programs, and what they mean in terms of the good governance of educational practices in Mexico.

Finally, as individual initiatives, LSAs represent different interests, solutions and thus potential outcomes. In this study, these are understood as the result of differently located agents with different degrees of power, who seek to influence and shape how different features of the education sector are governed. These issues matter because different large-scale assessments and their sponsoring bodies have distinct agendas and as well as the capacity to mobilize power around particular purposes in pursuit of specific outcomes. Given that "education is a human right, how it is funded and governed, by whom and for what, matters" (Robertson & Dale, 2013, p. 6).

2 Large-scale Assessment Arrangements in a Global Context

Over the past few decades, it has become increasingly frequent to come across the co-existence of multiple large-scale assessment surveys within national, subnational, or local settings. Despite the overlapping of tests, time, efforts, and economic resources invested in these "assessment assemblages", much remains to be learned about their origins, development, tensions, frictions, outcomes, and challenges. This book delves into these issues via a critical lens and offers a case in point against which readers can place their own situations. In other words, it serves as an empirically grounded thinking toolbox to help readers problematize emerging, ongoing, or upcoming challenges related to their large-scale assessment settings.

The rise and development of multi-scalar assessment arrangements around the world is undeniable, more so during the late XX century. This section will shed light on a few examples from different regions. It is important to note that this is not a comprehensive nor exhaustive list of all countries and assessment programs; its purpose is merely illustrative of what has been occurring in this realm.

Firstly, in line with the Latin-American tradition of employing multiple assessment programs, Argentina and Colombia have been developing arrangements like Mexico. With regards to the first, Argentina launched in 1993 their national large-scale assessment namely ONE, for its acronym in Spanish. In 2016, this program was replaced with a new survey called APRENDER. At the regional scale, they participate in ERCE, and at the global scale they participate in PISA. Notably, in 2014 and 2015, they partook in TIMSS and PIRLS as well. On the other hand, Colombia also participates in PISA and ERCE, and currently administers its national survey called SABER, introduced in 1997.

The African continent has several assessment arrangements of its own. For instance, concerning English-speaking countries, Zambia administers their National Assessment Survey (NAS), issued since 1998; at the regional level, they take part in the Southern and Eastern Africa Consortium for Monitoring Educational Quality Survey (SEACMEQ); and at the global scale, they have opted for participating in the Program for International Student Assessment for Development (PISA-D). With regards to French-speaking countries, Senegal takes part in the PISA-D at the global scale, the Program for the Analysis of Education Systems (PASEC for its acronym in French) at the regional scale, and since 1996, their National System for the Evaluation of School Results (SNERS for its acronym in French). Nearby, Jordan and the United Arab Emirates are two examples from the middle east that participate in TIMSS, PIRLS, and PISA while administering their own national large-scale assessment programs (Ababneh et al., 2016).

Asian nations such as Japan, South Korea, and Singapore participate in PISA, TIMSS and PIRLS at the global scale. At the same time, they administer their national programs, such as the National Assessment of Academic Ability (NAAA) survey in Japan (Kuramoto & Kiozumi, 2018) and the National Assessment of Education Achievement (NAEA) in South Korea. More recently, other Asian countries like Malaysia and the Philippines, apart from participating in global assessment programs, also take part in regional assessment initiatives, such as the Southeast Asia Primary Learning Metrics (SEA-PLM).

Finally, western countries like Canada, Australia, and the United States of America have a longstanding tradition of applying several large-scale assessments. For instance, Canada participates in PISA, TIMSS, and PIRLS at the global scale, and they administer their national program, namely Pan Canadian Assessment Program (PCAP). Australia also takes part in the same international large-scale assessments as Canada and administers its National Assessment Program – Literacy and Numeracy (NAPLAN). In the United States, following the Every Student Succeeds Act (ESSA), subnational states decide their large-scale assessment routes; however, at the federal level, the National Assessment of Educational Progress (NAEP) does test a representative sample of students from across the USA.

As we can note, multi-scalar large-scale assessment arrangements are commonplace worldwide. Cresswell, Schwantner and Waters (2015) and others have provided detailed descriptions of such arrangements; however, there is still a lack of critical readings and accounts concerning the implications, outcomes, and challenges of such assemblages to regional, national, subnational, and local education systems. To uncritical audiences, it may seem that all large-scale assessments share a common task and are compatible; nonetheless, as this book will show, they differ in program ontology and goals. Ultimately, this matters because program ontologies are likely to support, endorse, challenge, or oppose broader social, political, and economic agendas.

3 Large-scale Assessment and Governance Literatures

The large corpus of research which has been conducted around the world on large-scale assessments is overwhelming, to say the least. In an attempt to grasp and classify large-scale assessment studies, I have circled around the substantive literature and themes that leading researchers and organizations linked to this field have developed in order to generate some categories that might enable us to engage in a degree of complexity reduction. As a result of this exercise, four common threads, or domains of investigation, were identified and are discussed in further detail in Chapters 2 and 3. This classification of thus body of literature is neither fixed nor exhaustive, however for my purposes it is useful for approaching, organizing and studying this body of work.

The four domains are comprised of investigations that variously address: (1) studies associated with a concern for student achievement; (2) large-scale assessment comparison studies; (3) structural, technical, and chronological aspects of LSAs; and (4) large-scale assessments and governance.

With regards to the first domain, studies associated with a concern for student achievement, there are a large number of researchers who address a wide array of internal and external cultural, political, social and economic issues and practices related to schooling to help explain the differences between student achievement on LSAs (Barber & Mourshed, 2007; Darling-Hammond & Rothman, 2011; Deng & Gopinathan, 2016; Fullan, 2011; Leithwood et al., 2019; Sahlberg, 2007). Some of these issues range from high-quality teacher training, expectations for student learning, successful school leardeship, motivated teachers, teacher social recognition, high-quality supervision, training in situ, and recruiting the best students for teaching.

The second domain, large-scale assessment comparison studies, is also quite extensive and includes several variants. These range from investigations that compare: (1) distinct assessments programs, e.g. PISA and TIMMS (Gronmo & Olson, 2008); (2) test rounds amongst one or two programs, e.g. PISA 2003 and PISA 2009 (Gamboa & Wittenberg, 2012); (3) contrast between groups of test takers, e.g. female vs male (Liu & Wilson, 2009), and what appears to be the most widespread theme; and (4) comparisons between countries, territories, sub-national states and regions. Like the former domain, this domain is also concerned with variation in school performance, but with an emphasis on comparison of groups and their performance on assessment rounds over time.

The third domain of investigations, structural, technical and chronological aspects of LSAs, is far-reaching, and includes inquiries linked to the chronological and political development of both domestic and international LSAs (Pidgeon, 1969; Popham, 2001a), as well the structural and technical aspects of these (Goldstein, 2004; Goldstein, 2017; Rutkowski & Prusinki, 2011; Rutkowski & Rutkowski, 2016; Spaull, 2018). These inquiries feature a wide range of findings which sit between a dichotomy of critique versus detailed descriptive accounts.

The fourth and last domain identified in the literature review is concerned with large-scale assessments and their governance. Within the huge scope of investigations that center on different features of this enterprise, two distinctive issues can be noted. First, there is special emphasis on the role of the OECD and their PISA program (Meyer & Benavot, 2013; Sellar & Lingard, 2014). This focus is grounded in the argument that this assessment tool has become the most influential of our time (Grek, 2012; Meyer & Benavot, 2013; Waldow, Takayama, & Sung, 2014). In this respect, PISA is viewed as a technology which encourages, provides support for, legitimatizes, and mediates a form of soft governance to pressure national states into implementing educational reforms linked to human capital discourses and market-based rationalities (Morgan & Volante, 2016). Within this framework of literatures, Green (2015, 2019) has recently raised concerns regarding the lack of a direct and visible relationship between PISA and particular policies in national settings as the result of governance activities.

The second major issue from LSAs and governance literatures is that it draws mainly upon arguments which revolve around governing by numbers and the use of comparison (Grek, 2009; Lewis, 2017; Martens, 2007). Here, Martens (2007) argues that "Comparison as a form of governance implies a scientific approach to political decision making (...). The parties evaluated are implicitly pressured to converge towards those practices, forms of organization, or behaviors that are regarded as best" (p. 42). In this respect, numbers play an important role, acting as the primary source or basis on which comparisons are executed. Both of these theoretical advancements are relevant but insufficient. More recent arguments developed by Sorensen and Robertson (2020) focus on the OECD's Teaching and Learning International Survey (TALIS), to show that governing through statistical reasoning has been around for a while and that what is new is a modality of comparison they refer to as ordinality. These vertically arranged ordinal systems propel this new system of value and

worth through the ways in which competition and learning to win are fundamental to the program ontology.

It is important to notice here that although comparison explains the overall
action of how governing occurs, it does not offer details and explications as to
how the comparisons are made possible, enabled, or enhanced. At the most
general level this book aims to contribute to the discussions regarding the particular gaps illustrated by Green, and Sorensen and Robertson. First, it seeks to
shed light on, and thus make more visible, the relationships between LSAs and
particular policies within national settings. Second, it aims to offer explications
regarding the ways in which comparisons, statistical reasoning and numbers
are enhanced, enabled and empowered so as to govern education systems and
the actors within them. For this, it will make use of the conceptual grammar
advanced by Robertson (2012a, 2017) and Fourcade (2016), which shows how
processes of levelling to remove differences – (or flattening), practices of comparison to produce competition (competitive comparison) and the principles
of classificatory judgment (what to locate where and thus value or not) are at
play in framing beliefs and views about education, learning and assessments.
In working very closely with data on large-scale testing collected at multiple
scales of governing of the education system in Mexico, I hope to contribute to
debates on comparison as a mode of governance.

4   Purpose of the Research

This book is the outcome of research developed between 2016 and 2020. As
educational researchers, we have a responsibility to ask about the arrangements that constitute the current education evaluation ensemble in Mexico,
the issues this presents, and what this means for how we diagnose the state of
learning. We also need to ask about the nature and scope of the current regime
of accountability in Mexico regarding such large investments of time, personnel, and funding, especially given the influence that LSAs have on policies and
education practice.

This book is thus concerned with studying large-scale assessments and governance at the national, sub-national and local scales in Mexico. This country
represents a setting where three assessments with distinct ontologies operate
simultaneously and where many issues with regards to this enterprise remain
under-researched and under-discussed. Drawing on the broad disciplines that
contribute to critical education policy analysis, specifically sociology and politics, this book aims to: (1) Provide a multi-scalar account of the different ways
in which current large-scale assessment programs in Mexico are organized as

a means of governing education; (2) Explore the governance dynamics in four distinct units at three political scales within the Mexican context between large-scale assessments and their aspirations of generating data so as to aid policy decisions and contribute to education practice improvement; (3) Reveal some of the unintended consequences produced by the large-scale assessments at the national, sub-national and local scales in Mexico; (4) Uncover the presence or not of frictions, tensions, and conflicts from this sort of governance arrangement, and how the outcomes of this enterprise affect education governance Mexico; and (5) Explain how large-scale assessment programs make use of socio-technical tools to govern distinct aspects and scales of education.

The conceivable scope of this book is immense. There are various issues that can be addressed. In order to ensure that the investigation for this book was manageable, it embraced five broad research questions that help clarify, guide and delimitate the issues and scope of the study in mind. These questions are:

a. What are the histories, politics and governance arrangements of the current large-scale assessment regimen in Mexico aimed at supplying evidence for aiding policy decisions and education practice improvement?

b. How do large-scale assessments aid education practice improvement and policy decisions at different political scales in Mexico?

c. What are some of the unintended consequences of the assessment regime in Mexico, and why do these matter?

d. What frictions, tensions and contradictions can be detected amongst large-scale assessment programs, and how are they addressed and mediated?

e. Through what tools are LSA governing relationships mediated, and why do they matter?

The first research question focuses on constructing the history and profile of the assessment arrangement in Mexico, and of each large-scale assessment addressed in the study. This helps us understand how this enterprise came about and who were involved. Furthermore, it brings light to the ontological view of each program and anchors them to particular organizations, their overall missions and common aspirations. Addressing this question supports the development of the rest of the research and grounds the empirical work needed in order to surpass a theoretical research approach. The second question helps to open up a means to illustrate how large-scale assessments make use of their aspirations to participate in the governing of the education sector in Mexico at different scales and through distinct cases or units. The third question focuses on issues that are at times overlooked. These are the unintended consequences of assessments. Examining the unintended consequences is helpful for raising questions regarding the appropriateness and suitability of large-scale assessments, their outcomes and actual reaches.

It is assumed that different assessments with distinct aims and scopes reinforce and support one another. But is this really so? In the Mexican case, early readings and analysis suggest tensions and contradictions amongst programs. How these are addressed and resolved matter because they are key to education governance. In this respect, the fourth research question looks into these problematic situations and whether and how they are mediated or not. Finally, the fifth question looks into the details and particularities regarding the socio-technical tools that are enabling, framing and supporting certain forms of governing education in Mexico.

This book should be understood in the broadest sense as a contribution to the investigations and discussions concerning large-scale assessments and governance. Drawing upon a multi-scalar approach, this research hopes to offer a modest but meaningful contribution to understanding the distinct scales involved in the implementation of LSAs. Overall, it proposes an original entry point and approach to researching LSAs and governance focused on the education evaluation ensemble in Mexico, where a thread of horizontal assessment programs – PISA, ERCE and PLANEA – overlaps and operates within vertical settings at distinct political scales – national, subnational and local – in national boundaries.

5   Theoretical and Methodological Approach

This book deploys a series of theoretical and methodological resources for accessing the complex topic of large-scale assessments and governance in Mexico (see Chapter 4). In this section I will emphasize the theoretical orientation of this study as a way to offer the reader a particular lens to approach and understand the way in which this book views large-scale assessments.

One of the main features of this study is that it adopts critical theory as meta-theory. In the realm of research paradigms, critical theory is conceived as an alternative paradigm that transcends classical positivistic and interpretive theoretical premises, including their scope and claims. On the one hand, it aims to overcome the uncritical exploration and construction of cultural meaning developed by the interpretive research tradition (Crotty, 1998). On the other hand, it goes well beyond the classical objective apprehension and generalization of reality developed by the positivistic convention. In this book I employ as a meta-theory a form critical theory advanced by three authors.

First, the broad theoretical approach of Cox (1981), which enables a distinct form of envisioning and inquiring social phenomena. Second, the work of Robertson and Dale (2009), who develop a critical theory framework with particular focus on education policy analysis and governance. Before addressing this distinct vision of critical theory, I will briefly reflect upon its general antecedents and context.

Critical theory has its roots embedded in the Institute for Social Research of the University of Frankfurt in the early twentieth century, later on baptized as the Frankfurt School (Crotty, 1998; Horkheimer, 1972). This scholarly tradition drew upon the work of German classics, such as Hegel, Weber, and Marx (Kincheloe & McLaren 2002; McLaren, 2016), and continued to expand its scope into new arenas and fields of study. It developed as a philosophical and theoretical apparatus for generating new questions, categories, and forms of exploring emerging social phenomena that exceeded the limits of classical research paradigms. In this sense, Bronner (2011) argues that "critical theory insists that it must respond to the new problems and the new possibilities for liberation that arise from changing historical circumstances" (p. 2).

Although many authors within this theoretical and philosophical tradition (Adorno, Leppert, & Gillespie, 2002; Apple, Au, & Gandin, 2009; Giroux, 1983; Horkheimer, 1972; Kincheloe & McLaren, 2002; McLaren & Giarelli, 1995; Tripp, 1992) argue that critical theory is a contested concept, they do agree on a wide set of parameters grounded on the following characteristics: critical theory is (a) concerned with issues of power, values and justice; (b) aims to expose the hidden or imperceptible forms of subjugation and oppression; (c) sets its interests on studying the relations of cultural, historical, political and economic issues in contemporary and emerging social phenomenon; (d) criticizes and challenges the existing social structures of society and asks about how power, authority and domination shape social relationships and (e) it aims to achieve social emancipation and social transformation.

In this respect, critical theory is constituted as a loose amalgam of philosophical principles rather than a neatly packaged system or methodological recipe (Buck-Morss, 1977). As I outlined above, for this book I will mainly employ a form of critical theory elaborated by Cox (1981) and expanded into education policy work by Robertson and Dale (2009), amongst others.

Originally, Cox developed his arguments by contrasting problem-solving theory against critical theory. Cox claims that problem-solving theory takes the world as it is, and thus does not question issues of power and domination; rather it provides solutions to existing problems within the prevailing frame. By way of contrast, critical theory is concerned with understanding how and why such a state of affairs came into being, and what therefore might need to change if we want to alter the existing social order. It therefore looks into matters of structure, agency and power, and the role that these issues play in the production, reproduction, circulation and transformation of emerging social phenomena.

By employing critical theory as a meta-theory, both ontological assumptions and epistemological premises are driven by this advancement. Critical theory as ontology departs from the notion that "nature cannot be seen as it 'really is' or 'really works' except through a value window. If values do enter into every inquiry, then the question immediately arises as to what values and whose values shall govern" (Guba, 1990, p. 24). In this respect, the ontological assumptions of this research revolve around the notion that large-scale assessments are not merely objective assessment tools, and nor are they value free. On the contrary, each LSA that currently operates in Mexico was developed on a particular and distinctive platform of values and principles, which are bound to reproduce themselves through the evaluative and political processes and outcomes of these programs.

The use of critical theory as ontology for this research will allow us to overcome the framing of dominant large-scale assessment discourses, which neglect viewing and raising vital questions regarding relations of power, values and interests concerning the origins, functions and effects of large-scale assessment programs. A good example of this negligence can be found in a special report sponsored by the OECD and the World Bank, and developed by Cresswell et al. (2015), who barely dedicate four and a half pages in a 244 page-long report to addressing the use of large-scale assessments in policy decisions and education practices around the world. Moreover, they totally avoid discussing the effects and their unintended consequences, tensions, frictions and contradictions concerning the different LSA programs that exist around the world. By way of contrast, this book puts these matters into the center of this study.

With regards to epistemology, the task of critical theory as an epistemological paradigm "is, by definition, to raise people (the oppressed) to a level of true consciousness. Once they appreciate how oppressed they are, they can act to transform the world" (Guba, 1990, p. 24). With critical theory as the driving epistemological paradigm, this research is framed by the following premises and understandings:

a.   Large-scale assessments are driven by forces greater than national states. Hence we must question and reveal what are the underlying beliefs, values and agendas linked to these programs and that of those organizations who created them. This, in order to understand why and how these technologies act, in favor of whom and for what? And what this means for different aspects of the education sector (e.g., policy, practices, governance, etc.).

b.   Large-scale assessments programs provoke consequences that extend beyond their intended aims and aspirations. This in turn impacts the lives of students, teachers and schools. Hence, these consequences require close scrutiny and reporting in order to develop better understandings of what is occurring in these settings?

Both of these premises will require collecting quantitative and qualitative data from actors at distinct scales and settings and in relation to different education processes. This data must reflect the outcomes of conversations regarding the experiences of large-scale assessment data on policy decisions and education practices.

The set of ontological assumptions and epistemological premises outlined above, in addition with the research aims and questions of the proposed research, lean to a critical theory paradigm. Further motives for selecting critical theory as a meta-theory are related to my interest to modify the impassive or uncritical way in which many of my colleagues in Mexico look at the current assessment regime (Bazan, Backhoff, & Turullols, 2016; Jimenez, 2016; Martinez-Rizo & Guerrero-Silva, 2016).

Coming back to the particular variant of critical theory employed for this book. The work of Robertson and Dale (2009) is fundamental to this research as it supports the case of making visible the complex, distinct though overlapping governance relationships involved in shaping and implementing large-scale assessment ensemble in Mexico. It also interrogates those organizations and their projects whose missions and interests cannot be taken for granted; the OECD, UNESCO-OREALC, INEE and SEP. Lastly, the framework advanced by these authors allows this research to go beyond conventional understandings which view the development and enforcement of policies in Mexico as a national matter, and, permits this study to analyze the role and interaction of external and internal forces as the outcomes of this enterprise in current policies and practices in Mexico.

The research design of this book is a multi-scalar case study. The investigation focuses on large-scale assessments and governance at three distinct scales (national, subnational and local) and four particular units (cases) of analysis within the Mexican context. Each unit of analysis employs a multiphase mixed-methods design. According to Creswell (2012) the "multiphase design builds on the basic mixed methods designs and adds to these designs multiple phases or projects conducted over time. Any one phase may have a combination of convergent, explanatory, exploratory, and embedded mixed methods design" (p. 547).

Such a complex research design required gathering both qualitative and quantitative data. At different scales, units and phases, I collected evidence using three main methods: (a) documents, (b) survey, and (c) semi-structured interviews. Two main strategies were followed for analysis; the quantitative resources were subject to a frequencies and non-parametric data analysis, whereas a five-phase thematic adaptive analysis approach grounded on the work of Clarke and Braun (2013) was employed both for documents and interviews.

6   Layout of the Book

This book is structured into three parts which together hold 9 chapters. Part 1 is made up of Chapters 1 to 4. The first chapter locates the problem that this research addresses. It also offers an introduction to the main theoretical and methodological components of the book. Chapter 2 focuses mainly on revising the origin and development of large-scale assessments and their linkages to broader efforts to improve education systems. Chapter 3 develops an extensive literature review regarding LSAs studies, with special emphasis on investigations concerning governance. Furthermore, it discusses the main concepts and theoretical tools employed in this study. The first part of this volume finalizes with Chapter 4, which introduces each of the three assessments currently operating in Mexico and develops a detailed analysis with regards to the aspirations invoked by these programs.

Part 2 entails Chapters 5 to 7 which together present and discuss the results of the empirical part of this study. Chapter 5 addresses the local scale of the research which examines one substantial and complex unit of analysis focused on the aspiration of large-scale assessments of generating data for aiding education practice improvement. Chapter 6, the sub-national, studies a unit of analysis developed by education agents at the sub-national scale, and applied in the preschool education level. Chapter 7 deals with the national scale of this book. This scale addresses two units, one that entails legislators from the Honorable Congress on the Union in Mexico, and the other which involves officials and collaborators from the Secretariat of Education. Both of these units focus on the aspiration claimed by assessment programs of generating data for adding policy decisions.

Part 3 is comprised of Chapters 8 to 9. Chapter 8 seeks to theorize these governing technologies and outcomes arising from the education evaluation ensemble in Mexico. Finally, Chapter 9 presents a summary of the findings and analysis of the research data in light of the wider literature. It puts into conversation large-scale assessments and governance at distinct scales in Mexico and what the insights gathered from this study could represent to the broader theoretical understandings of this field.

The Rise and Development of Large-scale Assessments as Tools for Governing

In the opening chapter of this book, I suggested that one way in which we might understand contemporary large-scale assessments which operate in Mexico today is to see them as both evaluation and political tools that are deployed for the purposes of governing of education practices and policies. This is broadly in line with critical accounts of large-scale assessments – though where this book will differ is in exploring the similarities, differences, historical trajectories, and forms of engagement by different education sector actors in Mexico. In this Chapter I will review some of the main literatures on large-scale assessments (LSAs) and reflect on their role over time, as education policy instruments, intended to effect change in the system. This task will require that we grasp the broader array of historical and political processes from which LSAs have emerged, as well as addressing the distinct and different discussions regarding the concepts linked to this enterprise.

This chapter has three main objectives. First, in my review of the main literatures on LSAs, I will focus on their origins, purposes and effects. Here, there is special emphasis on the work of Popham (2001a) so as to bring into view two fundamental characteristics of LSAs: first their roots in, and linkages to, the recruitment of army officers; and second, their initial mission and efforts to prioritize education policy framings and practice outcomes in what, following John Prunty (1984), may best be described as the authoritative allocation of values. My focus on the means to make visible, and in doing so focus attention on, aspects of education which bring to the fore the notion that education policy is not simply technocratic but is, indeed, profoundly political. In essence, the act of valuing some agents and activity over others is political in that what follows is typically a means of selectively allocating resources, opportunities and worth. Second, I will discuss what the various researchers of large-scale assessments argue is at play and at stake in relation to the project to improve national education systems in countries around the globe through such tools. Third, I will review the rise, expansion, and extension of neoliberalism as a political project beginning in the 1980s, its connections to the shift from government to governance, and the parallel preference for large-scale assessments as a mode of governing education at multiple scales. My purpose in doing this is to draw attention to the precise nature of the values that are being promoted through large-scale testing, particularly by the OECD's PISA tests, UNESCO's ERCE, as well as Mexico's PLANEA.

1 Understanding Large-scale Assessments

In order to begin to understand large-scale assessments, it is vital to reflect upon their origins, forms of development and intended as well as unintended outcomes. This means raising questions regarding how they emerged, where, for what purposes, functions, and in favor of whom or what. Large-scale assessments, in other words, are tools that act as a means of structural and strategic selectivity (Jessop, 2005). By this I mean that large-scale assessments are intended to change the structural selectivities of education systems so as to bring them into line with a different set of purposes and outcomes. This demands that we inquire into how these public policy instruments are conceptualized over time, as well as what their current scope and limitations might be. This is because all forms of selectivity operate through principles of inclusion and exclusion. These issues will be addressed in the coming sections.

1.1 *Brief History of LSAs*

W. James Popham, Emeritus Professor from University of California, Los Angeles, and world-renowned specialist in education assessment, offers a detailed explanation regarding the origin of large-scale assessments in the context of the United States of America. This historical account constitutes an important reference point for this research. The narrative developed by this author, *The Truth about Testing,* links the advancement of large-scale assessments to recruitment activities of officers in World War I. Popham (2001a) argues that during this period, the US military sought to create a combat front of grand size. In the realization of this immense task, the army needed to recruit more officers. The military's particular challenge here was how best to identify those individuals within an army troop with the most likely attributes to become officers.

The army was aware of the existence of an intelligence test developed in 1905 by the French psychologist, Alfred Binet, who could help them with this task. However, this test had to be administered on a one-to-one basis. This was an impossible task given that the army needed to test large groups of people in a short period of time. The army turned to the American Psychological Association (APA), then led by Robert M. Yerkes, to see if this group was able to develop a test administrable to large quantities of people. The purpose of this test was to identify those candidates with the ideal qualities for succeeding the officer's training program and becoming officers of the US army.

In 1917, after a week's work at the New Jersey's Vineland Training School, a committee of eight specialists appointed by Yerkes came up with ten different subtests which collectively became to be known as the first large-scale assessment – "Army Alpha". The instrument, similar to the test that was advanced by Binet to measure practical IQ, aimed to discriminate between those applicants who could follow instructions, identify proper analogies, and engage in mathematical reasoning. These were all aspects assumed to be components of intelligence. It is estimated that during the remaining war period, the Army Alpha tested more than 1.7 million troops; an outcome which they viewed as evidence of great success. According to Popham (2001a), the Alpha Army Test "represented the first truly large-scale use of multiple-choice test items, and its items were subject to all sorts of statistical analyses that allowed the test's five forms to do their comparative assessment job well" (p. 41).

Popham (2001a) argues that after the end of World War I, countless new tests in the US mimicked the Army's Alpha Strategy, with the primary purpose of conducting comparisons amongst test applicants by contrasting their results to outcomes from a normed group. Many of the education tests that emerged after World War I period did not simply focus on measuring intelligence, instead they also emphasized how best to gauge student achievement. For instance, one of the earliest examples of a focus on achievement was the Stanford Achievement Test (SAT), first published in 1923, and which continues to be applied to this day. In the words of Popham, the Alpha Strategy became "the template for almost all of the nation's subsequent standardized testing, irrespective of whatever that testing was supposed to serve as an aptitude assessment or an achievement assessment" (Popham, 2001a, p. 42).

Popham goes on to argue that the overall purposes of standardized tests nowadays do not differ substantially from the mission of the alpha test. At their most basic, these tests consist of a set of multiple-choice test items which enable what are viewed by those developing and advocating for such tests as objective and precise comparisons of intellectual capability and the potential for achievement amongst test applicants.

However, an issue that is highly relevant for my purposes in this book, yet overlooked by Popham (2001a), is the fact that the Army Alpha laid out parallel references for future assessments not only as evaluative instruments but also as political ones. Viewed through a political lens, it can be argued that the Army Alpha tests generated a new kind of authority as to what (and who) might be valued in relation to education, and therefore what opportunities and resources might be made available to some groups over others as a result. For instance, each contender's outputs on this test would determine which applicants would be considered for the officer's training program, and who would be disregarded. Those successful candidates who became officers also became authority figures enacting those attributes seen as valuable, with those unsuccessful candidates now placed in a hierarchical relationship of power exercised by these now superior army officers and thus expected to follow commands.

Current national and international large-scale assessments not only resemble, but reproduce in important and powerful ways, the Army Alpha power relation dynamic. For example, those schools, sub-national states, national economies, and their related education systems, who achieve high scores are portrayed as more worthy and worth emulating by those below. In essence, they have been differentially valued with those constructed as low performing expected to learn from them, irrespective of their needs and aims. A good example of this practice is embedded in the following statement by the OECD (2016a):

> PISA results reveal what is possible in education by showing what students in the highest-performing and most rapidly improving education systems can do. The findings allow policymakers around the world to gauge the knowledge and skills of students in their own countries in comparison with those in other countries, set policy targets against measurable goals achieved by other education systems, and learn from policies and practices applied elsewhere. (p. 25)

In this respect, the OECD, through developing and promoting instruments to measure and identify (peer reviews) high performing countries, their policies and practices, what Sellar and Lingard (2014) refer to as "epistemic governance", is creating a policy agenda and deploying a set of tools that can be seen as authoritatively allocating value. Those countries that are successful in turn acquire a certain form of soft authority (Rutkowski, 2007), to reinforce those policy formulas and education practices which should be replicated, emulated or copied, though it is clear that the assumed link between OECD policy agendas and the needs of any one locale may be well off the mark. Martens (2007) argues that in this sort of context the "parties evaluated are implicitly pressured to converge towards those practices, forms of organization, or behaviors that are regarded as best" (p. 42). This is a preferred *modus operandi* of the OECD, their assessment PISA, and to a varied extent, national LSAs which draw upon PISA.

The initial mission of the Army Alpha may sound rather instrumental. Yet what I have argued so far is that what is involved here are a series of embedded and relational practices of power. First and foremost, it discriminates – on the basis of one test – who is worthy and who is unworthy. It also institutional-izes a chain of command whereby unsuccessful candidates are then provided with a clear sign of what it is that they must do to improve; that is, emulate the capabilities of those above them as identified by the test. This book will explore whether and how the essence of these dynamics was transferred to the education field through practices of education policy governance. It will also examine and explore variants of them at play with distinct scalar features in the Mexican context.

2 Large-scale Assessments Today, a Complex and Neglected Concept

I have suggested in the previous section that one of the first large-scale assess-ments to be developed in the educational field was the SAT test. Indeed 90 years after its foundation, many of its published documents and webpage define this assessment in instrumental terms of what it does, and not what it is. For instance, Pearson (2011) states that

> The Stanford Achievement 10 provides the valid and reliable data needed for an objective measure of student progress toward content standards and high expectations. This multiple-choice assessment helps to identify student strengths and needs leading to effective placement and instruc-tional planning. (p. 1)

Similar to the Stanford Achievement Test, current large-scale assessments, such as those that are promoted by the OECD, seem to take their core concept for granted.

Three major problems have been encountered when searching for in-depth comprehensive concepts of large-scale assessments. First, many concep-tualizations correspond to previous periods of time. Second, they are too generic. By this I mean that they mainly revolve around the claim that they are "multiple-choice assessments", "assessments administered to large popula-tions" or "standardized test". Third, they tend to focus mainly on purpose and rarely discuss their substance, such as in the case cited above regarding the Stanford Achievement. In order to delve into this topic, I will outline and elab-orate a few of the main concepts of large-scale assessments.

Bennett (1998) defines large-scale assessments as "those tests administered to sizeable numbers of people for such purposes as placement, course credit, graduation, educational admissions, and school accountability. It includes group-administered, standardized tests used most often in the secondary through postsecondary years" (p. 7). If we analyze this concept within the context of the early 90s, it may seem accurate. However, nowadays such a definition faces several limitations, of which three are easily spotted. First, their purpose. Although some current large-scale assessments continue to operate with the purposes outlined by Bennett above in mind, others have embraced more ambitious purposes, such as adding policy decisions and practice improvement suggestions as a way to realize more ideal outcomes. Second, regarding population, we can see that current large-scale assessments are not limited to the secondary and postsecondary years.

As this research will show, LSAs are becoming commonplace in levels of education often regarded as off-limits to testing, such as preschool. Third, their scope. Several contemporary large-scale assessments surpass the classical scope of simple tests. For example, PISA and TIMSS are labelled as surveys (Prais, 2004). Labelling these assessments as surveys reflects the fact that their methodological features are much more bound to the nature of surveys than to classroom exams or other forms of tests traditionally carried out in schools. One of the main methodological features of surveys, which has been embraced by LSAs, is the imputation of students' answers. In the case of PISA and PLANEA, students are given different questionnaire booklets, which contain distinct questions and tasks. Even though students do not answer all questions, they are awarded a mark or score which is imputed (Jerrim, 2014). This strategy is certainly not a practice amongst traditional tests carried out in classrooms, at least in Mexico.

Other conceptualizations of large-scale assessments, such as the one provided by Thompson et al. (2001), claim that they are "used at local, state, and national levels to measure the progress of schools toward the achievement of educational standards" (p. 1). This conceptualization seems to be constrained by the purposes of domestic LSAs which tend to be curriculum based and revolve around gauging students' and schools' achievement of national standards. It is also restricted in contrast to what some current international LSAs such as PISA claim they do, which consist of measuring students' abilities to confront real life problems.

Simon et al. (2010) define large-scale assessments as "standardized assessments conducted on a regional, national or international scale involving large student populations" (p. 1). This view is a clear example as to how some concepts can be too generic. Furthermore, its focus on "involving large student populations", could be challenged by today's OECD's assessment PISA-for-Schools. This large-scale assessment involves small student samples from particular schools, which can be contrasted against the larger international PISA community (Lewis, 2017).

Tobin et al. (2016) claim that large-scale assessments can "be viewed as a tool for monitoring the quality of education systems through a focus on education system outputs, namely student learning outcomes, in contrast to other development indicators which focus on educational inputs, such as access and resourcing" (p. 579). The focus of this concept lies on the capacity of large-scale assessments to scrutinize the quality of education through student learning outcomes, or what can also be referred to as its accountability nature. This draws attention to the accountability nature of many current LSAs which downplays the political dimension of large-scale assessments as discussed earlier in this chapter.

In addition to the issues previously highlighted, current assessment discussions seem to be missing conversations regarding what might be referred to as the program ontology of the specific assessment in question. The work of Pawson and Tilley is particularly helpful here. In the advancement of a framework for program evaluation, these authors argue that programs are theories, embedded, active and parts of open systems (Pawson & Tilley, 1997). Thus, each particular initiative has its own theory or "conception of how programs actually work" (Pawson, 2002, p. 341); this is referred to as program ontology. Pawson (2002) argues that the "vital ingredients of program ontology are thus its 'generative mechanisms' and its 'contiguous context'" (p. 342). Both of these features are distinctive for each large-scale assessment program, as briefly mentioned ahead, and discussed in further detail in Chapter 4.

While it is true that many LSAs today share common methodological aspects, some of them also differ quite considerably in relation to their aspirations, purposes and underlying logics. For instance, the current evaluation regime in Mexico is comprised of three distinct large-scale assessments, namely PISA, ERCE and PLANEA. PISA is a program auspicated by the OECD, driven by human capital theory and market-based logics and interests. In broad terms, it promotes the generation of data for fueling competition amongst countries, which is supposed to contribute to education improvement, which in turn is viewed as a proxy for bringing about economic growth. Quite oppositely, ERCE is a program developed by LLECE-UNESCO. This LSA is driven by a human rights logic. It promotes data development for the purposes of cooperation and learning amongst countries of particular regions and common conditions. This cooperation was originally viewed as source to expand education to all, given that at the time of its development (1994), many countries in that particular region were still struggling with universal access to basic education. Lastly, PLANEA, Mexico's national large-scale assessment can be seen as holding a public accountability logic, which promotes data production for the purposes of providing inputs to system members that can assist them in learning how to be certain types of leaders, teachers, students and so on, accordingly to the particular values of the Mexican system. Current large-scale assessments in Mexico, help exemplify the theoretical abstraction of program ontology coined by Pawson and Tilley (1997), used to explain that programs implicitly hold theories of how they work.

As the result of the limitations identified in the current literature regarding large-scale assessment concepts, and for the purpose of this study, I present a set of current characteristics drawn from previous concepts and components from PISA, ERCE and PLANEA to define what this book means by large-scale assessments or LSA programs. Whilst this is neither a finished nor exhausted list, it is nevertheless helpful for establishing a common grammar for readers.

Contemporary large-scale assessments which focus on student learning are survey-tests administered to varied proportions of participants and could:

a. Operate through comparing entities against an imagined ideal;
b. be applied at different scales: international, regional, national, sub-national, local;
c. be applied at different education levels: pre-school, primary, secondary and upper secondary;
d. have a variety of political, social and pedagogical aims and aspirations;
e. be comprised of different highly complex instruments;
f. be processed employing complex statistical models;
g. measure students' competencies, skills, knowledge in different learning domains such as math, science, literacy, and other subjects or educational domains;
h. measure students' perceptions concerning their own learning and learning experiences;
i. measure students' achievement in relation to distinct frameworks, such as local, sub-national or national curriculums, regional core-common curriculums, and/or a set of desirable competencies;
j. measure teachers, head-teachers and parents' perceptions concerning their students' learning;
k. have intended and unintended consequences, as well as produce collateral damage;
l. transcend classical functions and reaches of large-scale assessments; and
m. focus on generating and offering data for (a) aiding policy decisions, (b) aiding education practice improvement, (c) informing the public opinion about the state of learning of their education systems and (d) developing indicator databases for accountability, comparative and research purposes.

Two issues must be noted here. First, contemporary large-scale assessments in Mexico stretch beyond the classic or traditional view of "test administered to a large-scale population". Second, the previous list is an attempt to grasp the range of purposes and effects of current LSAs, but the field is not limited to these qualities. As mentioned above, it serves the purpose of offering a framework as to what and how this research views and refers to large-scale assessments. Establishing a comprehensive concept of LSAs is a task yet to be developed. This task is important and should not be overlooked. Doing so puts at risk undermining or neglecting the complexity that these instruments represent for evaluation, policies, practices and education systems. Understating large-scale assessments is problematic as it can be misleading to the enormous politic power they entail.

3 Efforts to Improve Education Systems

The historical development of the underlying logics and mechanisms that frame current large-scale assessments in Mexico are viewed by this book as distinct strategies aimed at improving education systems. In this section I will argue that the linkages between warfare and large-scale surveys are not limited to their emergence as solutions to identifying officer talent in World War I. World War II also left its mark on this enterprise, mainly through the advancement of organizations focused initially on sustaining post-World War II peace and boosting development, where education features quite centrally (Grek, 2009; Robertson, 2012a).

The aftermath of World War II brought about a range of distinct and diverse organizations to help in the reconstruction of societies and their different sectors (Robertson, 2012a). In the field of policy, the United Nations (UN) was created. In the field of economy several organizations flourished, such as the International Monetary Fund (IMF), World Bank (WB) and the Organization for European Economic Co-operation (OEEC). In the field of education, the United Nations Educational, Scientific and Cultural Organization (UNESCO) was founded.

The first association to develop international large-scale assessments emerged out of UNESCO meetings (Husen, 1979 cited in Johansson, 2016; Tobin, Nugroho, & Lietz, 2016). This organization, which later came to be known as the International Association for the Evaluation of Educational Achievement (IEA), sought to provide facts that were believed could help in the improvement of educational systems (Pidgeon, 1969). The advancement of UNESCO, followed by the development of the IEA, both signify a key antecedent that underlies part of the current dynamics of LSAs and governance in Mexico. These events represent initial efforts to improve education through two central mechanisms: (a) systems of data for developing comparisons, and (b) the advancement of international large-scale assessments.

Half a century later, a second hallmark of international LSAs evolved from the OECD, which in turn came from the OEEC, an organization created in the aftermath of World War II. The large-scale assessment developed by the OECD, namely Program for International Student Assessment, can be viewed as a concerted effort by this organization to consolidate a new order of indicators and culture of statistics which would transcend the descriptive approach of UNESCO (Cussó & D'Amico, 2005). The PISA program was initially launched as an initiative to improve education, although with a special challenge for education to serve as a proxy for economic growth and development.

To understand the current evaluation arrangement in Mexico, requires exploring and raising questions concerning the evolvement of education statistics, the development of IEA, and the advancement of the OECD's PISA. These fundamental antecedents frame and underpin the logics and mechanisms which the current evaluation regimen in Mexico draws upon.

3.1   *Rise of Education Statistics at UNESCO*

The rise of education statistics at UNESCO is mainly documented and studied by Cussó and D'Amico (2005). These authors argue: "Since its creation, the United Nations (UN) – through its specialized agencies and commissions – has supported the development and standardization of national statistics" (p. 199). Thus, when its specialized agency, UNESCO –which focuses on education, science and culture – was created, they were delegated with the responsibility for establishing, collecting and circulating international education statistics of member states. This was carried out by the Division of Statistics, through administering standardized questionnaires aimed at collecting data from all education levels, and with regards to the expenditure on this sector.

The objective of the statistical program at UNESCO aimed towards the basic values of this agency, based on the right to education – with special emphasis on increasing literacy development (Cussó & D'Amico, 2005; Roberson, 2012a). Moreover, this program also aimed to contribute to the evolvement of national education systems. Robertson (2012a) argues that the early statistical approach of UNESCO took the view that the world was regional, hence some countries could learn better from others as they were similar. This perception of comparability reflected a certain approach to the dialogue between nations (Cussó & D'Amico, 2005). In this manner, a sense of comparison and cooperation seemed feasible for fueling change. Amongst the statistics that UNESCO was producing, there was practically no call for league tables or complex statistical analysis.

However, in the early 1980's, other organizations – such as the OECD and the WB who were starting to produce their own indicators and statistics – began to criticize the work that was being developed at UNESCO mainly due to what was seen to be their descriptive nature (Cussó & D'Amico, 2005). The rationale of these organizations was led by the belief that the shifting political, economic, and cultural needs of that historical moment (and the future) required more complex statistical analysis in order to develop ordinal mechanisms and judgments, as drivers for progress and growth.

3.2 *Development of the IEA and PISA*

Husen (1979, cited in Johansson, 2016) and Wagemaker (2014) trace the origins of international large-scale assessments in education back to a meeting at UNESCO in 1958. In this gathering, educational researchers discussed the benefits of these instruments. Following this reunion, the International Association for the Evaluation of Educational Achievement (IEA) was born. However, it was only until 1967 when it acquired legal status and established among their main goals to:

a. Undertake educational research on an international scale.
b. Promote research aimed at examining educational problems common to many countries, in order to provide facts which can help in the ultimate improvement of educational systems.
c. Provide within the framework of the association, the means whereby research centers which are members of the association can undertake co-operative projects. (Pidgeon, 1969, p. 213)

De Landsheere (1997) argues that Arnold Anderson, who had contacted UNESCO during this period, regarding the need of producing educational measures, pointed out that "it was not much interest to judge systems by the number of persons graduating, but what was important was how many knew how much" (p. 2). Thus, the IEA set to embark in this mission. With the rise of the IEA, the first international large-scale assessment came about in form of a twelve-nation pilot study in the year of 1960. Subsequently, the IEA conducted the First International Mathematics Study (FIMS) in 1964, and from 1970 to 1971 it applied the Six Subject Survey in which it incorporated the assessment of science, reading comprehension, literature, French as a foreign language, English as a foreign language and Civic Education (Husen & Postlethewaite, 1996; Niemann, Hartong, & Martens, 2018).

Since then, the IEA has conducted more than 30 assessments around the world in collaboration with other institutions in which they address different educational levels, subjects or knowledge domains, and contents (Husén & Postlethwaite, 1996; Schmidt & Burroughs, 2013; Wagemaker, 2014; Wendt et al., 2011).

The second case that is considered to be ground-breaking in the realm of international large-scale assessments is the Program for International Student Assessment (PISA), developed and advocated by the Organization for Economic Co-operation and Development (OECD). Since its inception in 1960, the OECD has advanced, configured and promoted their capacity as a think tank with global technical and enterprise for boosting economic development. It did not take long before education was brought into the limelight. Drawing upon the work of Papadopoulos (1994), Sellar and Lingard (2014) note that education initially, "had an 'inferred role' in the OECD's work" (p. 921), which was characterized as not having an independent space in the organization. As the result of several internal shifts, and as part of their objective to position education as a driver for manpower and social affairs, it was shifted from the Science Directorate and in 1974, and incorporated into the Directorate for Social Affairs, Manpower and Education in 1975 (Papadopoulos, 1994). By the year 2002, education had become an autonomous Directorate within the organization, thanks to a series of events such as the creation of the indicators of education system program (INES), the publication of *Education and a Glance*, and the development of PISA (Grek & Ydesen, 2021; Sellar & Lingard, 2014). It is argued that the latter was gestated as a mechanism aimed at complementing the information that was being generated in the mid 90s for *Education at a Glance* (OECD, 2002). Today, PISA has by far surpassed and overshadowed this indicator factbook.

PISA began its formal operation in 1997 (OECD, 1999), and conducted its first assessment in the year 2000. Early claims concerning the purposes of PISA indicate a threefold front that revolves around: (a) its public policy driven spirit; (b) the need of nation states for scientific and comparable evidence; and (c) gauging students' competencies at the end of compulsory education in order to see how well they are prepared for the challenges of the world. Yet, underlying this rhetoric over the years PISA and the OECD through their publications now and then remind us that their overall goals and values are linked to the initial mission of the organization, which is "to achieve the highest sustainable economic growth and employment and a rising standard of living in Member countries, while maintaining financial stability, and thus to contribute to the development of the world economy" (OECD, 1999, p. 1).

A total of eight PISA editions have been carried out in three-year cycles over a 22-year period. The program started with 43 participating countries in the year 2000, and currently stands with approximately 90 nations or sub-national applicants in the 2021–2022 round; meaning that after eight testing rounds, PISA has doubled in number of participants. It is important to note that due to the spread of COVID-19, the 2021 PISA test administration was delayed, finally taking place in spring of 2022.

The authority and symbolic power that PISA has today was developed over the past 22 years as the consequence of multiple factors. For instance, the narrative of human capital, lifelong learning and economization of education rooted in OECD discourses has made PISA attractive for developed and developing countries (Lingard & Rawolle, 2011; Sellar & Lingard, 2014). The recognition and approval of PISA over other assessments, such as those offered by IEA, has sent a global message amongst European countries regarding its relevance, legitimacy and prioritization. For Grek (2012) "PISA represents an 'institutional order', which has brought together all the actors who took part in the construction of the problems and, subsequently, the solutions PISA offered" (p. 244).

Both the IEA – its assessments – and PISA proceed from organizations created in the aftermath of World War II. Both of these entities also sought to develop these instruments for improving education systems, although the reasons underlying this latter aspiration are distinct from each other. IEA on the one hand initially seemed to be committed to improving education system in the spirit of the core values of UNESCO. Whereas PISA – from its inception – is committed to improving education as a pathway for economic development. Lascoumes and Le Gales, (2007) note two fundamental issues about public policy instruments, such as large-scale assessments: first, that every instrument constitutes a condensed form of knowledge about social control and ways of exercising it; and second, that these instruments are not neutral devices: they produce specific effects, independently of the objective pursued.

This book is concerned with the current Mexican arrangement, in which three distinct large-scale assessments – which are public policy instruments – operate concurrently. Particularly, (a) what this represents in terms of governance for the different scales in which they operate, (b) in relation to the objectives that these assessments pursue (aiding policy decisions and practice improvement) and, (c) with regards to the unintended effects they produce. These issues will be picked up and unpacked in the following chapters.

4   Governing the Education Sector

Over time, the governing of education has been driven by different, distinct, complex and at times contradictory logics. For instance, following the post-war period, UNESCO developed its statistical program with the impetus of collecting data on education systems and by these means helping nation states develop their national education systems, which would eventually lead to education for all. Their improvement logic was founded on the premise that statistical data could be useful for developing cooperation between regions and nations and could help improve education systems. Today, a far different logic dominates the governing of many education systems around the world.

Contrary to the view developed by UNESCO, the OECD promotes an improving logic with an emphasis on competition as a main driver for system change. Robertson (2012a) argues that this is the result of the implementation of neoliberalism as a political project and its values founded on dynamics of free-market, competition, free trade, and so on.

One of the main arguments of this book is that over the past 20 years, large-scale assessments have played a fundamentally important role in the governing of the education sector not only in Mexico but more widely. To comprehend how these public policy instruments have been at work, it is essential to explore their core concepts, their main driving mechanisms, and evidence of outcomes over time. This includes raising questions regarding the rise of neoliberalism as a political project, and how this particular project is linked to the transition from governing at national and sub-national settings to governing at the global scale. This in turn also requires exploring the shifting dynamics regarding the "scales – or rescaling – from which education is governed, with growing power being concentrated in globally-influential actors and agencies" (Robertson & Dale, 2013, p. 2). In doing so, several issues are made visible. For instance, the ideological bases which underlie the current evaluation ensemble in Mexico, its main vehicle to access and govern the sector, and broad characteristics and relationships between these two matters.

4.1   *Emergence of Neoliberalism as a Political Project and the Rise of Global Governance*

Understanding global governance requires recognizing and reviewing the essential social, cultural, political and economic transformations from which this modality of governing has emerged (Robertson, 2012a). In this respect, it concerns the advancement of neoliberalism as a political project. Harvey (2005) argues that neoliberalism is "a theory of political economic practices that proposes that human well-being can best be advanced by liberating individual entrepreneurial freedoms and skills within an institutional framework characterized by strong private property rights, free markets, and free trade" (p. 2). Neoliberalism as political project, linked to the Hayekian economic doctrine, was propelled forward in western hegemonic countries such as the

UK, US and Chile in the early 1980s. This project envisaged and advanced new forms of viewing and executing governing activities and processes. These new forms of desirable social life are implicated in a rescaling of governing activities and actors (Robertson & Dale, 2013). This maneuver brought into play within national settings an array of supranational organizations and agents. Along with this advancement there was a distinctive shift concerning the locus of power from national to supranational entities (Lingard & Rawolle, 2011; Robertson, 2012a). The latter came to occupy dominating positions in the governing of education.

In the past it was assumed that national governments alone carried out all governing activities related to the provision, regulation, and funding of the education sector. Nevertheless Dale (1997), along with others, shows that this has mostly not been the case, and that looking back in history, different groups and agents – from those considered market actors to those located in the community, have also engaged in a range of education activity across time and scales. However, the presence of other actors and organizations in these matters were for the most part discreet. What the neoliberal project proposed was, on the one hand, an open and public exhibition of the growing and shared participation of non-governmental and governmental agents in this sector, and on the other, the gradual transfer-transition of governing activities to private and non-governmental entities of historically known tasks largely carried out by national states.

Dale (1997) explains that education governance as we know it nowadays came about as a consequence of a series of changes in the global economy and structural adjustments in a post Reagan-Thatcher period, which caused a shift from governments carrying out most of education activities, to an arrangement in which non-governmental institutions and agents extended their participations with regards to the funding, regulation and provision of education services (Dale, 1997; Grek et al., 2009). Robertson (2012a) identifies early linkages with regards to the expansion of global governance with the end of World War II and the settlement of the Bretton Woods agreement. This event, an essential antecedent of neoliberalism, gave birth to the International Monetary Fund (IMF) and the World Bank (WB). Both of these institutions became key organizations in the global governance of many sectors, including education, as they enrolled poor and developing countries into the adoption and implementation of structural reforms and policies based on neoliberal principles. Furthermore, the recent expansion of global governance is mainly associated with the decline of the Keynesian welfare-state era, the post-cold war period and the proliferation of neoliberal projects among western countries, especially the US and UK (Adamson et al., 2016; Dale, 1997).

As national states around the world were – and continue to be – increasingly persuaded and pressured to shift away from welfare-state arrangements so as to embrace education projects shaped by neo-liberal principles: a range of different agents, roles, processes, programs and institutions have begun to emerge which in turn reshaped the modes, mechanisms, and practices by which we organize societies (Harvey, 2005). Within this context, concepts such as global governance emerged to describe the shifts in the locus of power as the result of a rescaling of the governing of education (Robertson, 2012a), in which supranational agents and organizations started to usurp the role and functions historically developed by national and subnational states.

4.2   *What Is Global Governance?*

Exploring the notion of global governance requires the acknowledgment and previous discussion of the term of governance itself. This concept, which is employed by this book to help explain how large-scale assessments have been at play in the governing of the education sector, is complex and has evolved over time. Early versions of governance refer to it as "a new method by which society is governed" (Rhodes, 1996, p. 1246). More recent definitions claim that it can be considered as "forms of political organization and processes of policy-making that may involve formal and vertical governance, thus so-called hard governance, as well as informal and horizontal modes of regulating social processes, known as soft governance" (Bieber, 2016, p. 47). Robertson and Dale (2013) point out that whilst the concept of governance is useful because it "alerts us to governing as being more than a state activity" (p. 6), it does not "help us understand what parts of the education enterprise are subject to what form of governing. Nor does it differentiate between different kinds of actors, or the scales on which governing might take place" (p. 6).

Thus, the concepts of global governance and education governance frameworks come in handy here, as they can help illuminate and cover the gaps illustrated by Robertson and Dale on the one hand, whilst on the other they enable a better understanding of the nature of the relationships amongst large-scale assessment programs and the governing of the education sector, on the other.

Robertson (2012a) argues that

> governance can be described as the sum of the many ways in which individuals and institutions, public and private, manage their daily affairs, whilst global governance refers to a range of actors – from inter-governmental to non-governmental, citizens' movements and multinational corporations, who exercise authority and engage in political action across state boundaries. (p. 3; see also Keohane, 2003)

In this book, large-scale assessments are viewed as public policy instruments which are employed to exercise authority and engage in political action within and across state boundaries and political scales. The different ways in which this has occurred is yet to be explored in Chapter 3, and the distinct forms in which it is occurring in the Mexican context will be explored in the thematic chapters of this book (Chapters 5 to 7).

The concept of education governance coined by Dale (1997) and Robertson and Dale (2013), has been used to "describe the governing activity that is increasingly carried out not by government alone, but also by non-governmental actors" (p. 5). These authors argue that education governance is delivered through the informal authority of public, private and volunteer agents and institutions. This concept is particularly helpful for this research in two broad ways. First, it frames the overall relationships between large-scale assessments and the governing of the sector. Second, as it precedes the notion of education governance frameworks, which function as a basic structure in this book for posing questions regarding the actors, scales and parts of the education sector that are being governed by large-scale assessments. Furthermore, it invites us to adopt a critical theory stance and to raise question about why and how this particular state of affairs came into being.

5   Conclusions

In this chapter, I have developed a theoretical and conceptual framework for studying large-scale assessments and governance in Mexico. This has required discussing the origin of these public policy instruments with a particular focus on their warfare roots. This historical context constitutes the pioneering and main theoretical references for future large-scale assessments in relation to how they initially allocate value and acquire authority, and how they currently function both as evaluative and political instruments. I have also pointed out the negligence of large-scale assessments and the literature to provide a comprehensive concept from which to draw upon. This has led to the development of a working framework to inform how this research views and puts this concept to work. I also discussed that these public policy instruments have been employed as the result of a new scale of governing, namely the global, which in turn has emerged as a result of neoliberalism as a political project. Lastly, I have discussed the development of two hallmark entities of international large-scale assessments, who constitute two distinct reference points and illustrate that their public policy instruments are not neutral devices.

Expanding Our Understandings of Large-scale Assessments and Governance

Similar to the previous chapter of this book, this chapter addresses, analyzes and discusses leading large-scale assessment research. However, it differentiates itself from Chapter 2 in two broad ways. First, it studies the effects that these public policy instruments have on a range of diverse processes, actors, and settings, and discusses how large-scale assessments work in terms of governance as a means to achieve these effects. Second, whilst Chapter 2 elaborates relational accounts of large-scale assessments and their expansion over time, spaces and scales, Chapter 3 focuses on reviewing their current manifestations in the field of education, with the aim of pointing out major discussions, their concerns, and what are remaining gaps.

This chapter is divided into two main sections. First, I analyze large-scale assessments and governance literatures, with particular emphasis on their effects on policies and practices in national settings, and on their governing trajectories. Second, I introduce a set of theoretical tools which will be employed by this book together with the evidence from Chapters 5 to 7 to help explain how large-scale assessments have both historically and at the current time mediated governing relationships at diverse scales in Mexico.

1 Large-scale Assessments and Governance

The major question in this section is not if large-scale assessments are influencing governing, policies and practices, but rather, how, where, by which means and in what forms this has been occurring. With regards to this question, a growing body of literature has been produced over the past ten years, some of which I explore in detail below. Fischman et al. (2019) found 86 publications that range from the year 2000 to 2017 in English, Spanish and Portuguese in popular data bases that addressed the effects of ILSAs on education policies. By way of contrast, I have identified nine key publications produced in the past six years in the form of journal issues and books on this matter (Lewis & Lingard, 2015; Lietz & Tobin, 2016; Lingard et al., 2013; Martens, Niemann & Taltemann, 2016; Meyer & Benavot, 2013; Steiner-Khamsi & Waldow, 2018; Volante, 2016, 2017; Sorenson et al., 2021). These publications sum up 79 articles and book chapters. They constitute the main literature reference for this section and are examined to reveal the experiences of large-scale assessments and governance amongst both developing and developed countries, such as the cases of: Mexico, Chile, Jordan, United States, Germany, Japan, Spain, England and others.

1.1 *Effects of Large-scale Assessments on Policies*

The effects of international and national large-scale assessment programs on policies in the United States of America have been argued to be limited. This is mainly attributed to the fact that education decisions have traditionally been made at the local levels (Schmidt & Burroughs, 2016). Thus, it is argued that external mechanisms appear to have minor influences and impacts on local policies. Schmidt and Burroughs (2016) suggest that "the principal use of state assessments has not been to create a mechanism upon which to base policy but as a policy instrument of its own" (p. 568). With regard to international large-scale assessments, these authors argue that TIMSS has, to some extent, influenced policies, specifically the implementation of national learning standards, opening in path to the application of value-added models and student growth percentile models.

Baker and O'Neil (2016) argue that

> there is one more general and perhaps more important source of change in educational policy and practice that evolves from international studies. That influence comes from what can be learned from the methodology and the measures used in the study itself. (p. 130)

These authors suggest that the most useful part of these assessments lies in their methodological and measurement features which function as pedagogical devices for shifting attention and discussion to accountability concerns, and for infiltrating classroom practices. With regards to the latter, it is argued that high-stake large-scale assessments have led many schools and teachers in the US to embrace an array of different cheating practices (Nichols & Berliner, 2007). More recent publications by Niemann et al. (2018) argue that PISA results from early rounds (2000 to 2009) were mainly employed by educational state authorities for

> strategic projection-making for state-led benchmarking, standardization, and accountability policies .... Whereas results from 2012 and 2015 caused the federal government to refer to PISA to (post) legitimize the new reform paths that were taken to boost educational performance. (p. 600)

Another case in point is Chile. This nation initially employed neoliberalism as a political project during the Pinochet dictatorship (Budds, 2013), which, continues to be deeply embedded, despite recent efforts to de-privatize. The tradition of Chile's participation in ILSAs is longstanding and can be dated back to the 1960s. Cox and Meckes (2016) have identified and classified the direct and indirect forms in which large-scale assessments have exercised influence on policies in this nation. These modalities of influence have been labelled as: (a) reflexivity through discovery, which, is carried out mainly by offering data against which Chile is compared to developed countries, and thus arouses reflexivity concerning the need for reform; (b) capacity building, which, is linked to the enrichment in terms of knowledge and skills of distinct actors and teams of politicians, bureaucrats and technicians, involved in policy development and decisions making; (c) political leverage viewed as the forms in which the outcomes of these instruments are employed by different governance agents to pressure towards certain forms of policy-making, and (d) norms and governmental programs which refer to normative tools and programs, such as curriculum and assessment frameworks, which in turn play a fundamental role in reproducing assessment logics in other projects. Even though this country has participated in different assessments, Cox and Meckes (2016) claim that mainly the IEA and PISA assessments have caused visible effects on their national education policy. Finally, according to these authors, the transformations that have been triggered in Chile as the result of large-scale assessments consist of curricular modifications, implementation of learning standards, and attempts of reforming teacher education to comply with international surveys. Furthermore, international large-scale assessments have influenced methodological and technical issues of Chilean national assessment programs.

With regards to the European continent, there was an unexpected backlash in the German context when their results suggested that its system was not performing well (albeit it on PISA tests). Before PISA, large-scale assessments and comparative analysis figured modestly in the field of policy in Germany (Niemann et al., 2018). However, as the result of what came to be known as a "PISA shock" – in which the population of this country found their results to be mediocre in comparison to their peers – significant changes were put into place across the entire educational system, amongst them: the introduction of learning standards, reinforcing early childhood education, emphasizing on socio-economic disadvantaged students, and application of measures of evidence-based policy-making (Grek, 2009; Knodel et al., 2013).

Grek et al. (2009) explore the impact of early rounds of PISA (2000–2006) on national policies in several European nations, amongst them, England. Given this country's decent results in early editions of PISA, no specific actions were taken. However, this story changed drastically proceeding the 2009 PISA results. Thomas et al. (2016) argue that after the publications of this PISA round, England's results were regarded as declining. This evidence was used by former Secretariat of Education, Michael Gove, as an alibi for justifying the actions taken by his government especially in relation to the revision of the national curriculum and its assessments, and to policies regarding school resources for disadvantaged pupils.

As to the case of Spain, Choi and Jerrim (2016) argue that PISA has illuminated the necessity for educational reform at secondary education level. However, further studies revealed that learning problems originate at the primary level, which interestingly was not targeted by this reform. In this respect, it is argued that these policies were attacking the consequences and not the sources of learning problems in Spain. Fischman et al. (2019) argue that the shifts in Spain as the result of ILSAs focused on curriculum reform with an emphasis on competence-based learning, foreign languages and technology-communications.

In the Asian context, Japan also suffered a PISA shock following the 2003 PISA results (Sellar & Lingard, 2013b; Takayama, 2008). As a result, the Prime Minister implemented a series of actions legitimized by PISA outcomes. This included: (i) a market-based management model; (ii) national achievement testing; (iii) the publication of school-by-school test scores; and (d) a program of school choice (Takayama, 2008).

Sellar and Lingard (2013b) observe that following the outstanding performance of Shanghai in PISA 2009, Finland lost its place as the global educational reference. This caused the United States of America and England to commission reports from the OECD in order to detect what could be learned from Shanghai. In Australia, the government – through an appointed committee – commissioned reports to deliver the insights of the Asian success. Although no specific policies were mentioned as the outcomes of these actions during this period, Sellar and Lingard (2013b) consider them to be modes of influencing policy making in these countries, mainly by "using this new reference society as a form of 'externalisation' to push internal reform agendas in respect of their schooling systems" (p. 479).

In a more recent publication, Sellar and Lingard (2018) suggest that the PISA shock in Australia which came about as the result of declining test scores and the overachievement of Shanghai, generated several consequences and notably proliferating diverse policy narratives amongst federal administrations and affective response overall linked to Australia's economic future. One of the concrete outcomes of this enterprise was settling that Australia would achieve a place amongst the top five performers by PISA 2025. Masters (2017) argues that in response to declining PISA scores amongst students, the Australian Council for Educational Research published a series of guides to mathematic, reading and science literacy as a means to improve classroom practices in Australia. This can be seen as part of government policy focus of STEM in schools (Sellar & Lingard, 2018).

Breakspear (2012) authored a working paper for the OECD in which the influence of PISA 2009 on national policies in 37 countries was analyzed. He finds that Australia, France and Canada claim that PISA's impact in their countries has been moderate; however, Japan, Korea, Hungary, and Austria claim that in their cases it has been high or extreme. The ways in which PISA is influencing national policies in these countries is similar to what has already been discussed above consisting of three broad strategies: (i) the development and enforcement of learning standards; (ii) the implementation of competence-based curriculum; and (iii) the development and strengthening of national evaluation programs.

In relation to those countries who have produced less data on this matter, Ababneh et al. (2016) document the experience of Jordan. The results of this nation in TIMSS and PISA show that male students perform better than female counterparts. This situation has influenced new legislations aimed at reducing gender performance differences and elevating general scores in all large-scale assessments. The government in this country plans to achieve these goals by reforming their curriculum, improving teacher training, and developing national large-scale assessment programs.

Martínez-Rizo and Silva-Guerrero (2016) offer relevant insights regarding the effects of large-scale assessments on policies in Mexico. According to these authors, LSAs have had two important functions throughout time: first, as policies per se from 1970s to 1990s, and second, since the year 2000, as tools for aiding policy decision-making. Jimenez-Moreno (2016) has additionally highlighted the current accountability functions of these programs in Mexico. According to Martinez-Rizo and Silva-Guerrero (2016), the most influential large-scale assessment programs in Mexico have been EXCALE, a former national assessment program, and PISA.

The main influence of EXCALE on national policies consists of triggering a strong financial investment into a television-based secondary education system named "Tele-secundarias" (Televised Secondary Schools). The government decided to focus on this sub-system for two mains reasons. First, most of these schools are located in rural parts of Mexico; these are geographical locations known for providing poor quality of education. Second, these schools were attaining the lowest scores in national and international assessment programs. Hence, it was a strategy that targeted the low performers with the intention of raising test scores.

Martínez-Rizo and Silva-Guerrero (2016) argue that the results from early PISA rounds caused a media shock that pressured the national government to include, as an official policy, the raising of PISA tests scores in future rounds (also see Fischman et al., 2019). In addition, the national secretariat for public education implemented a new national competence-based PISA-orientated curriculum from preschool to upper secondary.

The previous accounts concerning the United States of America, Chile, Germany, England, Japan, Jordan, Chile, Mexico, and other countries, address important issues with regard to the influence of large-scale assessments on national policies. However, four important issues must be noted. First, many of these accounts fail to acknowledge and inform us of the ways in which parallel national and international large-scale assessment programs that coexist in a same context interact in terms of their governing activities, and what this means in relation to their outcomes on policies and practices. Second, they do not give us nuanced readings of what occurs at the distinct scales in which these public policy instruments operate. In other words, much research tends to center on the national scale, leaving the sub-national and local settings under-researched. Third, Green (2015, 2019) has recently raised concerns regarding the lack of direct and visible relationships between PISA and particular policies, as the result of governance activities. Last, Komatsu and Rappleye (2021) note that far too often this body of literature oscillates between those that are against and those that are in favor of large-scale assessments. This dichotomic framing is problematic because discussions tend to remain within these borders, when in fact, we need to expand our understandings concerning the intersections between LSAs and governance.

1.2 Governing Trajectories and Mechanisms

A second issue of interest in this section is concerned with the trajectories and mechanisms through which large-scale assessments have carried out governing activities. The literatures with regard to these issues share two main characteristics. First, they mainly address the role of the OECD in this enterprise. Second, they mainly focus on the PISA assessment.

Morgan and Shahjahan (2016) claim that the OECD has made use of three mechanisms in order to secure recognition, reputation, and legitimization in the arena of education governance. These are (i) building on its past successes, (ii) assembling knowledge, and the (iii) deployment of its bureaucratic resources. Through these means the OECD offers recommendations in education governance on a global scale. Morgan and Volante (2016), who draw largely upon the work of Woodward (2009), add to this discussion that the OECD has made use of surveys, such as PISA and TALIS, to consolidate its participation in governance agendas by promoting and spreading its norms, ideas, language, knowledge and values. Lastly, Breakspear (2012) argues that PISA results are on the one hand "used as an external trigger for large-scale public debate on education" (p. 15) and on the other "as evidence to argue that national performance requires improvement" (Breakspear, 2014, p. 7). The latter can be noted in the 2013 education reform in Mexico, in which PISA results and Mexico's positions on league tables are brought up in the national context and contrasted against those top performers who are also viewed as competing economies (Senado de la Republica, 2012). This may be seen as maneuver to highlight the "critical" state of learning in Mexico, and therefore a trigger to boost reform.

Sellar and Lingard (2013a) suggest that through PISA, the OECD employs a self-perpetuating dynamic through which the latter "prescribes education policy approaches and assesses the performance of national education systems in these terms" (p. 723). It is argued that this contributes to epistemological governance as it frames the beliefs of the actors that mediate reforms in national settings (Sellar and Lingard, 2014). This strategy was employed in Mexico as part of the latest education reform. Cuevas and Moreno (2016) point out that as a result of Mexico's low scores in all of the PISA rounds, the federal government commissioned a series of policy recommendation reports from the OECD. The suggestions endorsed by the 2012–2013 education reform bill from these documents can be easily spotted (OECD, 2010b, 2011).

Similarly, Meyer and Benavot (2013) claim that PISA has enabled the OECD to "assume a new institutional role as arbiter of global education governance, simultaneously acting as diagnostician, judge and policy advisor to the world's school system" (p. 5). These authors suggest that PISA encourages, provides support, legitimatizes, soft governance to pressure national states into implementing educational reforms deliberately designed and enhanced by a human capital and market rationality (Grek et al., 2009; Grek, 2012). Meyer and Benavot (2013) are, as a result, concerned that a non-academic organization and program is replacing the role of national governments. Commentators note that UNESCO suggests that some of these issues should be more country-driven (Auld et al., 2019).

More recent publications address the governance expansion attempt of the OECD and PISA through new modalities of this program. Such is the case advanced by Addey (2017), who argues the OECD took advantage of the adjustment developed by UNESCO when Education for All was replaced with Education 2030 and the Sustainable Development Goals (SDG). Through these means the OECD has sought to expand its reach into low and middle-income countries through its PISA for Development (PISA-D). The introduction and expansion of this program was advanced through a strategy that (i) prompted the OECD to align national and international assessments; (ii) ensure the technical capacity of making PISA and PISA-D results comparable; and (iii) secured the interlocking aims of PISA, PISA-D, the Education and Skills Directorate and the SDG. This maneuver is presumed to amplify and perpetuate the core values linked to this organization. In this sense, PISA-D is employed as a sort of modern expertise troy horse for spreading the OECD's values.

A good example of this expansion is outlined by Auld et al. (2019). These authors discuss the strategic partnership that the OECD and the World Bank have developed in the case of Cambodia. The OECD had claimed that PISA-D was developed on demand of low and middle-income countries due to their interest to participate in the international community. Nevertheless, this was not so much the case of Cambodia which, according to the evidence shared by these authors, show several points and issues of tension and overall small national interest in international large-scale assessments. Nonetheless, this did not prevent the OECD and its partners, including the World Bank, from promoting PISA-D as the main metric for tracking the realization of the SDG in Cambodia.

Another addition to the PISA suit of tools is PISA for schools launched in 2013 in the USA. In this respect, Lewis (2017) argues that "schools are, for the first time, able to interact directly with the policies and discourses of the OECD, but without the intervening presence of governments" (p. 282). PISA for schools is a test similar to main PISA but in this case, it compares particular school outcomes against local, sub-national and national systems (Lingard & Lewis, 2017) and offers to participant schools a set of best international practices, from high-performing education systems such as Japan, Shanghai, Finland, Singapore, amongst others. Through these means, the values of the OECD are now directly injected into schools in forms of "best international practices" on the one hand, and in the form of school assessment and accountability culture on the other.

The previous paragraphs address literatures that discuss the effects of LSAs in national settings and particularly the trajectories and mechanisms through which they govern. In other words, it offers insights regarding the intersections between these public policy instruments and the particular forms of political relationships entailed by global governance. This conversation contributes to answering the question: "what" has occurred in this enterprise? Meanwhile, it also offers broad insights concerning the discussions of "how" such turn of events came into being.

I would like to close this section by analyzing those literatures that discuss mainstream mechanisms which detail how the intersection between large-scale assessments and governance has been enhanced or boosted. In this terrain, the work developed by Martens (2007) with regards to governing by comparisons is milestone. The central premise of this work is founded on the following argument: "Comparison as a form of governance implies a scientific approach to political decision making" (p. 42). Furthermore, the author suggests that "The parties evaluated are implicitly pressured to converge towards those practices, forms of organization, or behaviors that are regarded as best" (p. 42). The "comparative turn" in education governance is widely referred to focus on those governing activities carried out by numerous international organizations which make use of assessments or evaluations in order to govern (Gorur, 2016; Grek, 2009; Pons, 2016; Robertson, 2012a).

Grek (2009) applies part of Marten's work regarding governing through comparison to the OECD and the PISA effect in Europe. The author argues that "policy instruments such as indicators and the whole audit and performance-monitoring nexus have become a significant element of the shift from government to the governance of national education systems" (Grek, 2009, p. 25). Although the paper is called "governing by numbers", there is a lack of explications as to how numbers were employed to cause the effects and shifts that are argued to have been set in place. In the concluding remarks, the author claims that: "In particular, PISA data are used to justify change or provide support for existing policy direction in both the domestic and the European contexts" (Grek, 2009, p. 34).

2   Thinking and Pedagogical Tools

Recent insights by Sorensen and Robertson (2020) raise two important concerns regarding the intersection between governing and large-scale assessments. First, that whilst governing through comparisons, numbers and statistical reasoning has been around for quite a while (see Desrosières, 1998; Lingard, 2013), the ontology of comparisons as a mode of governance still requires further explanation given that it remains under-theorized in the literature. Second, recent theoretical advancements in the field of sociology (Fourcade, 2016) have generated a conceptual grammar to talk about comparison, focusing particularly on "ordinality". This variant is viewed as a preferred mode of comparisons as it seeks to establish and perpetuate commensuration practices as a mean for developing systems of endless hierarchical ordering of people, groups, and things. This particular form of comparisons has become popular and dominating because of its linkages to political liberalism and its fundamental values of individual liberty.

This book makes use of three main theoretical thinking tools to contribute to the discussions regarding the ontology of comparisons as a mode of governance. By "thinking tool" I mean theories that enable us to think and theorize about particular issues and problems. These tools are namely: (a) competitive comparison, (b) flattening and (c) principles of classificatory judgment. In order to reach its purpose, this book draws upon, and puts these tools to analytical work at distinct scales inside the Mexican context in relation to the LSA aspirations of adding policy decisions and education practice improvement, which will be explained in further detail in the following Chapter 4.

Robertson (2012a) argues that "broadly, all governing practices are pedagogical in that they involve the selective acquisition of particular knowledge and practices" (p. 588). The thinking tools that this book draws upon are viewed as pedagogical tools in that they contribute to the framing, advancement and enhancement of the governing activities and practices developed by the particular large-scale assessments which operate in Mexico. In the following sub-sections, I will introduce these theoretical abstractions, which will be picked up in the thematic chapters of this book (see Chapters 5 to 7).

2.1   *Competitive Comparison*

The first thinking tool is proposed by Robertson (2012a) and is called competitive comparison. According to this author, the reach of competitive comparison is enabled when four features are mobilized as complex modalities of power. These modalities of power consist of: (a) the ordering of space hierarchically; (b) the nature of the temporal rhythms, (c) the evaluative domain and its implied repair work; and (d) scale. The author draws upon the case in point of TALIS to illustrate her point as follows:

> competitive comparison, as a powerful spatial framer and lever for allocating status, pitches one country and its teachers against another in terms of a global hierarchical ordering of performers and underperformers; second, it is enabled through ratchetting up the temporal dimension to comparison, such as regular cycles of data collection. This provides space for learning to improve, to do better the next time, and the time after, while keeping sufficient tension within the system. Third, an evaluative/moral dynamic provides the basis of judging where a country lies on each teacher policy area – from "not present" to "fully developed", as we can see in the World Bank's project. Countries and teachers are to learn from this evaluative element about how to act in ways specified by this framing of the good teacher. Fourth, embedding the governing

> strategy in national, regional, and global projects in turn amplifies its
> effects and, therefore, power. (Robertson, 2012a, p. 602)

Although Robertson (2012a) focuses on the case of OECD's TALIS to develop
her argument, the practices of competitive comparisons can be extrapolated to
those large-scale assessments that focus on student learning, such as the ones
currently operating in Mexico. For example, different features of competitive
comparison are at play in the Mexican national assessment PLANEA and can
be noted in their national reports and ontology. For instance, PLANEA pitches
sub-national entities, their teachers and students against other sub-national
entities in terms of hierarchical ordering, from the 1st to the 32nd place. The
creators of PLANEA have integrated into the inherent characteristics of this
program regular 3-year and 1-year data collection cycles, consequently ratch-
etting up the temporal dimension to comparison. This period of time is supposed to be sufficient to keep tension between participants on the one hand,
whilst on the other it represents an alleged acceptable period for entities and
schools to raise scores. Student outcomes enable an evaluative/moral dynamic
which judges where students, schools and sub-national stand in terms of
learning domains, from insufficient to outstanding. However, in this case, they
have a temporal value; in one cycle they can be labelled as insufficient and in
the following cycle as outstanding. This additional feature contributes to the
tensions and pressures for entities to at least not fall behind, and better still
either sustaining the same level or continuously pushing for higher levels of
achievement. And last but not least, features of PLANEA are embedded into
different scales and projects of the education system, which in return amplifies its effects.

PISA and PLANEA in Mexico employ features of competitive comparison.
The forms in which they are at play within the Mexican context, will be discussed in more detail in the thematic chapters of this book (see Chapters 5 to 7).

2.2 *Flattening*

The second tool in this research, also proposed by Robertson (2017), is flattening; this occurs when people, spaces, cultural practices, beliefs, values, qualities, activities, schools, systems, data and so on, are flattened for the purpose of
conducting comparisons or building upon the outcomes of these comparisons
for distinct purposes. Unlike commensuration, which seeks to embrace and
establish a common scale, flattening is viewed more as an action that com-
presses, erases or flattens particularities in order to create equivalences to
meet the criteria of comparability, and interpret, mediate, supply or enforce
indistinctively outcomes, policies and practices derived from this enterprise.

There are many examples of flattening practices. In what follows, I briefly illustrate some.

First, the audiences for which assessment data is directed to are flattened. Assessment programs claim that they aspire to aid policy decisions. However, policy decision-makers vary in type and function. For example, legislators make policy decisions, insofar, Secretariat officials who develop a new curriculum do as well. However, it is the same LSA data and publications available for these two distinct audiences despite their different needs. In terms described by Mortimore (1999), each of these groups operates and interacts in different currencies, which makes it particularly difficult for a flat and generic form of evidence as large-scale assessment data to function properly for both of them. Furthermore, if we examine the needs and functions of other audiences to which LSAs are directed to, this enterprise becomes more and more complicated.

Second, Legislators from different countries are also viewed through a singular or flat lens, and in that sense each political system is seen as the same. In this respect, different historically produced political arrangements are erased. For instance, legislators from Mexico and Brazil are treated as equivalents to legislators from Finland and Singapore. Some of the corrupted practices by which legislators are elected in Mexico and the benevolent dictatorship in Singapore (Friedman, 1990) are simply neglected. Despite that the outcomes of both of these national settings and particularities are bound to have some impact on the ways in which education matters are conducted. In this instance, LSAs claim that they generate data for adding policy decisions. However, they overlook that politics are conducted by distinct people, in a wide variety of ways, within different sets of cultural and political habits, values and motives. This kind of cultural and political flattening in turn reduces the world of differences, to a world of similarities.

Third, assessment rounds are flattened and treated as equivalents. For instance, the PISA 2006 round is made equivalent to the 2018, despite the social, political and economic differences within countries, not to mention the own technical and methodological differences amongst tests rounds. The OECD draws upon flattening to advance important judgments to try to publicly shame nations, this can be noted in the following statement: "it is disappointing that, for the majority of countries with comparable data, science performance in PISA remained virtually unchanged since 2006" (OECD, 2016a, p. 3). In addition to pitching some countries against others, it is also more common to see the pitching of countries against themselves.

Fourth, important indicators amongst countries such as poverty are flattened. For instance, the particularities of poverty in Finland are made equivalent to the particularities of poverty in Mexico and Brazil. However, the issues linked to poverty in Mexico such as drug trafficking, large-scale murders, and corruption, are distinct to the issues – both in form and in scale – linked to the sources of violence in Finland.

Fifth, schools themselves are viewed in such a way that their differences are erased because of the flattening processes. In the variant of PISA-for-schools, all participating schools are given a report. The first part of the report accounts for the school's performance. The second part of the document provides 17 best world practices, which are the same for all schools irrespective of their particular features, such as: country, type of school, social, economic and cultural backgrounds (Lewis, 2017).

Flattening practices can be identified and linked to dominant large-scale assessments from the very beginning of their development and enforcement. As mentioned in the Introduction to this book, despite this diversity within and amongst large-scale assessments, these instruments function by seeing or projecting the spaces or territories of governing in ontologically flat ways, in turn they intervene by proposing generic one size fits solutions of how to improve. This double flattening of space and solution, of populations and purpose, are deeply problematic in the education system in that in a structural sense they make inequalities invisible, in turn producing new inequalities.

It would seem that this theoretical notion – of flattening – has been largely overshadowed by quantitative practices, and a strong focus on commensuration studies (Addey, 2017; Auld, Rappleye, & Morris, 2019; Lewis & Holloway, 2019; Sellar & Lingard, 2014). However, in this research flattening practices are viewed as having a relevant role in global education governance in Mexico. This is not to say that commensuration is not at play in the Mexican context, or that it is unimportant. Moreover, I see flattening and commensuration at times working alongside each other. The ways in which this occurs will be explored in the upcoming chapters of this book.

2.3 *Principles of Classificatory Judgement*

Fourcade (2016) introduces the principles of classificatory judgment. She argues that these principles have been key in carrying out comparisons amongst people and things throughout the history of humankind. The first principle is namely nominal, which is defined in relation to the nature and essence of what people or things are, thus it is linked to their ontology. This principle is qualitative. Fourcade (2016) argues that "we can think of the pure, ideal-typical nominal topology as a flat and horizontal map: Entities are simply distributed across space without any assumption of hierarchy between them" (p. 177). Nominal judgments are common in large-scale scale assessment literature.

For example, they are as simple as labelling students or education systems as high performers or low performers. According to the author, these judgments matter because they are "articulated with claims of identity, authenticity, and value" (p. 182).

The second principle refers to cardinality, which, is related to quantities, proportions, or the idea of accumulation. In this respect, Fourcade (2016) suggests that "cardinal judgments allow for comparison but solely in terms of an underlying number of elements" (p. 177). This principle is also commonplace amongst large-scale assessment programs. For instance, the phrase: "In PISA 2012, Mexican students achieved a national mean of 413 points in math, whereas in the 2015 round, they achieved a national mean of 408 points in this same domain" implies a cardinal judgment. The difference between these two rounds is a 5-point spread. In this case, the relevance is on the overall aggregation or degradation of the mean. In some instances, cardinality becomes a fixation, in these cases, aggregation is usually employed as an ends per se, whereas higher purposes for aggregating are undermined or overlooked.

The third principle proposed by Fourcade (2016) is ordinality. This principle is bound to the ordering into a hierarchy between things, people or qualities. The author argues that

> unlike nominal differences, ordinal relations imply different valuations, a distinction of (at minimum) two levels, highest and lowest, above and below ... unlike cardinal judgments, which focus on magnitudes, ordinal judgments are interested in relative ranks, no matter the size of the difference. (Fourcade, 2016, p. 178)

Ordinal judgments seek numerical commensuration as a form to avoid the subjectivity of issues revolving around the criteria for comparison, hence reducing the process to a mere quantification exercise. This principle is at play in large-scale assessment programs, especially in the ranking of students, schools and education systems, based solely on the numeric scores obtained in different domains. For instance, Singapore occupies the first place in the 2015 PISA round regarding both math and science, whereas Dominican Republic occupies the 72nd position (last place) amongst both OECD and non-OECD members (OECD, 2016a).

Finally, Fourcade (2016) argues that all three of these principles enable comparisons within the larger society. Some comparisons also come about as the result of the intersection between these principles. In this book I will be arguing that these principles and the practices outlined above are key elements to be found in the governance practices at distinct scales in Mexico.

3 Conclusions

In this chapter I have presented and discussed a wide and varied array of literatures regarding large-scale assessments. The main focus of this chapter was the analysis of publications that focus particularly on the intersection between governance and large-scale assessments. This analysis revealed two big issues: (a) the effects of these intersections on policies in national settings, and (b) the mechanisms through which large-scale assessments have carried out governing activities. Whilst these literatures are important, I have argued that the field requires further and detailed explication regarding: (1) nuanced understandings of how this is occurring at distinct scales within national settings, not only at the national scale; (2) the implications for governing in contexts where several large-scale assessments with distinct ontologies coexist; and (3) more detailed explication regarding the ontology of comparisons as a mode of governing. Finally, in an attempt to contribute to these discussions, I have introduced a set of theoretical resources which will be deployed by this research to help explain how is it that they figure as pedagogical tools in the enhancement of large-scale assessment as governing tools at distinct scales within the Mexican context.

Mexico's Cacophony or Harmony of Large-scale Assessments?

Large-scale assessment programs such as PISA, ERCE and PLANEA, which operate in Mexico today, and which focus upon student achievement, would appear to coincide to a noticeable degree with the aspirations agreed for the data they each produce. These aspirations can be sorted into four main purposes according to their claims: generating data so as to (a) aid policy decisions; (b) contribute to education practice improvement; (c) inform public opinion about the state of learning of their education systems; and (d) develop indicator databases for accountability, and for wider research purposes.

Keeping in mind the aims and questions of this book, I focus on the first two of the purposes outlined above. Specifically, I ask what assumptions and claims are made regarding how these large-scale tests might aid policy, on the one hand, and how might they contribute to improvements in education practice, on the other. This chapter offers important insights for research question one: What are the histories, politics and governance arrangements of the current large-scale assessment regimen in Mexico aimed at supplying evidence for aiding policy decisions and education practice improvement?

The aim of this chapter will be threefold. I will begin by introducing and discussing each of the LSAs implicated in this book, with particular emphasis on what, following Pawson and Tilly (1997), call their program ontology. Second, I will engage in an extensive review of the publications from each assessment program so as to identify and discuss assumptions and evidence regarding large-scale assessments aiding policy decisions and contributing to education practice improvement. Third, I will discuss how the notions of "policy decisions" and "education practices" have been embraced by large-scale assessments, yet at the same time these programs have avoided discussing and defining them. Furthermore, I will reflect on what this enterprise could be a case of, and how I have framed these concepts for conducting the empirical part of this book.

1   Large-scale Assessment Programs in Mexico

The first national large-scale assessments within the field of education in Mexico date back to 1972. During this period, variants of these tools were used as a means for selecting students for admissions to post-secondary schools (Martinez-Rizo & Silva-Guerrero, 2016). In 1984 the federal government began employing large-scale tests in some schools to gauge students' achievement levels at the end of each compulsory education stage: preschool, primary and lower secondary (INEE, 2015).

The 1990s can be understood as an important period in the field of international large-scale assessments for this Aztec nation. First, in 1995 Mexico participated for the first and only time in the Trends in International Mathematics and Science Study (TIMSS), developed by the International Association for the Evaluation of Educational Achievement (IEA). This was then followed by Mexico's participation in the first Regional Comparative and Explanatory Study round (PERCE for its acronym in Spanish), conducted by Latin American Laboratory for Assessment of the Quality of Education (LLECE for its acronym in Spanish) under the auspices of the Regional Office for Latin America and the Caribbean of the United Nations Educational, Scientific and Cultural Organization (OREALC-UNESCO). Finally, in 1997 Mexico joined the Program for International Student Assessment (PISA) consortium under the auspices of the Organization for Economic Cooperation and Development (OECD). It conducted its first PISA round in the year 2000.

Since the 1990s, Mexico has participated actively in two international large-scale assessment programs: ERCE at the regional Latin-American scale, and PISA at the global scale. In addition, since 2004, Mexico has operated and conducted its own formal and periodic national assessments carried out by the Secretariat for Public Education (SEP for its acronym in Spanish), the now extinct National Institute for Education Evaluation (INEE for its acronym in Spanish), and the National Commission for the Continuous Improvement of Education (MEJOREDU INEE for its acronym in Spanish). The current national large-scale assessment is administered under the name of National Plan for Learning Assessment (PLANEA for its acronym in Spanish). Table 4.1 provides further details regarding these assessments.

Table 4.1 illustrates the scale, sponsor-organizations, targeted populations, application rounds, assessment domains and most importantly, what could best be described as their program ontology (Pawson & Tilly, 1997), that is to say the logic of how this program is to work. Despite the remarkably similar aspirations claimed for the data they produce, each of these assessments espouses a distinctive program ontology; for instance, human rights, human capital and public accountability.

As it was discussed in Chapter 2, this book draws upon the work of Pawson and Tilley (1997) regarding the idea of program ontology. According to Pawson (2008), program ontologies are shaped by two features: (1) generative mechanisms, that

TABLE 4.1   Large-scale assessment programs in Mexico

Program	Population	Round	Domains assessed	Program ontology
PISA International OECD	15.3–16.2 year-olds 9th and 10th grade	2000, 2003, 2006, 2009, 2012, 2015, 2018, 2021–2022	Literacy Math Science	Human Capital
ERCE Regional OREALC- UNESCO	3rd & 4th grade 3rd & 6th grade 3rd & 6th grade 3rd & 6th grade	PERCE 1997 SERCE 2006 TERCE 2013 ERCE 2019	Reading Writing Math Science Socio and emotional	Human Rights
PLANEA National SEP-INEE	3rd, 6th, 9th & 12th grade	2015, 2016, 2017, 2018, 2019, 2022	Literacy Math	Public Accountability or Educational Accountability

is the reasoning, resources and restraints that lead to action; and (2) contiguous contexts. Given that each assessment program in Mexico has a distinct ontology, and these are likely to influence the ways in which they operate and their outcomes at distinct scales regarding policy decisions and education practices, I will elaborate on this feature of each program in the following paragraphs.

First, I will address the program ontology of PISA – that of human capital – which is tightly linked to the ethos of the OECD and rests on their assumptions about the causes of economic growth and wider societal wellbeing (OECD, 1999). This relationship must be understood in the light of the aftermath of World War II, and the development of its key organizations (see Chapter 2). In this regard, Bürgi and Tröhler (2018) argue that during the post-war period, and through strategic organizations such as RAND, OEEC and later on the OECD, "education was conceptualized as one of the central keys for development and progress" (p. 77). It is important to notice that development and progress in this context were largely viewed and promoted as equivalents to economic growth and expansion.

Further key events and publications from the early 1960s – such as Techniques for Forecasting Future Requirements of Scientific and Technical

Personnel – made the case that the development and progress of nations into the future would strongly rely on their technological and scientific capacity. Thus, education and education policy were viewed as central so as to foster the development of these capacities, skills and knowledges (Bürgi & Tröhler, 2018).

The principles and reasoning embraced by the project erected in the post-World War II order were boosted by human capital theory. With regard to this development, Tikly and Barrett (2011) argue that in promoting a human capital approach the "rationale for investing in education (including more recently education quality) lies in the contribution that education quality can make to economic growth" (p. 4). Half a century earlier, Schultz (1961) had promoted the idea that "the quality of human effort can be greatly improved and its productivity enhanced" (p. 1), mainly through education. Furthermore, Schultz asserted that human capital is in great part "the product of investment and, combined with other human investment, predominantly accounts for the productive superiority of the technically advanced countries" (Schultz, 1961, p. 3). These ideas regarding the 'expenditure' or 'investment' in people and relying on their 'returns' in favor of economic growth were embraced by the OEEC and were put to work as part of their economic development agenda.

In the transition from the OEEC to the OECD in 1961, many of the core values, attributes, principles, and agenda of the first were transferred onto the latter (Bürgi & Tröhler, 2018), especially those associated with economic affairs. Robertson et al. (2007) argue that for the large influential multilateral agencies "human capital theory remains the dominant theory that provides the justification for much of the activity of the World Bank in the education sector and the OECD" (p. 19). This book argues that human capital is not only the dominant theory in the OECD but, moreover, it constitutes the program ontology of one of the most important assets of this organization today; that of PISA. This can be noted in several of their publications. For instance, in the initial set of PISA readings concerning the opening round (2000), the very first paragraph of the first content page states that:

> Compelling incentives for individuals, economies and societies to raise levels of education have been the driving force for governments to improve the quality of educational services. The prosperity of countries now derives to a large extent from their human capital and the opportunities available for their citizens to acquire knowledge and skills that will enable them to continue learning throughout their lives.
>
> All stakeholders – parents, students, those who teach and run education systems as well as the general public – need to be informed on how well their education systems prepare students to meet the challenges of the future.

> In response to the need for cross-nationally comparable evidence on student performance, the OECD has launched the Program for International Student Assessment (PISA). PISA represents a new commitment by governments to monitor the outcomes of education systems in terms of student achievement on a regular basis and within an internationally accepted common framework. PISA aims to provide a new basis for policy dialogue and for collaboration in defining and operationalizing educational goals – in innovative ways that reflect judgements about the skills that are relevant to adult life. (OECD, 2003b, p. 3)

In these opening statements, we can see that the OECD (a) "normalizes" their human capital stance, referring to it as a driving force that (b) creates a necessity for stakeholders to be informed; and (c) offers a solution, based on its instrument PISA. Moreover, it justifies the existence and relevance of PISA in terms of what it can do for building human capital and thus the "prosperity" of nations. It is also important to note that the rhetoric regarding "meeting the challenges of the future", "prosperity of countries", and notions of "human capital" are in line with the discourses developed for the role of education in this process.

Early notions of human capital, such as those embraced by Schultz (1961), are viewed as strongly influenced by the work of Adam Smith in that they believed that workers' individual capabilities are some kind of capital which could be enhanced through appropriate stimulus (Keeley, 2007). Today, the OECD (1999, 2001b) claims to have embraced a broader conception of human capital which they define as "The knowledge, skills, competencies and attributes embodied in individuals that facilitate the creation of personal, social and economic well-being" (Keeley, 2007, p. 29; OECD, 2001b, p. 18). This definition is viewed as overcoming the limitations of those linked to previous assumptions about homo-economicus. However, it can be argued that many of the actions carried out by the OECD continue to make visible and amplify a strong emphasis towards human capital as expenditure on people for the sake of economic growth and financial expansion (Aghion et al., 2009; Schultz, 1961). For instance, this can be noted in their PISA program, and their focus on assessing and prioritizing literacy, along with science and mathematical skills, so as to give rise to scientific and technological knowledges as a means for being globally competitive. Furthermore, it can also be identified in a deeply rooted rhetoric across its reports which promotes the need for highly trained and skilled people in the specific domains that they assess, and which stand as a proxy for economic growth.

The ontology of ERCE-LLECE, that of human rights, is linked to its sponsor body, UNESCO, and its early mission of developing indicators for ensuring collaboration amongst common blocks of nations as a means for spreading education for all and achieving general wellbeing (Cussó & D'Amico, 2005; Roberson,

2012a). Tikly and Barrett (2011) argue that a human rights approach in the field of education is mostly "interested in the role of education in securing rights to education, rights in education and rights through education" (p. 5). These features can be identified in the publication of the second ERCE round of results. In this publication, it is argued that: "The evaluation and comparison of school performance developed by the Second Regional Comparative and Explanatory Study (SERCE) are assumed from the conceptualization of Education as a fundamental human right, as an inalienable public good and indispensable for the full development of the human being (UNESCO-OREALC, 2008b, p. 14). ERCE-LLECE reasoning estimates that by aligning themselves behind this principle, the countries of the Latin-American region adhere to, and share, what is collected and promoted by various international treaties, such as the Universal Declaration of Human Rights (UN General Assembly, 1948). In this respect, ERCE is promoted as a collaborative effort of Latin American countries to achieve human rights through education, on the one hand, and to offer insights and monitor the realization of the right to education, on the other.

Lastly, PLANEA's program ontology is not as evident as its counterparts. This requires a close and careful review of its purposes and aims in order to identify this feature. In this respect, INEE (2015) states that the general purpose of PLANEA is to "inform the extent to which students achieve mastery of a set of essential learnings at different times in compulsory education" (p. 11). Furthermore, INEE argues that the outcomes from this assessment will contribute to education improvement through: (a) informing society about the state of learning of students; (b) providing education authorities with relevant information for the monitoring, planning, programming and operation of the education system and its schools; (c) providing pertinent, timely and contextualized information to schools and teachers, to help improve their teaching practices and the learning of all their students; and (d) contributing through relevant information to the development of data-based guidelines for education improvement (INEE, 2015, p. 11). Based on the purpose and aims of PLANEA outlined above, I consider that this program's ontology is linked to public accountability in education theory or educational accountability (Anderson, 2005; Ranson, 1986).

During the Thatcherism era in England, 1979 to 1990, assumptions regarding accountability as a means for improving school performance began to emerge which drew upon the idea that "performance would improve if information about achievement is provided for the consumers of the service. Their reflective choices would serve to challenge weak institutions and confirm and reinforce successful schools" (Ranson, 1986, p. 77). Today, all four central aims of PLANEA revolve around the idea of 'being held to account' for the levels of mastery regarding essential learnings to different audiences, in other words what Ranson (2003) terms "Performative Accountability". In this enterprise, being accountable to and accounting for is viewed as the main trigger for bringing about a desired state of affairs. Here, it is important to note that Ranson (2003) makes an important distinction between accountability as "giving an account" or "being held to account". The first refers to the discursive relationships, whereas the latter implies providing reasons for one's actions along with the normative grounds where these are supported on (see also Giddens, 1984).

By way of contrast, PISA also relies strongly on its public accountability features, however its dominating and driving force for action is based on human capital which is a proxy for economic development. In the case of PLANEA, public accountability is seen as the main mediator for bringing about system change in terms of education quality. This in turn is viewed as the maximum goal (education quality), whereas in the case of PISA and ERCE, economic development or the full development of the human being are seen as the ultimate goal. Seemingly, PLANEA's ontology is largely instrumental.

Anderson (2005) draws attention to three forms of education accountability to which teachers have been subject to in current times. These are: (a) compliance with regulations, also orientated to meeting formal norms, regulations and bureaucracy; (b) adherence to professional norms, or in other words compliance with principles of social conventions concerning peers; and lastly, (c) results driven, better known as accountable to the broader public regarding students learning. Anderson notes that education agents are more and more concerned with results-based accountability. In results-based systems, students' learning failures are attributed to weaknesses in educational programs and practices rather than to students' characteristics and backgrounds (Anderson, 2005). High quality information is therefore portrayed as the solution to the system's problem.

All three current assessment programs, and in the national case its predecessors, have been operating concurrently since the mid 90s. Although they advocate similar and generic aspirations for the data they produce, their program ontology differs. In some cases, it may be argued that these ontological approaches are either incompatible at worst, or in tension or in conflict with each other, at best. For instance, human capital has a strong emphasis or inclination towards economic growth. The human capital part here means that human beings through education and learning are regarded as generating/driving economic productivity and financial expansion; an approach not always aligned with conceptions of education for the purposes of human development and as a human right. In the case of PISA and PLANEA, their program ontologies are compatible and can at times work together across distinct scales towards the achievement of a particular project. This will be discussed in more detail later on in this book (see Chapter 8).

The assessment arrangement that currently stands in Mexico is comprised of three LSAs with distinct ontologies, which coexist in the same context. In doing so, they raise many questions regarding their purposes, not to mention how they overcome their differences, and the nature of the outcomes of this arrangement on policy decisions and education practices. These and other concerns are central to this research and will be addressed latter on in this book. Before I do this, I will introduce each assessment program in the following sections of this chapter.

2   PISA

PISA was developed and launched by the OECD in 1997 (OECD, 2003a). The OECD (1999) argues that this program came about as a response to the demand from Member States for reliable and comparable indicators for monitoring learning amongst their education systems. Currently, PISA is operated by the Directorate for Education and Skills at the OECD, led by Dr Andreas Schleicher.

This program is comprised of a series of surveys that are administered to students, head-teachers and parents, in a three-year cycle, from OECD member and non-member countries. Surveys are applied to a national representative sample of schools per country or particular entity like a city (e.g. Toronto or Shanghai). In some cases, sub-national states or national regions participate as individual economies for the purposes of gaining the results of their particular setting. For instance, in the case of Mexico, all states participate in the national sample; however, in early PISA rounds some of them also paid the consortium for assessing an extra number of schools from their state so as to gain insights from this particular entity in relation to the overall framework. Other examples of this practice can be noted in the case of China, where Shanghai, Macao and Hong Kong participate in PISA as economies.

PISA evaluates students who are from 15- and 3-month-old to 16- and 2-month-old, and enrolled in formal secondary and upper secondary schools. The OECD considers that by assessing this age; "knowledge, skills and attitudes accumulated over approximately ten years of education is gained from an assessment at this time" (OECD, 2006, p. 7). This stage also constitutes, on average, the end of the compulsory education cycle amongst participating countries.

The exact number of students and schools who participate in PISA varies amongst countries, and from round to round. PISA mainly evaluates a range of different generic math, science and literacy key competencies and skills. In the latest PISA rounds, the OECD has introduced new components and

TABLE 4.2   Mexican PISA scores per round 2000–2015

	2000	2003	2006	2009	2012	2015	2018
Math	387	385	406	419	413	408	409
Ranking	35th	36th	45th	46th	50th	59th	61st
Science	422	405	410	416	415	416	419
Ranking	34th	37th	47th	46th	52nd	61st	57th
Reading	422	400	410	425	424	423	420
Ranking	34th	37th	42nd	44th	49th	58th	53rd

Note: The 2000 PISA round was carried out with 32 participating nations, in 2002 11 more participants were tested. PISA 2003 round involved 41 countries; PISA 2006 round involved 57 countries; PISA 2009 round involved 65 countries; PISA 2012 round involved 65 countries; PISA 2015 round involved 73 countries; PISA 2018 involved 79.
SOURCE: PISA REPORTS (2000–2018), ORGANIZATION FOR ECONOMIC COOPERATION AND DEVELOPMENT

allied competencies, such as those related to financial education, and global citizenship.

There has now been a total of seven rounds of PISA since the year 2000. Table 4.2 shows the Mexican national mean scores in PISA per domain from the 2000 to the 2018 rounds.

2.1   *PISA Aspirations*

PISA is a special case because it emerges as a strong instrument with firm policy aims. It also brands itself as a global education system evaluator, based on assessing accumulated student competencies acquired throughout the entire compulsory education cycle (OECD, 1990, 2001a). This aim for the program has been clear and upfront since its beginning. However, as it will be discussed later, ever since its early publications, this OECD assessment has been gradually incorporating new discursive dimensions suggesting the aspiration to aid education improvement practices as well.

One of the first PISA framings can be found in Measuring Students Knowledge and Skills, A New Framework for Assessment (OECD, 1999). This publication was released one year before the first PISA testing round. The document offers key insights into PISA's aspirations, which are later picked up and elaborated in further OECD publications. In relation to its main aspiration of generating data for aiding policy decisions, the OECD (1999) claims that:

> While it is expected that many individuals in participating countries, including professionals and lay-persons, will use the – PISA – survey results

for a variety of purposes, the primary reason for developing and conducting this large-scale international assessment is to provide empirically grounded information which will inform policy decisions. (OECD, 1999, p. 7)

According to this statement, it can be noted that the OECD is clear that the primary reason of its assessment is to provide information so as to inform policy decisions regarding education in national settings. Nonetheless, there is also the additional acknowledgement and hope that the survey will also assist many people and many purposes. In reference to this, the OECD (1999) argues that comparative international analysis can:

> provide direction for schools' instructional efforts and for students' learning as well as insights into curriculum strengths and weaknesses. Coupled with appropriate incentives, they can motivate students to learn better, teachers to teach better and schools to be more effective. (OECD, 1999, p. 7)

In this second quotation, the OECD does not exactly claim that PISA, or the insights to be drawn from the comparative features that emerge from PISA, will enable these features. However, they do use this argument in their rationale and report, leaving this matter up for interpretation for those involved in school instruction and student learning. This move can be seen as an attempt on behalf of the OECD to try to inflate PISA's reach, or as a 'fishing' strategy to see what uses can be found for their PISA data.

In the set of reports concerning the 2000 PISA round, a strong emphasis on its policy aspirations can be noted. For instance, the first report (OECD, 2001a) includes a section, How PISA can inform policy. In this section it is argued that:

> PISA provides a broad assessment of comparative learning outcomes towards the end of compulsory schooling, which can both guide policy decisions and resource allocations, and provide insights into the factors that contribute to the development of knowledge and skills ... The international perspective of PISA offers policy-makers a lens through which to recognize the strengths and weaknesses of their own systems. (OECD, 2001, pp. 27–28)

Two years after this first report was issued, the OECD (2003b) released an extended version of this document. The new publication included an important addition; a focus on elaborating and highlighting the policy function of

PISA. This feature has since been maintained and forms a key part of all PISA results publications to date. It states; "the main features driving the development of PISA have been its: policy orientation, with design and reporting methods determined by the need of governments to draw policy lessons" (OECD, 2003b, p. 16). Interestingly, the section, How PISA can inform policy, included in the first report, was not integrated in any further publications. Seemingly, it was replaced by the latter.

Whilst the 2003 PISA reports incorporated important features in other areas, their stance concerning program aspirations has remained virtually the same as the 2000 extended report (OECD, 2004). In a significant breakthrough, the 2006 PISA results report comments that:

> In order to provide answers to these questions – e.g. to what extent have students learned fundamental scientific concepts and theories? – for policy makers and educators and to assist them with improving the teaching and learning of science, PISA provides a series of international benchmarks. (OECD, 2007, p. 32)

This is the first time in PISA publications where the OECD explicitly states that one of its intentions is assisting educators with improving teaching practices through PISA and the provision of benchmarks. From this moment, the OECD concentrated its efforts on projecting PISA as a multipurpose instrument.

With regards to PISA 2009, the document which accounts for the framework of this round, states: "In anticipating a range of options for reporting, the PISA reading literacy framework and assessment are designed to provide an array of data capable of richly informing the work of policy makers, educators, and researchers" (OECD, 2009, p. 78). Here the OECD recognizes a predetermined intention of generating data so as to inform the work of educators.

In the 2009 PISA Volume 1 publication of its results, the OECD acknowledges for the first time that their assessment cannot identify cause-and-effect relationships between inputs, processes and educational outcomes. However, they argue that "it can highlight key features in which education systems are similar and different, sharing those findings with educators, policy makers and the general public" (OECD, 2010a, p. 20). Educators are mentioned at this point again. However, the purpose of sharing findings with these audiences is not made explicit. Further on in this same document the OECD argues that: "As difficult as international comparisons are, they are important for educators" (OECD, 2010a, p. 34). In both of these quotations, the OECD emphasizes the relevance of their data for educators, although it does not mention for what purposes. However, in the 2012 PISA Volume 1 report, this matter is cleared up as the OECD (2014) claims that:

> Over the past decade, the OECD Program for International Student Assessment, PISA, has become the world's premier yardstick for evaluating the quality, equity and efficiency of school systems. But the evidence base that PISA has produced goes well beyond statistical benchmarking. By identifying the characteristics of high-performing education systems PISA allows governments and educators to identify effective policies that they can then adapt to their local contexts. (OECD, 2014, p. 3)

In this sense, the purpose of sharing comparisons, findings and policies is based on the assumption that policy makers and educators can adapt them to their local context. The OECD continues to elaborate on this matter and affirms that PISA is:

> an ongoing program that offers insights for education policy and practice, and that helps monitor trends in students' acquisition of knowledge and skills across countries and in different demographic subgroups within each country. PISA results reveal what is possible in education by showing what students in the highest-performing and most rapidly improving education systems can do. The findings allow policy makers around the world to gauge the knowledge and skills of students in their own countries in comparison with those in other countries, set policy targets against measurable goals achieved by other education systems, and learn from policies and practices applied elsewhere. (OECD, 2014, p. 24)

In this 2012 PISA report the OECD (2014) advances a dual aspiration; that of generating and providing data both for policy, on the one hand, and for teachers and their practices, on the other. This second component is now clearly visible alongside the policy aim. In the 2015 PISA reports, the OECD continues with a similar discourse, arguments and rationale advanced in the 2012 series (OECD, 2016a).

Noteworthy, PISA's aspirations of generating data for aiding teachers and practice improvement is clearer in the 2016 OECD publication, Ten Questions for Mathematics Teachers (...) and how PISA can help answer them. This publication claims that:

> While many national centers and governments try to ensure that the schools and teachers participating in the assessments get constructive

> feedback based on PISA results, most of the key messages published in
> the PISA reports don't make it back to the classroom, to the teachers who
> are preparing their country's students every day. Until now. (OECD, 2016b,
> p. 3)

This booklet is the first of its kind published by the OECD. It is a reading dedicated to educators aimed at helping them improve their practices. The publication takes findings from the 2012 PISA round then analyzes and organizes them
into ten questions which discuss what is known about mathematics teaching
and learning around the world and how this data might help teachers in their
mathematics classes. The questions incorporate teaching strategies, student
learning strategies, curriculum coverage and various student characteristics,
and how they are related to student achievement in mathematics and to each
other. The booklet concludes with a section entitled "What can teachers do?"
that provides concrete, evidence-based suggestions to help them develop their
mathematics teaching practice (OECD, 2016b).

In the PISA 2018 results report, the OECD argues that their initial intention
with PISA was not to create an accountability apparatus, but to help policy
makers and educators to look outwards to other systems, schools, and teachers
as a means to bring about change. In this regard, they claim that; "In essence,
PISA counts what counts, and makes that information available to educators
and policy makers so they can make more informed decisions" (OECD, 2019b,
p. 5). This narrative puts forward important discursive issues that deserve
unpacking, particularly with regard to the idea that the OECD "counts what
counts"; this will be picked up in further chapters when I talk about vertical
vision.

This short review of the aims of the OECD's PISA over time illustrates relevant features concerning its aspirations around what and how change is to
come about. In terms of policy orientation aims, PISA has been more or less
consistent with its discourse. Whereas in relation to its aspirations for education practice improvement, these have been somewhat ambiguous and have
evolved over PISA cycles. Earlier on in the book I asked two fundamental questions. First, what type of assessment does PISA claim that it is? And, second,
does PISA imply that it generates data for aiding decision-making concerning
policy and practice improvement? For the first question, we can conclude that
PISA is a highly ambitious program which has tactically employed an ambiguous discourse, positioning itself first as school system evaluator, and from
there to extend its reach into the classroom and in relation to teacher practice.
This provides the answer to the second question; that through data on system
performance, teachers can alter their teaching practices.

3   ERCE-LLECE

Initial meetings that led to the creation of the consortium known as the Latin American Laboratory for Assessment of the Quality of Education, LLECE for its acronym in Spanish, were held in Mexico City in 1994, by UNESCO's Regional Bureau for Education in Latin America and the Caribbean – OREALC for its acronym in Spanish – (OREALC-UNESCO, 1998). LLECE is overviewed by a Governing Board comprised of one representative from each participating nation and members of OREALC and UNESCO. The laboratory has administered four test rounds during the past 27 years; First Regional Comparative and Explanatory Study (PERCE) from 1995 to 1997, with a participation of 11 countries; Second Regional Comparative and Explanatory study (SERCE) in 2006, with a participation of 16 countries and the sub-national state of Nuevo Leon in Mexico as an economy; the Third Regional Comparative and Explanatory Study (TERCE) in 2013, with the participation of 15 countries, and also the special involvement of the state of Nuevo Leon; and the fourth Regional Comparative and Explanatory study (ERCE), with the participation of 16 countries. The Governing Board has decided that from this last evaluation onwards, the name will remain the same, ERCE, for its acronym in Spanish. In this respect, ERCE is the assessment and LLECE is the group or consortium that develops it, whereas OREALC-UNESCO is the sponsor body who overviews the enterprise.

PERCE assessed students from third and fourth grade of primary school. However, in SERCE the focus shifted to third and sixth graders. Subsequent testing rounds carried on assessing these latter grades. ERCE is applied to a representative sample of primary schools in each participating country. Since the third ERCE round – TERCE – the main test was accompanied by a series of contextual questionnaires for students, parents, teachers and head teachers. This program assesses contents and competencies developed from a core common curriculum in Latin America, taking into account knowledge domains such as reading, writing, math, and natural science. Noteworthy, for the first time ever ERCE 2019 assessed a range of social and emotional skills linked to empathy, school self-regulation and openness to diversity (OREALC-UNESCO, 2021). The results of Mexico in this program are presented in Tables 4.3 and 4.4.

3.1   *ERCE-LLECE Aspirations*

The evidence produced by LLECE in all of its ERCE testing rounds targets an audience comprised of policy makers, head teachers, educators, parents, and educational researchers. This can be noted in the first PERCE report namely, First International Comparative Study on Language and Mathematics, and

TABLE 4.3   PERCE results in math and language 1997

Subject	Math		Language	
School year	3rd	4th	3rd	4th
PERCE	236	256	232	252
PERCE average	245	259	247	264

Note: PERCE only evaluated the areas of math and language.
SOURCE: OREALC-UNESCO (1998)

TABLE 4.4   SERCE, TERCE, ERCE results in math, reading, writing and science (2006, 2013)

Subject	Math		Reading		Writing		Science	
School year	3rd	6th	3rd	6th	3rd	6th	3rd	6th
SERCE 2006	532.1	541.6	530.4	529.9	n.a.	n.a.	n.a.	510.6
SERCE average	490.6	492.1	491.2	494.2	n.a.	n.a.	n.a.	479.8
TERCE 2013	741	768	718	735	2.91	3.26	n.a.	732
TERCE average	700	700	700	700	2.86	3.19	n.a.	700
ERCE 2019	722	758	713	726	n.a.	n.a.	n.a.	726
ERCE average	798	697	696	796	n.a.	n.a.	n.a.	702

Note: SERCE and TERCE incorporated the evaluation of additional subjects. However, Mexico does not participate in third grade science. The grading system has changed from PERCE to SERCE.

Associated Factors in Third and Fourth Grades. In this respect, OREALC-UNESCO (1998) claims that:

> The First Comparative Study has been designed to be of benefit to a number of groups. Three come immediately to mind. The first consists of education policy makers in respective countries. The study provides useful information for the creation or modification of policies which produce qualitative improvements in education within the Region. The second group is comprised of people involved in education within the ambit of families, schools and the classroom. School directors, teachers, parents and students will discover where their country lies within the regional Latin American education context. We expect that the study will be

especially meaningful for school directors and teachers, providing them with the basis to learn about and to improve the education of their students, based on the successes and limitations identified not only in their own countries, but within the other countries in the Region as well. (pp. 8–9)

According to the previous segment of the LLECE-PERCE report, its aspirations are focused on two issues: (a) supporting diverse groups and agents linked to the creation and modification of policies (in other words, policy decisions), and (b) contributing to the improvement of the education of their students, which can be understood as the improvement of education practices. These aspirations are narrowed down and refined in the first report of SERCE – the second LLECE round. The discourse in the first SERCE publication is more explicit as to the functions that this program aspires. Here, OREALC-UNESCO (2008) states that:

> One of the central activities of the Regional Bureau – LLECE – is generating and disseminating knowledge to inform decision-making on initiatives that promote educational policies and practices aimed at strengthening the quality of education in the various countries … The major findings of SERCE's Second Regional Comparative and Explanatory Study (SERCE, 2002–2008), are presented in this report. We hope they will facilitate decision-making and foster the implementation of educational policies and practices that make possible a faster and more assertive transition to quality education without exclusion in the region. (p. 5)

As mentioned above, this statement is much more upfront and clear about the aspirations of ERCE. In the third LLECE round, namely TERCE, the main report reinforces the arguments previously advanced in PERCE and SERCE, but it now incorporates two important additions. In this regard, the TERCE results report comments that this assessment:

> not only aims to provide information regarding the quality of education in the region, but also focuses on raising information that can identify the factors that are associated with learning and, from there, generate inputs to feed decision-making, the design and improvement of policies and practices in education. (OREALC-UNESCO, 2016a, p. 9)

One of the important additions of the third ERCE (TERCE) round is a set of four booklets. This material was created aiming to directly help teachers with their instructional practices. In this respect, OREALC-UNESCO (2016c) claims that:

> There is a broad consensus that ratifies that teachers are the most important actors in student learning achievement. For this reason, the OREALC / UNESCO Santiago presents the collection Contributions for Teaching, in the four pedagogical areas covered by the TERCE (Reading, Writing, Mathematics and Natural Sciences). These publications constitute a powerful tool for the strengthening of the teaching capacities, by providing orientations to this important group that allows them to adjust their pedagogical practices in the classroom. (p. 5)

The second addition advanced in the TERCE assessment round consists of a document entitled Recommendations for Educational Policies in Latin America based on TERCE. This document is presented as a technical instrument to support decision-making in educational policy matters (OREALC-UNESCO, 2016b, p. 14).

The ERCE website provides some hints that publications concerning their fourth testing round remain in production. However, those that have been released present a noticeable degree of consistency with earlier publications but, recontextualized in the light of recent advancements. In this regard, OREALC-UNESCO (2021) claim that:

> we are committed to continuing to strengthen cooperation between countries and to fostering the generation of knowledge and information to guide education policies. This, with the aim of advancing towards quality education with equity in the region, as established in Development Goal 4 of the 2030 Agenda. (p. 4)

In sum, it can be noted that in distinction to PISA, LLECE – even in the release of the first PERCE report is unambiguous as to its aspirations concerning aiding policy and practice. Like PISA, these aspirations have been refined as the program has evolved.

4   PLANEA and Predecessors

In the year 2015 the Secretary of Public Education (SEP) in Mexico, in collaboration with the National Institute for Education Evaluation (INEE), launched its new national large-scale assessment program – PLANEA (for its acronym in Spanish), translated into English it would read "National Plan for Learning Assessment". PLANEA's role was to take over the function of two previous large-scale assessment programs in Mexico namely: Educational Quality and Achievement Tests (EXCALE) and National Assessment of Academic Achievement in Schools (ENLACE). These programs were cancelled as a result of allegations of the negative impact on schools that included teaching to the test, copying during tests, asking low performing students to not attend school during examination week, and introducing a system of performance-based pay which did not result in substantial improvements to the education system (Backhoff & Contreras, 2014).

Similar to PISA and ERCE, PLANEA is comprised of a main test or series of tests administered to students, along with a set of contextual questionnaires for students, teachers and head teachers. There are three modalities in which PLANEA is administered to students in Mexico. The main modality of PLANEA (ELSEN) and which is the central variant focus of this research is applied nation-wide at the end of each compulsory education level, from kindergarten to upper secondary schools. Specifically, this involves the (a) third grade of kindergarten, (b) sixth grade of primary school, (c) third grade of secondary school, and (d) sixth semester or third grade of upper secondary schools. This program assesses levels of achievement regarding curriculum competencies and learning standards on two learning domains: (a) mathematics and (b) literacy. The two additional formats in which PLANEA is administered (INEE, 2015a, 2016) to schools and students are briefly outlined:

a.   ELSEN (Achievement Evaluation referred to the National Education System). This format is applied by INEE to representative sub-national and national samples of students and schools at the end of each compulsory education level in 3-year cycles.

b.   ELCE (Achievement Evaluation referred to Schools). This format is applied by the National Secretariat of Education in coordination with the Sub-National Secretariats. It is administered annually to samples of 35 students from those grades that comprise the end of each compulsory education level.

c.   EDC (Census Diagnostic Evaluation). This format is applied by primary schools at the beginning of the school year to all students that pass to fourth grade of primary school.

Although there are three different formats of PLANEA, only the ELSEN results are made public nationally. Given that PLANEA ELCE and EDC are applied by

TABLE 4.5   PLANEA ELSEN national scores

LSAS program	6th grade		9th grade		12th grade	
Knowledge domain	Literacy	Math	Literacy	Math	Literacy	Math
National mean 2015	500.0	500.0	500.0	500.0	n.a.	n.a.
National mean 2017	n.d.	n.d.	495	497	500	500
National mean 2018	501	503	n.a.	n.a.	n.a.	n.a.
National mean 2019	n.a.	n.a.	n.a.	n.a.	n.a.	n.a.
National mean 2020	n.a.	n.a.	n.a.	n.a.	n.a.	n.a.

Note: (a) This table only contains results from the ELSEN PLANEA variant; (b) PLANEA for preschool (3rd grade) was applied in the 2017–2018 school year, but results were not published due to a shift in federal administration.
SOURCE: HTTP://PLANEA.SEP.GOB.MX

local agents and institutions, national authorities consider that these formats lack the rigor and reliability for comparability and accountability purposes (INEE, 2015). Hence, these are only accessible to schools and local education agents. To date there has been at least one PLANEA ELSEN application in each compulsory education level in Mexico. The mean results have been released in different dates and years. Table 4.5 shows the main results per grade age and knowledge domain.

4.1   PLANEA *Aspirations*

As mentioned above, before PLANEA, there were two concurrent national large-scale assessments, namely EXCALE and ENLACE. Both of these programs shared some common objectives and aspirations (Martinez-Rizo, 2015a). The EXCALE program was founded in 2004 and its first test was administered in 2005. This assessment was produced by the INEE with the purpose of:

> enhancing the diagnosis of student performance as a whole, not individually. It also aims to provide an assessment of education status at the national scale. It is a macro initiative at the national level sought to influence: public policies, the updating and adaptation of study plans – curriculum-, psycho-pedagogical mediations, teacher training programs, and support and promote academic activities and the lives of students, teachers, parents and authorities. (Martinez-Rizo, 2015b, p. 44)

As opposed to EXCALE, ENLACE was developed by the National Secretariat of Education in Mexico. With regards to this program, Martinez-Rizo (2015c) argues that:

> The decision to develop these tests was taken with the idea that they would serve above all so that teachers and parents of elementary and secondary students could have information about the level of learning of each child in a few important topics of two areas key to the curriculum. Aiming to timely address the support needs of each one of them. (p. 28)

ENLACE's aspirations initially were mostly focused on the micro level. However, this did not remain for long. Shortly after this assessment was enforced, its results were employed as key information so as to decide the entrance and promotion to a program for salary increments for teachers in the Magisterial Career. In this regard, the OECD (2011) has argued that since the first assessment round in 2006, the yearly census-based ENLACE assessment has become a cornerstone of public accountability and school improvement efforts in Mexico. The Ministry of Education also explored the use of student achievement results from ENLACE for developing school-level value-added initiatives.

Both ENLACE and EXCALE were cancelled in 2014 following allegations of education corruption. Proponents argued that the tests had become corrupted because of: (a) teaching to the test practices; (b) variety of cheating during tests practices; (c) test score inflation; and (d) misuse of test outcomes. In 2015, the National Secretariat of Education in collaboration with the National Institute for Education Evaluation launched a new joint program named PLANEA. This assessment was advertised as a next-generation large-scale assessment program, which took into account the best of ENLACE and EXCALE whilst leaving behind their undesirable defects and habits.

Similar to PISA and ERCE, but at a national scale, PLANEA has made public its aspirations. These can be reviewed in different leaflets, posters and official documents. PLANEA claims that it aims to:

> (a) inform society about the state of learning of students; (b) provide education authorities with relevant information for the monitoring, planning, programming and operation of the education system and its schools; (c) provide pertinent, timely and contextualized information to schools and teachers, to help improve their teaching practices and the learning of all their students; and (d) contribute through relevant information to the development of data-based guidelines for education improvement. (INEE, 2015a, p. 11; 2016a, p. 9)

PLANEA has been operating in Mexico since 2015. It is a fairly recent assessment, so that its overall aspirations have remained virtually the same since its launch. However, as it is in effect a renewed and improved version of its predecessors – ENLACE and EXCALE – its consequences on policies and practices will require much scrutiny and discussions.

5   LSAs and Claims to Aiding Policy Decisions and Education Practices

An interesting finding that is common to all of the three large-scale assessment programs addressed in this study is their vagueness around what they mean by policy decisions and education practices. PISA, ERCE and PLANEA all claim that they aspire to aid policy decisions and education practices. However, they neither define nor discuss how these are envisaged. Given that there is an array of different forms of policy decisions and education practices, not defining them leads to the question – why? Is it that they fear treading on the toes of national education systems? Or is it that the solution is partly found in the instrument itself – that to improve means looking at those countries or schools which are above, or clustered together, as the answer to the question. Or is it that the program ontology – with its singular focus – provides the answer to the question, and that what is on offer is a one size fits all response to what are effectively diverse schools, with diverse populations and problems?

Not defining "policy decisions" and "education practices" is problematic from a governance stance because discussions around their political and contested nature are avoided and thus are projected as merely instrumental, with a false sense of objectivity. Education governance is concerned with the regulation, provision, and funding of education services (Dale, 1997). Large-scale assessments such as PISA, ERCE and PLANEA are viewed as governance instruments in that through influencing, shaping and mediating policy decisions and education practice they govern distinct aspects of the education sector. However, if policy decisions and education practices are not defined but instead employed loosely, it is difficult to track and question what these instruments are doing, how they are doing it, and for what purposes. One way of analyzing this situation is viewing it as a flattening maneuver. By flattening here, I mean the tendency by these LSA to view the world out there as a homogenous terrain. As a result, it now becomes difficult to examine their historical, political and ideological differences and agendas (Scott, 1998). That is, policy decisions are just policy decisions irrespective of what lies behind them in terms of beliefs and values, and what these are a proxy for. And education practices are seen ontologically flat (Robertson, 2012b) with no relations to higher purposes such as those linked to economic expansion or human development.

In response to this major negligence, and to inform the reader of this book how this research views and has inquired policy decisions and education practices as part of the empirical component of this book, at distinct scales and units of analysis inside the Mexican context, in the following paragraphs I will elaborate on this matter.

From a generic approach, Dente (2014) defines policy decisions as "the process of choice between alternative ways to solve a collective problem" (p. 8). This definition implies that the aim of policy decisions is in fact to solve problems; however, this is not always the case. For example, policy decisions can be made to reproduce or perpetuate certain views or the status quo (Robertson & Dale, 2015b). This by no means represents or guarantees a solution to a collective problem. The notion of policy decisions employed in this research is framed by the characteristics of education policies, which are conceived by Robertson and Dale (2015b) to be "understood as concerned with bringing about a desired state of affairs in the future (which may be the maintenance of the status quo) through re/shaping education activities (such as knowledge production/reproduction), outputs and outcomes" (p. 3). Hence, this research views policy decisions as the "choices" made by different governance actors for bringing about a desired state of affairs in the future through the re/shaping or not of activities, outputs and outcomes.

In relation to education practices, Carr (1987) claims that "it seems to be assumed that the meaning of educational practice is so straightforward and clear that we can safely rely on our common-sense understanding when we use the term" (p. 163). Carr continues to argue that the important conceptual distinctions between notions of practice rely on the different kinds of actions and the forms of knowledge appropriate to them (Carr, 1987). The notion of education practices employed for the empirical part of this research is linked to the actions and interactions carried out by head teachers and teachers aimed and enhancing instruction. These can include but are not limited to teaching-instructional strategies, student learning strategies, learning environment management, behavior management, motivation mediations, lesson planning, assessment for learning, amongst others.

6　　Conclusions

In this chapter I have shown that each large-scale assessment program operating in Mexico today prioritizes a different social ontology in its program –

though they all refer with more or less emphasis on policy and practice as to solution to realizing change. This is turn raises important questions as to their separate and combined effects on education governance, policy decisions and education practices in Mexico. That said, PISA is the program that has been most ambiguous concerning the aspiration to generate data for aiding practice improvement, whilst the other two programs – ERCE and PLANEA – have been a bit more consistent in this respect.

I have also argued that PISA, ERCE and PLANEA fail to define or theorize what they mean by policy decisions and education practices whilst also providing insights as to how this book views and embraces these features in relation to LSAs. The insights provided in this chapter, in synergy with the theoretical highlights of Chapters 2 and 3, complete the foundations for addressing and understanding Chapters 5 to 7.

Local Scale

Teachers

This chapter is the first of the following three that will address the units of analysis, or cases, of this book. Chapter 5 entails the local scale of this multi-scalar investigation, and represents the first empirical entry point to this research. In this unit I focus on addressing the underlying logics, interactions and outcomes amongst LSA programs, their aspirations to aid education practice improvement through involving local education agents, processes, and settings, such as schools, educators and education practices. This enterprise is viewed by this research as a matter of governance in the sense that it addresses or relates to issues of education provision and regulation. As I have pointed out in Chapter 2, these are key aspects of education governance (Dale, 1997).

Recognizing the vast amount of publications that PISA, ERCE-LLECE, PLANEA and its predecessors have generated in the past 25 years, it is only fair to acknowledge that these programs have indeed kept their promise of producing data. Lots of it, warranting in popular parlance, the term "big data". Nevertheless, there are three pivotal questions that will be explored in this and the following chapter. The first question concerns the extent to which the generated data actually serves the purpose of aiding practice improvement. The second asks about to the unintended or collateral effects that this enterprise visits upon educators, and shapes their views concerning education, and its practices. The third question concerns the matter of what both of these issues mean in terms of education governance for the Mexican context. The overall purpose is to offer inputs for responding research questions two to four outlined in Chapter 1.

I have divided the following chapter into six main sections with several subsections. The first two sections provide a description of the participants involved in this unit of analysis and their contexts. A third section revisits the literature regarding the particular LSA aspiration of aiding education practice improvement and discusses some of its implications for this level of education. Section four sketches out an account of educators' knowledge and usage habits concerning the more recent data derived from LSAs in Mexico. A fifth section explores and reflects upon the unintended effects produced by LSAs at the local scale of this research. The last section of this chapter is a brief conclusion that draws together the insights from the chapter as a whole.

1 Sources of Data for Unit One

The unit of analysis addressed in this chapter draws upon an original data set comprised of four main sources. First, a series of LSA related-documents. Second, a paper-based survey answered by 319 educators from 34 primary, secondary and upper secondary schools, in five different cities within one subnational entity in northern Mexico. The name of the particular state and cities have been withheld for ethical reasons. Thirdly, it reports on 29 semi-structured interviews with educators (22) and pedagogical leaders (7) from the same cohort of surveyed schools. Lastly, a fourth source is used to provide data to all units of this research. This is comprised of interviews with a group (4) of Mexican academics and previous large-scale assessment program representatives from INEE who serve as expert commentators regarding several key findings of this research. The field work for this unit was conducted from August 2017 to March 2018.

The particular subnational entity was selected as the geographical site to develop the local scale of this research based upon opportunistic criteria. I had been a resident of this entity and had experience working for the State Secretariat of Education in various posts, such as: area coordinator, teacher educator and teacher at different education levels and schools. Consequently, I possess the requisite broad social capital within this context which enabled me to establish contact with diverse education agents for negotiating access into schools and participants from the different municipalities. Tables 5.1, 5.2 and 5.3 offer a detailed account of the participants per city, school level and current role, in addition to the numbers of surveyed and interviewed participants for each school.

The schools and teachers who participated in this unit of analysis are all from urban contexts. No rural schools were taken into account, mainly because of access and security issues. Of the 34 institutions who comprise the sample, 31 are public schools, and three are private for-profit education institutions.

2 Context of the Local Unit of Analysis

2.1 *The Sub National Entity*

The sub national entity is situated in the northern part of Mexico. Its primary economic activity is manufacturing industries. The state's strategic geographical position below the US makes it an attractive site for many foreign offshore manufacturing companies. The GDP per capita ranges around 6,797 US dollars per year (INEGI, 2017).

TABLE 5.1   Total survey participants per city and school type

City	School type	Actors	No. surveys
Primary schools			
City 1	Primary school 1	Teachers	10
	Primary school 2	Teachers	10
	Primary school 3	Teachers	9
City 2	Primary school 4	Teachers	10
	Primary school 5	Teachers	25
	Primary school 6	Teachers	6
	Primary school 7	Teachers	6
	Primary school 8	Teachers	17
City 3	Primary school 9	Teachers	6
	Primary school 10	Teachers	7
	Primary school 11	Teachers	9
	Primary school 12	Teachers	5
City 4	Primary school 13	Teachers	11
Secondary schools			
City 1	Secondary school 1	Teachers	6
	Secondary school 2	Teachers	8
	Secondary school 3	Teachers	9
	Secondary school 4	Teachers	8
	Secondary school 5	Teachers	11
City 2	Secondary school 6	Teachers	3
	Secondary school 7	Teachers	13
	Secondary school 8	Teachers	6
City 3	Secondary school 9	Teachers	5
	Secondary school 10	Teachers	6
	Secondary school 11	Teachers	9
	Secondary school 12	Teachers	7
City 4	Secondary school 13	Teachers	3
City 5	Secondary school 14	Teachers	14
Upper secondary schools			
City 1	Upper secondary school 1	Teachers	11
	Upper secondary school 2	Teachers	10
City 2	Upper secondary school 3	Teachers	21
	Upper secondary school 4	Teachers	10
City 3	Upper secondary school 5	Teachers	6
	Upper secondary school 6	Teachers	6
	Upper secondary school 7	Teachers	16
	Total teachers surveyed		**319**

TABLE 5.2 Sample and population of teachers and schools in the subnational state

No.	City	Sampled teachers	Population of teachers	Sampled schools	Population of schools
1	City 2	117	17,864	10	1,161
2	City 1	92	11,779	10	746
3	City 3	82	6,428	11	548
4	City 4	14	1,400	2	110
5	City 5	14	1,356	1	105
	Total	319	38,827	34	2,670

Note: Total number of schools, teachers and student in primary, secondary and upper secondary schools.

SOURCE: BASED ON OFFICIAL DATA

TABLE 5.3 Total interview participants

City	School type	Actors	Total
City 1	Primary school 1	1 head teacher, 1 third grade teacher, 1 sixth grade teacher	3
City 2	Primary school 5	1 head teacher, 1 third grade teacher, 1 sixth grade teacher	3
City 3	Primary school 11	1 head teacher, 1 third grade teacher, 1 sixth grade teacher	3
City 3	Primary school 9	1 head teacher	1
City	Secondary school 3	1 academic head, 1 Math teacher, 1 Science teacher, 1 Literacy teacher	4
City 1	Secondary school 5	1 superintendent, 2 pedagogical advisors	3
City 1	Upper secondary 1	1 academic head, 2 Maths-Science teachers, 2 Literacy teachers	5
City 2	Upper secondary 3	1 academic head, 2 Maths-Science teachers, 2 Literacy teachers	5
City 3	Upper secondary 5	2 Math-Science teachers	2
			29

Note: It was only possible to interview educators and leaders from the largest three cities: City 1, City 2 and City 3.

SOURCE: BASED ON RESEARCH SAMPLE

TABLE 5.4   Total population per city

No.	City	General population
1	City 2	1,641,570
2	City 1	988,417
3	City 3	486,639
4	City 4	102,406
5	City 5	96,734
	Total	3,315,766

SOURCE: INEGI (2017)

The population of this subnational entity is comprised of approximately three million inhabitants (INEGI, 2017). Table 5.4 shows an approximate distribution of habitants per city where this unit was developed.

2.2   *The Subnational Education System*

All 32 subnational entities in Mexico have their own State Secretariat of Education who, in collaboration with the national Secretariat (SEP), form a very complex architecture of education that is best described as a centralized-decentralized model (Mendoza, 2018; OECD, 2018b). To provide an example of this relationship, issues regarding curriculum design, decisions over participating in large-scale assessments, teacher evaluation and CPD, are decided and planned at the national level, whereas organizing, operating, and implementing aspects of these processes are left mainly to the sub-national entities. The latter have some discretion over local policy development. However, these must be applied parallel to national policies, and rarely can repeal or replace them. All of this is legally enshrined in the National Constitution of the United States of Mexico (3rd Article) and the General Law for Education.

The operation and running of schools is a responsibility of State Secretariats of Education, which are also organized in complex national-state-municipality model (Santiago et al., 2012). The State Secretariat at the subnational entity where the local scale was carried out is divided into the following sub secretariats namely for: (1) basic education; (2) middle and higher education; and (3) planning and administration. The sub secretariat for basic education is distributed into the directorates for: (a) preschool, (b) primary and (c) secondary education. Each municipality has its own respective department for preschool, primary and secondary education led by the state directorates. As to upper secondary education, there are eight different subsystems which are governed

TABLE 5.5   2016–2017 school year general statistics from the subnational

No.	City	Schools	Teachers	Students	General population
1	City 2	1,161	17,864	361,491	1,641,570
2	City 1	746	11,779	202,482	988,417
3	City 3	551	6,428	112,466	486,639
4	City 4	110	1,400	23,379	102,406
5	City 5	105	1,356	26,050	96,734
	Total	2,673	38,827	725,868	3,315,766

Note: Total number of schools, teachers and student in primary, secondary and upper secondary schools.
SOURCE: INEGI (2017)

TABLE 5.6   Schools per city and education level

No.	City	Primary	Secondary	Upper secondary	Total per city
1	City 2	680	286	195	1161
2	City 1	467	182	97	746
3	City 3	347	147	57	551
4	City 4	69	24	17	110
5	City 5	59	28	18	105
Total per level		1622	667	384	2673

SOURCE: OFFICIAL DATA FROM THE SUBNATIONAL STATE

in part by the sub-national state, and in part by the Federal level. Tables 5.5, 5.6 and 5.7 offer information regarding the number of schools, teachers, students and total population per each city in the subnational state where the local scale of this research was carried out.

3   Large-scale Assessments in the Subnational State

In relation to large-scale assessments, this subnational state willingly participated in all three ongoing programs in Mexico. The extent of its participation varies in

TABLE 5.7   Teachers per city and education level

No.	City	Primary	Secondary	Upper secondary	Total per city
1	City 2	6935	6058	4871	17864
2	City 1	4033	4441	3305	11779
3	City 3	2408	2167	1853	6428
4	City 4	492	444	464	1400
5	City 5	485	497	374	1356
Total per Level		14353	13607	10867	38827

Note: Total number of schools and teachers in primary, secondary and upper secondary schools per city.

SOURCE: OFFICIAL DATA FROM THE SUBNATIONAL STATE

TABLE 5.8   PISA scores

LSA program	PISA		
Knowledge domain	Math	Science	Literacy
Subnational mean 2003	384	401	391
National mean	385	405	400
Subnational mean 2006	411	412	416
National mean	406	410	410
Subnational mean 2009	416	415	429
National mean	419	416	425
Subnational mean 2012	415	417	428
National mean	413	415	424

SOURCE: MEXICO IN PISA (2012), INEE, PLANEA, GENERAL RESULTS (2015, 2017)

each case. For instance, this subnational entity has engaged in different versions of PLANEA and PISA (see Chapter 4). From 2003 to 2012 this state paid the PISA consortium an additional fee to test a larger sample of schools from this entity, so that aside from providing national scores, they could also offer the mean scores for the subnational entity. Tables 5.8, 5.9 and 5.10 show results from PISA 2003 to 2012, PLANEA from 2015 to 2017 and its predecessor, ENLACE, from 2006 to 2011. With regards to ERCE-LLECE, the subnational samples are small, thus, only national scores are provided, except for the case of the state Nuevo Leon.

TABLE 5.9   ENLACE scores

LSA program	Primary		Secondary	
Knowledge domain	Literacy	Math	Literacy	Math
Subnational mean 2006	498.3	495.9	n.a.	n.a.
National mean	500.0	500.0	n.a.	n.a.
Subnational mean 2007	512.3	507.9	n.a.	n.a.
National mean	507.8	509.3	n.a.	n.a.
Subnational mean 2008	517.1	507.1	n.a.	n.a.
National mean	513.8	512.8	n.a.	n.a.
Subnational mean 2009	528.5	522.9	497.5	493.9
National mean	520.4	522.6	504.5	506.0
Subnational mean 2010	540.7	533.9	476.9	490.5
National mean	532.2	529.5	488.6	510.7
Subnational mean 2011	545.6	536.3	475.8	491.5
National mean	542.6	544.1	485.6	513.0

SOURCE: HTTP://WWW.ENLACE.SEP.GOB.MX (WEBSITE NO LONGER ACTIVE)

TABLE 5.10   PLANEA ELSEN scores

LSA program	6th grade		9th grade		12th grade	
Knowledge domain	Literacy	Math	Literacy	Math	Literacy	Math
Subnational mean 2015	509.6	497.8	506.8	484.8	n.a.	n.a.
National mean	500.0	500.0	500.0	500.0	n.a.	n.a.
Subnational mean 2017	n.a.	n.a.	504	488	523	519
National mean	n.a.	n.a.	495	497	500	500
Subnational mean 2018	510	495	n.a.	n.a.	n.a.	n.a.
National mean	501	503	n.a.	n.a.	n.a.	n.a.
Subnational mean 2018	n.a.	n.a.	n.a.	n.a.	n.a.	n.a.
National mean	n.a.	n.a.	n.a.	n.a.	n.a.	n.a.

Note: This table only contains results from the modality of PLANEA named ELSEN, which is developed and applied by INEE.

SOURCE: HTTP://PLANEA.SEP.GOB.MX

After each assessment round, PISA and ERCE offer at least four types of publications which can be sorted into the following categories: (1) main results; (2) associated factors with student outcomes; (3) policy and practice recommendations; and (4) methodological and technical issues of surveys. These publications are mostly national and/or sub-national representations at best. Although it is not the main interest of this research, it is important to acknowledge that the variant of PISA-for-Schools does provide data per individual school (Lewis, 2017). However, this research focuses on, and considers only, the main PISA survey.

PLANEA differs from ERCE and PISA publication-wise. Considering that PLANEA is administered in three different variants (see Chapter 4), each one of these modalities has a set of different reports. For instance, after each PLANEA ELSEN round, MEJOREDU (previously INEE) and SEP publish a national report, which is not as extensive or detailed as the PISA or LLECE ones, but it does offer the main results per sub-national entity, service type, and overall scores. PLANEA ELCE releases a series of individual reports per group, school, municipality and state, which in addition to providing the main descriptive statistics of mean results, they also offer insights regarding those test items that were answered either correctly or incorrectly. Lastly, PLANEA ECD generates results per student. In this particular case it is important to notice that this variant of PLANEA is only applied to students from the fourth grade of primary school at the beginning of each schoolyear (INEE, 2016).

4   Large-scale Assessment Data for Aiding Practice Improvement

As discussed in Chapter 4, each large-scale assessment has its own unique program ontology, and a set of multiple aspirations for the data that they produce. The latter are extremely alike between programs. The unit of analysis addressed in this chapter is concerned with the particular LSA aspiration, which refers to generating data so as to inform education improvement practices. This aspiration is implied in all three ongoing programs in Mexico as discussed in detailed in Chapter 4 and synthesized in the following paragraphs.

Early signs of PISA's interest on generating data so as to aid education improvement practices can be noted in the main 2006 PISA results report. Here, the OECD insists that PISA provides an array of international benchmarks to assist policy makers and educators for improving the teaching and learning of science (OECD, 2007). This interest not only persisted but grew as the program evolved. The OECD finally opened up and went beyond their policy mediation role in a 2016 publication directed to math teachers (OECD, 2016b), in which this organization raises and answers a series of questions as a way of offering data to assist educators in improving their classroom practices. It is important to note that up until the moment of this publication, the OECD's approach to influencing change in terms of education practice was assumed to come about through policy mediation, much in line with their motto "Better policies for better lives". I argue that this publication (OECD, 2016b) paves the way into this new arena of influence for the OECD. Meanwhile ERCE, since its first round in 1997 (PERCE), affirms that their data will be "especially meaningful for school directors and teachers, providing them with the basis to learn about and to improve the education of their students" (OREALC-UNESCO, 1998, pp. 8–9). Similar to ERCE, PLANEA since its inception, maintains that it will "provide relevant, timely and contextualized information to schools and teachers, to help improve their practices of teaching and learning of their students" (INEE 2016, p. 9).

The previous claims might appear somewhat arrogant in the sense that they assert, without any hint of blushing, that they generate relevant and meaningful data so as to aid more insightful practice improvement. Given these statements, two sets of basic – though fundamental – questions come to mind. First, is this happening? If so, to what extent and how? Second, is large-scale assessment data meaningful for educators? And if so, in what ways? How is this manifested? What are the benefits and consequences of this? And what does this mean in terms of education governance? This set of questions will be addressed in the following sections of this chapter.

In essence, ERCE, PLANEA – and more recently PISA (OECD, 2016b), suggest that in order to improve education practices, educators and school leaders need data. Not surprisingly, this is the type of data that these programs happen to generate and offer. Large-scale assessment programs assume that educators will willingly search for their data, initiate a theoretical and technical dialogue with it, adapt it to their context and needs, and subsequently improve education practices. All of this, it might be pointed out, whilst carrying on with their already existing, often overloaded, daily work programs, without mentioning their more commandingly adverse work conditions (Chambers et al., 2019). Figure 5.1 displays visually the way in which large-scale assessment programs assume that their contribution to education practices functions.

As we will come to see, Figure 5.1 does not resemble accurately the reality of the large-scale assessment data-practice-improvement proposed model. The evidence collected from documents, the survey and interviews conducted at the local scale of this research suggest that the relationships between data, agents, processes and outcomes within this assessment arrangement are not linear at all. A more likely scenario to be found amongst schools and educators from this case is shown in Figure 5.2.

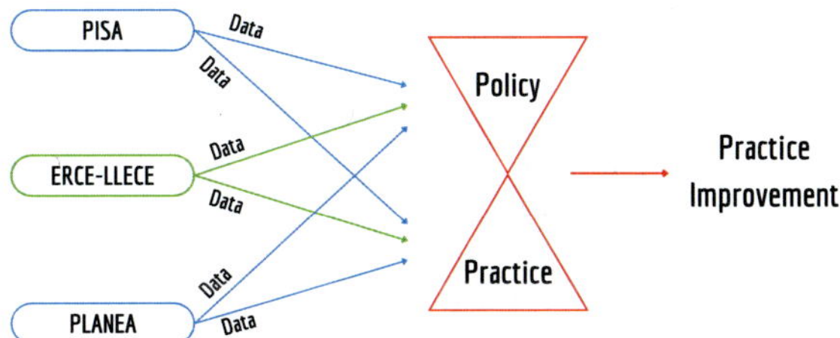

FIGURE 5.1   Assumed large-scale assessment education practice flux

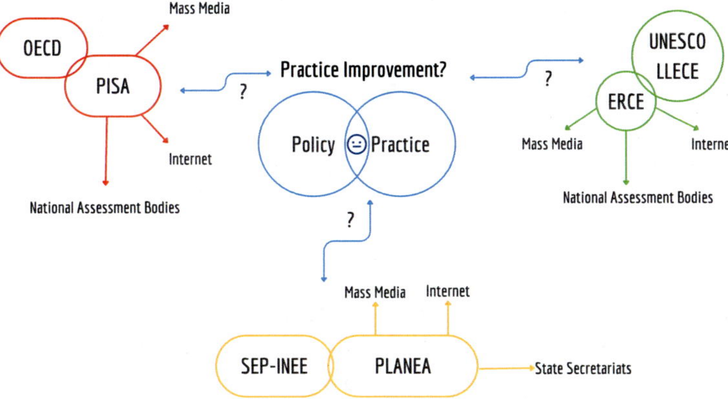

FIGURE 5.2   Large-scale assessment data for aiding practice improvement

Figure 5.2 was sketched taking into account the evidence collected from the research outlined above. This figure represents my interpretation of the dynamics occurring in the large-scale assessment ensemble in this particular subnational state. Furthermore, it illustrates several crucial and interesting findings. Considering the research's interest, here I emphasize three. First and foremost, large-scale assessment datasets arise and are put into circulation from multiple and distinct directions and timings, each of them with different degrees of resonance and capacity for reach, that in turn can mobilize and influence education. Second, even though large-scale assessment programs claim they generate data for aiding practice improvement, there is no clear or neatly ordered way in which this occurs. Assessment programs insist that lower-performing nations, education systems or schools can learn from high performing ones, and then adapt the "successful experiences or practices" to their own particular contexts (OECD, 2016a; INEE, 2016; OREALC-UNESCO, 1998). Nevertheless, neither of the programs that operate in Mexico offer specific guidelines, advice nor details on how to adequately or effectively develop this romantic adaptation. Mrs. Ema, an upper secondary science educator interviewed in this study, claimed that LSAs "only give you a sense of where you are, but they do not give you improvement strategies". Indeed, large-scale assessment programs do not provide improvement strategies. Educators are expected to generate them from the data LSAs produce, yet how this is supposed to come about, is ambiguous. Third, PISA, ERCE and PLANEA are far from neutral instruments. These programs play a key part in sustaining international and national organizations, each one of them with their own social, political, economic and cultural projects and agendas (Sorensen, 2017), which are developed from very different, and somewhat, contradictory sets of values and projects. The foundational principles and logics of these organizations are likely to permeate their programs, publications and data, thus influence the ways in which their arguments are built, and their beliefs and problems framed, defined, develop and put into circulation.

The issues presented and discussed in this section are likely to impact on how and what educators and education actors know about large-scale assessment programs. In the following sections, I will present, analyze and discuss some of the main findings from the survey and interviews carried out for this unit of analysis.

5   What Do Educators Know about Large-scale Assessments?

As discussed earlier, large-scale assessment programs in Mexico claim they generate key, relevant, and meaningful data for aiding education practice improvements. In the following sections, I will present the data and analyze this assumption by looking into what educators in this subnational entity used for this study actually know and have to say about current assessment programs, their data, publications and perceived usefulness.

5.1   *Participant Characteristics*
I will begin by presenting the general characteristics of the survey participants so as to put into context the respondents answers and their answering patterns. This is intended to provide a contrast between the study's sample and its population outlined above. Table 5.11 presents the distribution of participants per gender. Findings indicate that two thirds of survey participants are female (63.6%). This outcome resembles the profile of teachers in terms of gender in the national teacher census in compulsory education (INEE, 2015b, p. 33); 67.5 per cent of all educators in Mexico are female, in contrast with 32.5 per cent that are male.

Table 5.12 displays the distribution of participant by age. The sample's median group is the one that accounts for educators between 39 to 44 years old. This is also consistent with the 2015 teacher census which indicates that the mean age for primary and secondary school teachers is between 39 to 42 years old, and in upper secondary schools – from 40 to 44 years old (INEE, 2015b, pp. 35–37).

TABLE 5.11   Participant distribution by gender

	Female	Male	n
Participant Gender	203 (63.6%)	116 (36.4%)	319 (100%)

SOURCE: BASED ON SURVEY RESPONSES

TABLE 5.12   Participant distribution by age

	21–26	27–32	33–38	39–44	45–50	51–56	57 up	n
Participants by age	24 (7.5%)	53 (16.6%)	62 (19.4%)	74 (23.2%)	46 (14.4%)	39 (12.2%)	21 (6.6%)	319 (100%)

SOURCE: BASED ON SURVEY RESPONSES

TABLE 5.13   Participant distribution by seniority

Years	0 to 5	6 to 11	12 to 17	18 to 23	24 & up	n
Seniority	54 (16.9%)	89 (27.9%)	82 (25.7%)	53 (16.6%)	41 (12.9%)	319 (100%)

SOURCE: BASED ON SURVEY RESPONSES

Another important feature of the participants in this study is seniority in the teaching service. Table 5.13 provides an overview of this variable which indicates that slightly more than half of the participants (55.2%) from the sample have teaching experiences of over ten years.

Table 5.14 shows participants by education level in which they work, also known as workplace. This variable is divided into three categories: Primary, Secondary and Upper Secondary Schools. In Mexico, the primary education level is the largest by student and teacher population, followed by lower secondary and then upper secondary; the smallest education compulsory level is preschool (INEE, 2015b).

Table 5.15 presents the distribution of participants by the school subject they teach. The first two groups account for educators who work in primary education. Participants from these first two groups cannot be divided into subjects they teach because at this level, educators teach the entire set of subjects

TABLE 5.14   Distribution of participants by education level in which they work

	Primary	Secondary	Upper secondary	n
Education level in which participants work	131 (41.1%)	108 (33.9%)	80 (25.1%)	319 (100%)

SOURCE: BASED ON SURVEY RESPONSES

TABLE 5.15   Participant distribution by subject they teach

	All subjects 1st to 3rd grade	All subjects 4th to 6th grade	Literacy	Math	Science	n
Grade or subject taught	71 (22.3%)	60 (18.8%)	62 (19.4%)	60 (18.8%)	66 (20.7%)	319 (100%)

SOURCE: BASED ON SURVEY RESPONSES

indicated in the curriculum. The other three groups account for participants who teach literacy, mathematics, and science-related subjects, which are taught in secondary and upper secondary schools. These were not separated by school grade because most teachers work in a diversity of grades at both levels. The study only considered sampling educators from secondary and upper secondary institution who taught subjects that were traditionally evaluated by large-scale assessment programs. Hence no humanities, arts, or physical education teachers were taken into account by the sample.

Lastly, Table 5.16 shows participant distribution by city in which they work. This was a deliberate intention to sample a larger number of teachers from the most populated cities.

6   Program Knowledge, Depth and Acquaintance

The first issue addressed in this section could seem rather innocuous. However, neither national nor international academic work was found that looked into this topic. It would appear that assessment programs, researchers, and

TABLE 5.16   Participant distribution by city

	City 2	City 1	City 3	City 4	City 5	n
City	117 (36.7%)	92 (28.8%)	82 (25.7%)	14 (4.4%)	14 (4.4%)	319 (100%)

SOURCE: BASED ON SURVEY RESPONSES

TABLE 5.17   I know PISA, LLECE and PLANEA

	Yes	No	n
PISA	211 (66.1%)	108 (33.9%)	319 (100%)
ERCE-LLECE	5 (1.6%)	314 (98.4%)	319 (100%)
PLANEA	235 (73.7%)	84 (26.3%)	319 (100%)

SOURCE: BASED ON SURVEY RESPONSES

education ministries assume that all education actors are aware of the existence of large-scale assessment programs. The first issue here tackles whether educators *know about* PISA, ERCE-LLECE (PERCE, SERCE & TERCE) and PLANEA.

Table 5.17 shows that 73.7 per cent of research participants claim to know PLANEA, whereas 66.1 per cent claim to know PISA, whilst only 1.6 per cent of all participants claim to know ERCE assessments. It is worthwhile noting here that merely 55.17 per cent of all participants know both PLANEA and PISA.

Table 5.17 suggests a discrepancy regarding educators' knowledge of these programs. As mentioned earlier in this book (see Chapter 4), ERCE-LLECE is an assessment developed by OREALC-UNESCO aimed at providing Latin American countries with an exclusive comparison study of their own common conditions (OREALC-UNESCO, 1998). Despite the origins and aims of this assessment, the difference of acknowledgement between PISA and PLANEA, with LLECE, is striking. Given the low level of awareness of LLECE, it will not be included in the remaining analyses of this chapter. Nevertheless, it is an intriguing state of affairs and will be discussed further in Chapter 8 of this book.

Two Pearson chi-square test of independence were performed to assess whether a participant's seniority was associated with knowing PISA or PLANEA. Results show no significant association, χ^2 (4, n = 319) = 0.36, p = 0.98, χ^2 (4, n = 319) = 3.53, p = 0.47. Two additional Pearson chi-square test of independence were performed to assess whether the city in which the participants worked was associated with knowing PISA or PLANEA. Test results indicate no significant association, χ^2 (4, n = 319) = 8.19, p = 0.85, χ^2 (4, n = 319) = 7.30, p = 0.12.

A second issue linked with educators' awareness of LSAs is their perceived levels of knowledge regarding these programs. Table 5.18 indicates that, aside from PLANEA having a greater proportion of participants who know it compared to PISA, a larger number of educators also claim to have a more profound awareness of it.

The third and last issue in this section, explores the main channels through which participants found out about PLANEA and PISA. Table 5.19 reveals that educators became acquainted with these programs mainly via two channels:

TABLE 5.18   My knowledge of PISA and PLANEA

	No knowledge	Basic	Intermediate	Advanced	n
PISA	108 (33.9%)	120 (37.6%)	77 (24.1%)	14 (4.4%)	319 (100%)
PLANEA	84 (26.3%)	99 (31%)	101 (31.7.%)	35 (11.0%)	319 (100%)

SOURCE: BASED ON SURVEY RESPONSES

TABLE 5.19   How did you first hear of PISA and PLANEA?

	Media	Superintendent head teachers	Colleagues	Personal search	n
PISA	82 (25.7%)	63 (19.7%)	33 (10.3%)	33 (10.3%)	211 (66.1%)
PLANEA	82 (25.7%)	119 (37.3%)	16 (5.0%)	18 (5.6%)	235 (73.7%)

Note: Percentage matches cases that claim to know these programs.
SOURCE: BASED ON SURVEY RESPONSES

(a) secretariat officials through media (television, press and internet); and (b) superintendents or head teachers. Results suggest a modest acquaintance as a result of personal searching, or via colleagues, regarding both assessments. Interestingly, participants found out about PLANEA by means of what appears to be a vertical hierarchical communication string involving superintendents and head teachers, whereas in the case of PISA, media communication channels stand out.

Four chi-square test of independence were performed to assess whether the nature of the work place or the type of subject that participant taught was associated with how they first found out about PISA or PLANEA, no significant association was found, χ^2 (6, n = 211) = 1.81, p = 0.93, χ^2 (12, n = 211) = 8.61, p = 0.73, χ^2 (6, n = 235) = 11.84, p = 0.66, χ^2 (12, n = 235) = 11.27, p = 0.50.

7 Offering Data to Which Educators?

So far, research findings outlined above indicate that 73.7 per cent of research participants know PLANEA, whereas 66.1 per cent know PISA. Both of these assessments claim that one of their main aspirations is to contribute to education practice improvement through offering data to educators (see Chapter 4). The question that remains here is, to which educators is LSAs data directed to? In this section I shall reflect upon this issue, particularly in relation to PISA, departing from participants' awareness regarding large-scale assessments, their workplace and the school subject that they teach.

There are three fundamental claims about PISA made by the OECD regarding the topic addressed in this section. First, that it generates "a basic profile of knowledge and skills amongst students at the end of compulsory schooling" (OECD, 1999, p. 8). Second, that by evaluating 15 years-old "knowledge, skills and attitudes accumulated over approximately ten years of education is gained from an assessment at this time" (OECD, 2006, p. 7). Third, that educators can learn from this PISA data and apply it to their own context (OECD, 2016a). From these claims, one could infer that if PISA generates a basic profile comprised of accumulated knowledge, skills and attitudes gained from the entire compulsory schooling cycle, the data produced by PISA for educators should at least be equally known to those who comprise the compulsory schooling spectrum.

A Pearson chi-square test of independence was performed to assess whether the educational level which participants worked in was associated with their awareness of PISA. The results suggest a significant relationship between these variables, χ^2 (2, n = 319) = 16.13, p = 0.00. Table 5.20 indicates that the direction

TABLE 5.20   I know PISA

	Primary	Lower secondary	Upper secondary	n
No	61 (46.6%)	26 (24.1%)	21 (26.3%)	108 (33.9%)
Yes	70 (53.4%)	82 (75.9%)	59 (73.8%)	211 (66.1%)
Total	131 (100.0%)	108 (100.0%)	80 (100.0%)	319 (100.0%)

SOURCE: BASED ON SURVEY RESPONSES

of this relationship points to the fact for Primary School Teachers only 53.4 per cent of them knowing PISA, in contrast to Secondary School Teachers (75.9%) and Upper Secondary School Teachers (73.8%).[1] No significant relationship was found between this same variable and the awareness of PLANEA amongst participants, χ^2 (2, n = 319) = 5.59, p = 0.61.

A second Pearson chi-square test of independence was conducted to assess whether the subject that educators taught was associated with their awareness of PISA. The outcomes of this test also suggest a significant association, χ^2 (4, n = 319) = 21.98, p = 0.00. Table 5.21 indicates that participants who teach all subjects from first to third grade in primary education know PISA (45.1%), in contrast to the group of educators from fourth to sixth (63.3%), Literacy (74.2%), Science (71.2%), and Maths (80%) who know it.[2] No significant relationship

TABLE 5.21   I know PISA

	1st to 3rd	4th to 6th	Literacy	Science	Math	n
No	39 (54.9%)	22 (36.7%)	16 (25.8%)	19 (28.8%)	12 (20.0%)	108 (33.9%)
Yes	32 (45.1%)	38 (63.3%)	46 (74.2%)	47 (71.2%)	48 (80.0%)	211 (66.1%)
Total	71 (100.0%)	60 (100.0%)	62 (100.0%)	66 (100.0%)	60 (100.0%)	319 (100.0%)

SOURCE: BASED ON SURVEY RESPONSES

was found between this same variable and the awareness of PLANEA, χ^2 (4, n = 319) = 6.333, p = 0.17.

With regard to the preceding data, and as previously outlined above, the OECD claims that PISA offers relevant student learning insights to educators (OECD, 2007, 2016b, 2018). Nevertheless, this assumption is ambiguous in several ways. First, it is unclear which educators PISA sets out to benefit. In other words, the OECD does not specify if their insights for aiding education practices are directed to a general educator audience or if they are meant to address a particular educational level. Second, the OECD is also unclear as to whether their insights will be equally helpful to educators from all subjects and grades, or only to the ones their survey assesses. In a special publication (OECD, 2016b) directed at maths teachers, the OECD is vague as to which math teachers it refers to. This matters because whilst the evidence from this study shows that math educators from secondary education represent the group that is most aware of PISA (80%), math is taught across the entire education compulsory cycle, including the lower ends, where less than half of educators are aware of this program (45.1%).

Given that PISA presumes that it generates "a basic profile of knowledge and skills amongst students at the end of compulsory schooling" (OECD, 1999, p. 8), that is from preschool to upper secondary in the case of Mexico, it may be argued that the data they offer should be equally known at all of these education levels and across all teaching subjects. However, the Pearson chi-square tests of independence that were presented and explained in the previous paragraphs suggests quite the opposite. According to these statistical tests, the proportion of primary school teachers who know PISA statistically differ from groups of teachers from latter education levels. Despite the marked effort of the OECD since as early as 2001 in their *"Starting Strong"* series (OECD, 2001b, 2017a, 2017b), where they have relentlessly sought to raise awareness as to the importance and relevance of education in early childhood years, according to the evidence from this study, it would seem that educators who are teaching grades closer to these early years are less aware of or enaged with the OECD's main education informing tool (PISA).

Researchers and PISA architects may argue that it is obvious that educators from the early stages are not as aware of this program because it is administered at the upper end of the schooling cycle. This rationale is to some extent reasonable and understandable. However, it is nevertheless problematic in light of OECD claims, which state that PISA is an instrument which assesses accumulated knowledge from the full compulsory schooling cycle. Thus, it could be argued that it should at least be feeding data equally to all levels which comprise this cycle.

The findings presented above are not to suggest that the OECD should start testing students at the early stages of compulsory education. Not at all. What should be considered and drawn from these findings is a call for the OECD to adopt a more nuanced, measured and targetted approach for educators so that the link between findings and practice can be realised. In this respect, the OECD should explicitly claim which educators, and from what subjects and grades, their data could possibly aid. They should also be more nuanced as to the actual reach of their instruments in terms of aiding education practice improvement.

Lastly, it could also be argued that if the OECD were genuinely interested in aiding education practice improvement through PISA, they should try invest in further efforts to make their data and tools more visible and useful amongst educators at early stages. This is particularly so for challenging learning problems at these levels, and in helping prepare educators for future learning challenges. Teachers from the upper secondary school levels usually argue that they have little discretion and thus less influence over students' learning due to the fact that when students arrive in their classrooms, "they come with serious learning deficiencies" (Secondary School Math Teacher). A similar situation occurs in the Spanish context, where evidence suggests that policy intervention tends to focus on upper secondary levels, whilst learning deficiencies originate at the primary levels (Choi & Jerrim, 2016). The evidence from this study's survey shows that educators who have a greater awareness of the existence of PISA are those that are at the end of the compulsory education cycle, where, according to teachers, little can be done to amend these learning deficiencies. In contrast, educators who strive to take on those challenges facing those at the early years where learning problems can be anticipated, are less aware of this instrument. Furthermore, INEE "aiding materials" for teachers regarding how to address more effectively PISA competences are directed to Secondary and Upper Secondary educators (INEE, 2008b, 2012, 2014b).

8   PISA and PLANEA Publications

Aside from asking about general large-scale assessment program knowledge, educators were also questioned about their practices associated with consulting specific materials published by the OECD and INEE regarding PISA and PLANEA. This question sought to examine if educators had consulted large-scale assessment publications. If this had been the case, further questions are then raised as to which and how much.

Table 5.22 shows that out of the 66.1 per cent of participants who stated they knew PISA, only 31 per cent of them agreed to have read PISA materials

TABLE 5.22 Have you read, and what have you read of PISA publications from OECD or INEE?

	No	Yes	n	Observations
Have you read OECD text of PISA?	112 (35.1%)	99 (31.0%)	211 (66.1%)	
PISA 2012 results	34 (10.7%)	66 (20.7%)	100 (31.3%)	1 additional value aside from 99 that have read OECD
PISA 2015 results	28 (8.8%)	72 (22.6%)	100 (31.3%)	1 additional value aside from 99 that have read OECD
Have you read INEE texts of PISA?	158 (49.5%)	53 (16.6%)	211 (66.1%)	
Mexico in PISA 2012	17 (5.3%)	31 (9.7%)	52 (16.3%)	5 missing from the 53 that have read INEE
Mexico in PISA 2015	19 (6.0%)	33 (10.3%)	52 (16.3%)	1 missing from the 53 that have read INEE
How to read mix texts? PISA collection for teachers	25 (7.8%)	27 (8.5%)	52 (16.3%)	
PISA science in classrooms; PISA collection for teachers	31 (9.7%)	21 (6.6%)	52 (16.3%)	
Chores of mathematics in classrooms; PISA collection for teachers	31 (9.7%)	21 (6.6%)	52 (16.3%)	

SOURCE: BASED ON SURVEY RESPONSES

published by the OECD. In contrast, only 16.6 per cent of this same cohort agreed to have read PISA materials published by the INEE. This is important because PISA readings from the OECD are much more extensive and broader than INEE publications. Moreover, INEE publications are all in Spanish and directed to the diverse Mexican audiences, whereas OECD readings are mainly in English and directed to more international technical specialized publics.

Table 5.22 indicates that materials published by the OECD; namely *PISA 2012 Results and PISA 2015 Results*, were read by between 20.6 per cent and 22.6 per cent of participants, whereas resources such as *Mexico in PISA 2012* and *Mexico in PISA 2015* which were published by INEE, were only consulted by 9.7 per cent and 10.3 per cent of educators. Even more surprisingly, materials published by INEE, such as *How to Read Mixed Texts? PISA Collection for Teachers, PISA Science in Classrooms. PISA Collection for Teachers* and *Chores of Mathematics in Classrooms. PISA Collection for Teachers*, which were developed exclusively for educators' use in classrooms, were consulted by less than 9 per cent of all survey participants.

Table 5.23 shows frequencies concerning the extent to which educators read the publications outlined above. Findings show that less than 5 per cent of all participants have fully read PISA related documents published both by OECD and INEE. Four Pearson chi-square tests of independence were conducted to assess whether participants' workplace, or the subject that they were associated with, influenced reading PISA materials both from OECD and INEE. No significant relationship was found in any of these cases.[3]

Table 5.24 shows how many educators have consulted PLANEA publications and to what extent. According to these findings, 41.1 per cent of participants have read PLANEA documents published by INEE. The proportion of educators who have read PLANEA is slightly higher than the proportion of participants who have read PISA texts (31 per cent). Nevertheless, similar to the PISA case, PLANEA documents also present low rates regarding the number of participants who have read them to a full extent (3.8% and 5.6%).

TABLE 5.23   Extent to which PISA documents were read

	Fractions	Full	n	Observations
PISA 2012 results	60 (18.8%)	6 (1.9%)	66 (20.7%)	
PISA 2015 results	61 (19.1%)	11 (3.4%)	72 (22.6%)	
Mexico in PISA 2012	29 (9.1%)	2 (.6%)	31 (9.7%)	
Mexico in PISA 2015	27 (8.5%)	6 (1.9%)	33 (10.3%)	
How to read mix texts? PISA collection for teachers	21 (6.6%)	6 (1.9)	27 (8.5%)	
PISA science in classrooms; PISA collection for teachers	19 (6.0%)	1 (0.3%)	21 (6.6%)	Missing one value of 21

SOURCE: BASED ON SURVEY RESPONSES

TABLE 5.24   Have you read, and what have you read of PLANEA published by INEE?

	No	Yes	n	Observations
Have you read PLANEA publications from INEE?	102 (32.0%)	131 (41.1%)	233 (73.0%)	Two missing cases from the 235 participants that know PLANEA
PLANEA main document	50 (15.7%)	81 (25.4%)	131 (41.1%)	
PLANEA 2015 6th and 9th grade results	61 (19.1%)	71 (22.3%)	132 (41.4%)	One additional value

	Fractions	Full	n	Observations
PLANEA main document	70 (21.9%)	12 (3.8%)	82 (25.7%)	One additional value
PLANEA 2015 6th and 9th grade results	53 (16.6%)	18 (5.6%)	71 (22.3%)	

Following the results from the survey outlined above, educators who participated in the interviews were questioned about these findings. Some made the following comments regarding their reading experiences and practices:

> The report itself I have not read, but, suddenly I see the news, or a message on social networks, or on television ... there is more conversation about our place in the ranking than all the results in general. (Mr. Juan, upper secondary math teacher, on PISA)

> No, we've only reviewed the ones here in the school. They gave us the results of mathematics and literacy, and the comparison between other schools. (Mrs. Tulip, upper secondary education math teacher, on PLANEA)

> I can not give precise information because I did not put them into practice, I only read a bit, 10 per cent to say the truth. (Mrs. Josefina, upper secondary literacy teacher, on PISA)

> Not the entire report no, just a table with results ... No, as I told you, the only contact that I had with it, is a table in which Mexico is situated, a comparison table. (Mr. Caballero, upper secondary science teacher, on PLANEA)

> After every test application we are on the lookout to see in which level we are at, including how we're doing as a city, municipality, state and country. (Mr. Josefa, upper secondary literacy teacher, on PLANEA)

> I have read statistics of the results of PISA. We saw the level in which we were, below the average, not as low as Peru or Colombia but not as high as Chile. (Mrs. Emma, upper secondary science teacher)

> Yes, one of the publications was focused precisely on the results and the objectives it followed, for what purposes it was applied, but I tell you right now, I do not know. (Mrs. Josefa, upper secondary literacy teacher, on PISA)

These comments by participants reinforce the snapshot provided by the survey, which suggests moderate reading practices and acknowledgement amongst educators concerning large-scale assessment publications and data. Educators seem to focus their attention mainly on the tests results rather than the information disclosed in these publications related to effective or successful practices which could potentially help them improve their practices according to the logic of LSAs. When educators were questioned directly about specific large-scale assessment data, they provided responses that had little to do with the questions that were made to them.

Interviewee comments outlined above indicate a focus on particular aspects of large-scale assessments; for example, "results", their place on "rankings", their "comparisons" against other schools, "league tables", and "score average". For proponents of Human Capital theory, such as the OECD, such aspects can be viewed as competition drivers that will propel teachers to teach better (Robertson, 2012a). However, the particular way in which this is supposed to come about is unclear.

9 Perceived Usefulness of Large-scale Assessment Data

The last issue to be addressed regarding survey findings is related to participants' perceived usefulness of LSA data for enhancing assessment and lesson planning skills; two of the most basic skills involved in educators practices (Kauchak & Eggen, 2012). Table 5.25 shows that 30.1 per cent of educators agree that PISA data is 'useful' for enhancing assessment skills, whereas 43.3 per cent agree that PLANEA is useful for this same ends.

TABLE 5.25   LSA data is useful for enhancing assessment skills

	Don't know program	Agree	Disagree	Not sure	n
PISA	108 (33.9%)	96 (30.1%)	56 (17.6%)	59 (18.5%)	319 (100%)
PLANEA	84 (26.3%)	138 (43.3%)	44 (13.8%)	53 (16.6%)	319 (100%)

SOURCE: BASED ON SURVEY RESPONSES

TABLE 5.26   LSA data is useful for enhancing lesson planning skills

	Don't know program	Agree	Disagree	Not Sure	n
PISA	108 (33.9%)	111 (34.8%)	50 (15.7%)	50 (15.7%)	319 (100%)
PLANEA	84 (26.3%)	147 (46.1%)	44 (13.8%)	44 (13.8%)	319 (100%)

SOURCE: BASED ON SURVEY RESPONSES

Table 5.26 shows that 34.4 per cent of participants agree that PISA is useful for enhancing lesson planning skills, whereas for PLANEA, 46.1 per cent of educators agree on this same matter.

During interview sessions, participants were asked to elaborate further as to how LSA data helps them enhance or improve their lesson planning and assessment skills. With regard to PLANEA, some participants mentioned the following;

> Yes, in the sense that one has to adapt to the contents that must be seen, and make sure that they are learned, it's about adapting the activities and lesson planning situations to this type of test items ... At the beginning I was not very efficient at it, I have been improving because I started to present the classroom tasks in the form of the test items. (Mr. Juan, upper secondary math teacher)

> For assessing no. PLANEA influences in what I plan, in how I plan it, in what I include in my learning sequences, in what I scrap or to what

content I give more attention or time in the sequences, but it does not improve my skill. (Mr. Alex, six-grade primary school teacher)

Yes, because it tells you where students have more learning needs, in which area they are doing well and in which of them they are failing, so, that is where one realizes what should be prioritized at the moment of lesson planning. (Mrs. Sulema, third-year primary school teacher)

It gives me a parameter of questions, items and topics that I have to improve, so then, what I have to develop in my class must be grounded on these. (Mr. Alcatraz, upper secondary math teacher)

Yes, now I have to elaborate evaluation instruments focused on what PLANEA asks, which maybe should not be but, we're in this, right? (Mrs. Josefa, upper secondary literacy teacher)

Comments made by participants appear to focus more on how educators make use of assessments rather than on *how* large-scale assessment data helps them improve lesson planning skills, assessment skills, or improve education practices. Furthermore, comments provided by participants show some level of difficulty that educators have for providing coherent and reasonable arguments regarding the use of LSA data for its alleged purposes.

What educators confirm in these explanations is that it may be possible that little has changed regarding the use of large-scale assessment data from the previous national program – ENLACE – to the current one – PLANEA – given that framing practices around the test, continue to prevail. Federico, a pedagogical leader with more than 30 years of experience at the secondary level, observes that "the educational system has failed to strengthen some issues, the educational system has not been concerned at all with teaching educators how to make use of these instruments". Indeed, according to research findings something is failing in Mexico, it could be attributed to the education system. However, large-scale assessment programs have also been limited concerning more serious substantial and realistic ways, which go beyond publishing findings and expecting educators to engage with them, regarding how to help education agents make use of their data for improving education practices.

Linking together findings from the interviews and from Tables 5.25 and 5.26, it would seem that participants consider LSA data from PISA and PLANEA to be more useful for enhancing lesson planning skills in contrast to enhancing assessment skills. This may have to do with the fact that teachers dedicate time for elaborating and applying PISA and PLANEA-like items as part of their teaching strategies during formal classes according to the comments outlined above, and others shared in the following section.

Some unusual and paradoxical findings arise from the data outlined above. First, Tables 5.25 and 5.26 show that 43.3 per cent and 46.1 per cent of participants respectively agree that PLANEA data is useful for enhancing assessment and lesson planning skills. Yet, a lower proportion (41.1%) of participants agree that they have actually read PLANEA material published by INEE. Moreover, only 22.3 per cent of them claimed to have read PLANEA results from 2015, and just as few as 5.6 per cent agree they have read them to a fuller extent (see Tables 5.23 & 5.24). A similar scene is produced when PISA data is contrasted in a parallel way. Only 31.3 per cent of educators mentioned they had consulted PISA material from the OECD, and just 16.3 per cent of participants had consulted the materials of PISA published by INEE. However, a higher proportion of participants (34.8% and 30.1%) claim that PISA data is useful for enhancing assessment and lesson planning skills. These findings indicate that the proportion of educators who agree that PISA and PLANEA are useful for enhancing lesson planning and assessment skills is higher than the proportion of educators that claim to have actually read formal publications or materials from one or both of these programs.

This outcome could indicate several situations. Amongst them, it suggests that: (a) educators are receiving information from elsewhere – other than formal publications – which leads them to develop the belief that these materials are useful; (b) educators are providing expected responses, what is known as socially desirable responses; (c) educators are not being truthful; or (d) participants are reproducing a propagandistic slogan advanced by these assessments and their sponsor bodies. In relation to this matter, a former Mexican PISA representative whom I will call Professor Felix, was asked about his interpretations concerning educators' responses to this particular query, to which, he responded in the following way:

> Well, it may be an expected response, a bias. We Mexicans tend to say that everything is fine, that everything is useful, that everything serves to improve ... then, the answer, I can not generalize but, my intuition is that it serves very little for these purposes.

Despite that LSAs are not fulfilling their own expectations and aspirations according to the evidence presented in the four previous sections, they are nevertheless producing effects. Some of these effects are explored in the following section.

10 Unintended Large-scale Assessment Data Effects at the Local Scale

The local scale of this research focuses on the LSA aspiration concerned with generating data so as to contribute to education practice improvement. The findings outlined above regarding this scale do not suggest out a favorable landscape. Nonetheless, as Lascoumes and Le Gales (2007) argue, public policy instruments – such as LSAs – produce effects independently of the objective pursued. In this research, these effects involve unintended consequences which will be discussed in the following subsections.

10.1 *Teaching to the Test*

Teaching to the test is neither new in the field of large-scale assessments (Jennings & Bearak, 2014; Nichols & Berliner, 2007; Popham, 2001b), nor to the Mexican context. In fact, the preceding national large-scale assessment in Mexico, ENLACE, was cancelled following teaching to the test, score inflation and other malpractice allegations (Backhoff & Contreras, 2014; Martínez-Rizo & Silva-Guerrero, 2016). Despite this, the main findings from this study suggest that teaching to the test prevails amongst schools at the local scale of this research. Before continuing, it is worth noting that teaching to the test has been thoerized in different ways. For example, Popham (2001b) argues that teaching to the test implies organizaing instruction around actual test or look-alike items. For Jennings and Bearak (2014) teaching to the test is a "spectrum of instructional practices rather than a dichotomy typically used to describe it (i.e. teachers are or are not teaching to the test)" (p. 381). For these authors, teaching to the test can include: (a) test coaching or test preparation; (b) aligning instruction with test standards, (c) emphasizing on test standards; and (d) teaching skills in tested formats. Findings from the distinct scales of this research display different combinations of these practices. The ways in which this occurs, and some of its implications, will now be discussed.

According to interviewees who work at the primary, early secondary, or upper secondary education grades which comprise the range of grades and ages that PISA does not assess, in their experience teaching to the PISA test is something that has not happened to them, and is unlikely to occur to educators working outside of the PISA testing sample spectrum. Consistently, the participants who claim to have had some experience in teaching to the PISA test, were educators who taught the PISA assessing domain areas in schools that in the past had participated in PISA rounds. I was able to gain access to three different institutions who formed part of the 2015 or 2018 PISA sample. Their experiences are expressed in the following comments:

The PISA exam comes to us again at the end of April or beginning of May (2018). We are now starting a preparation task for students, working on PISA like exercises, as we call them, so that they arrive a bit better prepared for the exam … this consists of showing students the type of questions they are going to be subject to, and doing some exercises. (Mr. Caballero, upper secondary science educator)

In previous PISA rounds we provided information to teachers; exercises and everything, in order for them to work with their students. Also, we had meetings per domain area, for example, reading, writing and literature, and mathematics, in which we worked to develop exercises to be able to give support to students prior to the exam. (Mrs. Jazmin, upper secondary academic headteacher)

During two or three weeks that was my job; helping and preparing students for the examen. (Mr. Omar, upper secondary science educator)

In some schools they have the following strategy. They teach the core standards from all 5 study units of the entire maths, science and literacy syllabus up until April, and from this point onwards, educators use their time in developing and applying PISA like items. To help prepare students for this task, they use PISA questions from the 2015, 2012, 2009 and 2006 rounds. (Mr. Brambilla, science pedagogical leader for all technical secondary schools, and upper secondary science educator)

These comments share three commonalities: educators prepare students for the test, they apply what in their understandings are of "PISA like" exercises and questions from previous PISA rounds, and educators are concerned with familiarizing students with the PISA format and its variant of tests items. These practices and concerns will be discussed together with those from PLANEA. However, it is important to note that it was not possible to explore in further detail the sources or supply chains from which teachers or school leaders obtained PISA questions, this issue is proposed as an area for further research. Nevertheless, it is important to stress that there are several groups and institutions that amplify PISA items. For instance, the INEE dedicates an entire section of their webpage to this matter. In this particular website they facilitate past PISA items released by the OECD.[4] Also, private for profit higher education institutions, such as Technologic University of Monterrey (Tec de Monterrey), have developed their online PISA laboratory[5] as a means to aid schools and help students 'practice' for the test. And last but not least, the Carlos Slim foundation (CARSO Group), led by Carlos Slim, the tenth richest man in the world according to real time billionaires-Forbes, has also developed their PISA preparation tool,[6] where past PISA and PISA like items are made accessible to the public.

Unlike PISA, PLANEA is administered in different modalities and at distinct moments of the compulsory education cycle in Mexico (see Chapter 4). Thus, it may be expected that teaching to the PLANEA test could vary slightly. With regard to this phenomenon, some participants shared the following comments:

> In previous years, I have tried to address test items during classes at least once a week, in order to study topics that come in these exams but that do not form part of the third year secondary school syllabus ... I do not consider this practice unprofessional because I am acting in a way that helps students re-study what was not tested previously. (Mr. Albeiro, secondary math educator)

> As a result of my analysis regarding different evaluations, including this one – PLANEA – I had to make changes, I began to include theoretical aspects in the literacy and mathematics classes, so that students could achieve the practical tasks during the tests .... As I am carrying it out – practice of teaching to the test – I think it is complementary to the primary education learning program that I teach (...) we are expected to have positive results, to seek positive results, sometimes we have to go hand in hand with this assessment (PLANEA). (Mr. Alex, six grade primary school teacher)

> In the Writing and Reading courses I and II, I have to comply both with the course syllabus and the PLANEA syllabus. Luckily, they have some similarities. (Mrs. Josefina, upper secondary literacy educator)

In addition to these comments, the reader might also consider the statements from earlier sections of this chapter, as they also reflect similar issues. Taken together, these comments suggest that the case of PISA in this context, could be associated with practices of teaching to the test and preparing for the test, whereas in the case of PLANEA, in addition to this, it also incorporates an intention of alignment between standards, instruction and tests, given that some educators and school leaders are inclined to link test preparation with ordinary teaching and learning activities of the curriculum and its learning standards. Furthermore, it should also be noted that test preparation for PLANEA in some cases is permanent, as opposed to PISA, which is temporary.

Jennings and Bearak (2014) argue that not all teaching to the test practices generate negative consequences. According to these authors, some of these practices provoke experiential benefits, specially when they result in familiarizing students with the test format. However, comments made by participants in this study suggest that teaching to the test practices at the local scale of this research are narrowed to essentially two things: first, applying test like items, and second; making use of items or questions from previous tests rounds. Both of these practices are far from unproblematic. In the following paragraphs I explore why.

First and foremost, there is a great deal of ambiguity around the notion of test like items. According to findings from this research, educators have limited knowledge and readings of large-scale assessment programs and their data so as to elaborate or emulate these complex instruments or create test like items of their own. Hence, in many cases, applying test like items could merely be a reduction of teaching so as teach to the test practices which are activities solely based on answering multiple-choice questions.

Second, pedagogically PLANEA and PISA are fundamentally different. For instance, PLANEA is curriculum-based and takes its test items on content and skills from the national curriculum PISA does not design its test items on any particular curriculum but rather on a set of skills and knowledge which students are expected to acquire by the end the compulsory education cycle. Hence, teaching to the PISA test is unlikely to be the same as teaching to the PLANEA test.

Third, what is the value of practising questions from previous test round whilst, ignoring the reasons for why these questions were made public in the first place. In other words, past tests might not look like future tests, meaning wasted time; time which could have been spent on other learning.

Taking into consideration the issues outlined above, when some educators claim that by teaching to the test, they comply both with the syllabus and with the test preparation requirements, this raises many questions as to what is really occurring in those classrooms? Unfortunately I will not be able to explore this matter any further, however it is an interesting topic to consider for future research.

As it can be noted, teaching to the test is a complex issue. Some of the more common conflicts linked to this practice involve narrowing curriculum and instruction time to teaching topics associated with the test (Berliner, 2011; Comber, 2012). However, in the previous paragraphs, I have highlighted additional situations and issues which represent a challenge for this sort of practices. Together, these form part of the unintended consequences of large-scale assessments at the local scale.

10.2 *From Cheating to Institutionalized Practices*

During interviews, one headteacher revealed that a sub-system of upper secondary schools (n = 50) in this subnational state, which provides schooling for roughly around 40,000 students per school year (SEE, 2017), is formally dedicating instruction in class time to teaching to the PLANEA test. These comments were verified with other interviewees, and by teachers from other schools from this same subsystem. In this respect, Mr. Fernando, an upper secondary academic headteacher made the following statement:

> Educators from fifth and sixth semesters (12th grade) are mandated to work PLANEA with their students (...) for example, if the Reading and Writing Strategies course has a workload of three hours per week, one of those three hours must be dedicated to working PLANEA ... one hour in the area of literacy skills and another hour a week in mathematical ability. During this time, students carry out the tasks of reading PLANEA questions, answering and revising them with the rest of the group to check where they failed, or where they present major flaws. Students do this every week.

Despite that teaching to the test was condemned in the preceding national LSA and resulted in its cancellation, we can observe that this activity has been embraced for PLANEA. Furthermore, it can be argued that what has occurred here is a shift involving the institutionalization of teaching to the test practices. In the past, researchers found that schools were teaching to the ENLACE test (Backhoff & Contreras 2014; Martínez-Rizo & Silva-Guerrero, 2016). In many cases, educators carried out this task instructed (unofficially) by their headteachers; in other cases, they were driven by personal reasons. However, in both instances, this was officially not happening, or was denied or indeed covered up by schools. What is currently happening in the set of schools in this subnational state takes teaching to the test to a new category.

I argue that in this case, teaching to the test has been institutionalized because: (1) this subsystem has formally incorporated this activity into their structure; (2) this activity is overviewed and regulated by the subsystem; (3) all schools within this subsystem are required to instrument this activity; (4) it is compulsory for all educators from math and literacy courses to carry these tasks; and (5) this set of schools have committed to this activity as a measure to bring about a desired state of affairs.

The institutionalization of these practices however, is not unproblematic. For instance, despite the fact that LSA-related courses and subjects already benefit from most of the teaching hours within the syllabus, this has been narrowed even more as a result of teaching to the test. Students are in the final stage of the compulsory education, instead of fostering other skills related to adulthood or the labour market, students are investing their time in answering questionable teaching to the test like items. By enforcing these practices at this crucial stage of their lives, schools are transmitting and reproducing messages as to the validation of these practices as normal, natural and harmless. This in turn can lead to the acceptance, tolerance, and reproduction of these practices elsewhere. Overall, these risks can reproduce misleading ideas about learning and teaching, and in an extreme case can contribute to their potential institutionalization at different educational scales and sites. Moreover, for McLaren (2016) teaching to the test serves as an effective policing device for keeping oppositional discourses and practices out of the classroom.

Some people could argue that what is occurring in the set of schools in this subnational entity is a minor or insignificant activity. However, it is worthwhile noting and questioning how is it that an undesirable activity, such as teaching to the test, not only suddenly lost its stigma but became a must in this set of schools. To answer this, I will revisit part of the theoretical underpinnings of this research.

In Chapter 2, I drew upon the work of Prunty (1984) to argue that LSAs, such as PLANEA and PISA, are both evaluatitve and political instruments. They are political in that they have the authority to value some agents, education systems and activities over others. For instance, PISA values nations such as Mexico and Brazil as low-performers, whereas Singapore and Finland are regarded as high-performers. This in turn is followed by the selective allocation of resources, opportunities, worth and obligations. In this regard, given that Mexico's education system is regarded as less than, hence their obligation is to follow the example of other education systems who are regarded better. This in turn places pressures on resources and opportunities, such as implementing certain reform measures, establishing pacts, relationships or agreements with international institutions such as the OECD, WB and IMF, and so on.

For Prunty (1984), policy is viewed as the authoritative allocation of values. By this he means that, in the broadest of senses, LSAs as policy instruments can be regarded as instruments for defining, identifying and allocating attention and resources to those things that are seen to be valued. LSAs do this in different ways. For the moment I will focus on the case at hand regarding the set of schools in this study. From a curricular stance, it could be argued that what has occurred here is a redistribution and reallocation of teaching time; lecture time is taken from math and literacy subjects and is given or granted to teaching PLANEA. This is correct. However, behind this shift, and in terms of policy, what happened can be interpreted as an authoritative allocation of value in terms of learning and teaching, as the result of LSAs.

In order to understand what has been outlined above, one must ask: why did this set of schools have the need to employ this particular shift? First, because large-scale assessments exist, second because schools are valued in terms of their outcomes on LSAs, and third because schools value highly how they are valued by assessments. Thus, as a means to achieve a higher value, this set of shools sought to institutionalize teaching to the PLANEA test. In this case, teaching the syllabus was weighted against teaching to the test, the latter was viewed as more valuable in relation to what is valued by the school. This, in turn, brought about issues of opportunities and resources, particularly, the opportunity to teach and learn from the PLANEA test, and the resources in terms of teaching hours to do this.

11   Relevance of Large-scale Assessment Programs: What about the Bigger Picture?

The previous sections of this chapter show: (a) scarce knowledge amongst participants in terms of the awareness of LSAs; (b) diminutive depth of their knowledge regarding these programs; (c) modest reading habits of LSA publications; and (d) moderate perceived use for enhancing education practices. In an effort to stress participants' subjectivities, interviewees were questioned about the relevance and advantages of large-scale assessment programs in the broadest sense they could think of. Some of their answers are shared in the following comments:

> Yes, in fact, the information that is now found is important in helping us on how to increase results, and in supporting me on how my teaching domain can achieve higher learning standard levels. This is important to me. (Mrs. Rosa, upper secondary literacy teacher)

> They give us a starting point, which, pushes us to always want to be better. At that moment in which comparisons are shown to you, you think, I have to raise my levels, I have to raise my percentages, or I have to make students raise their understandings to this or that performance level. (Mrs. Jazmin, upper secondary academic head)

> When they give us the test results, we analyze where we are failing, in what type of questions, or in what type of answers, this helps us reinforce students, and focus on achieving better results in what is at the state level or at the national level. (Mr. Fernando, upper secondary academic headteacher)

The responses provided by participants regarding the relevance of LSAs revolve around some common concerns, amongst them: a focus on increasing results, achieving higher standards, pushing to be better, raising performance levels and so on. These features can be linked to the underlying reasons why educators comply with teaching to the test practices discussed above and are consistent with features outlined by participants regarding other questions.

However, an issue is the absence of responses linked to the higher purposes of large-scale scale assessment programs. In this respect, PISA, ERCE and PLANEA have historically evoked honorable causes and purposes, such as, (a) enabling long-life learning, (b) preparing students to adapt to society, (c) enhancing students to meet and embrace the challenges of the future, (d) realization of human rights, (e) spreading equality in terms of quality learning, (f) economic growth, and so on. (OECD, 2016a; OREALC-UNESCO, 2015; INEE, 2015b). Assessment programs advertise themselves as specialized technical tools linked to the accomplishment of certain wider social projects, as the ones mentioned above. Yet, it is difficult to trace these bigger purposes and aspirations within educators' responses, even when they are directly questioned about this.

Whilst the higher purposes of large-scale assessment programs are broadly advocated rhetorically, these features are simultaneously downplayed by educators' strong focus on raising standards. The landscape drawn from the comments provided by participants reflect that the main concerns regarding LSA data pivot around performativity (Ball, 2012) rather than the claimed aspirations for their data and the higher purposes evoked in their name.

12 Conclusions

Data presented in this chapter, which draws on the local practices, offers new insights into how the large-scale aspiration of contributing to education practice improvement has played out in a particular setting. This chapter reveals several statistically significant relationships between educators' workplace and their awareness and practices regarding LSAs. Interestingly, the proportion of educators from the early education years are less aware of these programs, in contrast to those at the upper education levels. This is viewed as problematic according to some educators because, at the end of the compulsory education cycle there is less they can do to amend early learning deficiencies.

In this chapter I have also reflected upon the unintended consequences produced by large-scale assessments at the local scale of this research, concerning teaching to the test practices, and discussed why these are problematic. This study discovered that a set of schools at the local scale of this research have institutionalized teaching to the test. I view this as a transition regarding how these practices are viewed; from cheating to normal institutionalized practices. Moreover, I discuss that this implicates much more than just relocating teaching time from one activity to the other. But rather what is at stake here, is an authoritative allocation of value, as the result of LSAs.

Lastly, I have argued that despite the evidence and knowledge produced by large-scale assessment programs over the past 25 years, many educators from this study's sample on the one hand ignore that these programs exist at all, and on on the other, very little LSA data actually gets to them. Moreover, those bits of data that make their way into educators' sights are rarely put into full extensive use by those who is intended to influence and for what it is expected to contribute to. Nonetheless, there are particularities of LSAs that can be identified in educators' statements and which figure significantly in their work according to them. These features focus on aspects such as rankings, comparisons, league tables, test scores and so on. In the final chapters of this book, I will link some of these findings with the governing tools explored in this study.

Notes

1   The direction of the relationship was determined by a post hoc test based on calculating residuals. The original p-value (p = 0.05) was modified using Bonferroni adjustment (p = 0.0083). The chi-square test result of educators from Primary Schools that don't know PISA is significant, χ^2 (1, n = 319) = 16.00, p = 0.000064.

2   The direction of the relationship was determined by a post hoc test based on calculating residuals. The original p-value (p = 0.05) was modified using Bonferroni adjustment (p = 0.0033). The chi-square test result of educators that teach all subjects from first to third grade and don't know PISA is significant, χ^2 (1, n = 319) = 18.15, p = 0.000020.

3   Workplace – read PISA by OECD χ^2 (2, n = 211) = 0.06, p = 0.97, Workplace – read PISA by INEE χ^2 (2, n = 211) = 4.79, p = 0.91, Grade or Subject taught – read PISA by OECD χ^2 (4, n = 211) = 0.765, p = 0.94, Grade or Subject taught – read PISA by INEE χ^2 (4, n = 211) = 8.686, p = 0.06.

4   See https://www.inee.edu.mx/evaluaciones/pisa/reactivos-liberados/

5   See http://www.cca.org.mx/profesores/reactivos_pisa/

6   See https://pruebat.org

Subnational Scale

Municipal and State Policymakers

In Chapter 4 I introduced the Mexican large-scale assessment namely, Educational Quality and Achievement Test, EXCALE for its acronym in Spanish. I argued that EXCALE was the first periodic Mexican large-scale assessment focused on gauging the achievement of learning standards amongst students at the end of each compulsory education level. Furthermore, I emphasized that in 2014 this assessment was cancelled and replaced with PLANEA, which absorbed many of its functions. In this Chapter 6 I turn to a policy, which for anonymity purposes I shall call EXCALE's use in kindergarten, to examine its pedagogical use. This policy was planned, developed and enforced during the 2016–2017 schoolyear in the same subnational state as the local scale. This initiative was advanced by and for the kindergarten education level and makes use of the EXCALE assessment in response to apparent curricular faults and weaknesses in initial teacher training concerning pupil assessment.

In Chapter 6 I explore the underlying logics, interactive dynamics, and outcomes between EXCALE and education agents at the subnational-municipal scale. This unit of analysis explores the design, development, and enforcement, of the EXCALE's use in kindergarten initiative. The advancement of this policy constitutes both the outcome of policy decisions and an effort to contribute to education practice improvement through measures such as: (a) replacing learning standards with test descriptors; (b) replacing descriptive assessments with proficiency tables; and (c) employing an "EXCALE like test" to track students' progress during their preschool education cycle. This unit shows that LSAs outcomes and effects, in some cases can outlive the programs from which they emerge.

This chapter is structured in seven parts which aim to address research questions two, three and four: RQ2) How do large-scale assessments aid education practice improvement and policy decisions at different political scales in Mexico? RQ3) What are some of the unintended consequences of the assessment regime in Mexico, and why do these matter? RQ4) What frictions, tensions and contradictions can be detected amongst large-scale assessment programs, and how are they addressed and mediated? In the first section I present some of the main characteristics regarding the data sources which inform this unit of analysis. In the second section I provide an overview of the

EXCALE program, with particular emphasis in its preschool education variant. In Section 3, I present the main statistics regarding the context in which the policy addressed in this chapter was developed and employed. In Section 4 I introduce the EXCALE's use in kindergarten initiative. Section 5 reflects upon and questions the use of EXCALE results in this initiative. The sixth section involves a detailed discussion regarding a widespread myth of math and literacy as milestones for learning, whilst the last section draws together the main findings and discussions of this chapter.

1   Sources of Data for the Subnational Case

First and foremost, it is important to note that preschool and kindergarten are treated as synonyms in the Mexican context, and they refer to the same education level. The unit of analysis addressed in this chapter draws upon an original data set comprised of three main sources: (1) documents related to the EXCALE assessment and to the preschool education curriculum; (2) 11 individual semi-structured interviews with subnational-municipal education authorities and educational leaders; and (3) two group semi-structured interviews with educators. A total of n = 23 education agents were participants in this aspect of the unit of analysis. Interviewees were divided into three groups. The first group was responsible for the design, development, and overview of the policy. The second group enforced this initiative at their schools; it includes teachers and head-teachers. The third group is comprised of participants who offer critical commentary on this initiative. Table 6.1 offers a summary of participant characteristics.

Table 6.1 shows a diverse group of research participants comprised of education authorities, educational leaders, and educators. Interviewees share important commonalities, such as initial teacher training in preschool education. However, they vary in seniority, posts, and postgraduate studies. It is important to note that the interview phase was developed using a top to bottom approach, which took place from January to March 2018. This top-to-bottom approach envisaged interviewing (i) initiative proponents who occupied top ranking positions within the internal hierarchy of the state education system (e.g. Chief of Sector and Department Chief), (ii) interviews with policy enforcers at the middle of the hierarchy, such as superintendents and head teachers; and (iii) teachers who are at the bottom of this schema.

The EXCALE's use in kindergarten initiative was selected as the unit to be addressed at the subnational scale of this multi-scalar research, based on a combination of diverse criteria that will be explained shortly. First and foremost,

TABLE 6.1   Participant characteristics

No.	Participant	Background
1	State Director of INEE; initiative proponent	Bachelor's in Education Sciences, Master's in Education Administration from local university. Has occupied different posts in the State Secretariat of Education.
2	Chief of Preschool Education Department in City 1; initiative proponent	Bachelor's in Psychology from local university, has occupied different posts in the State Secretariat of Education.
3	Chief of Sector; initiative proponent and enforcer	Basic normal training in Preschool Education, Master's in Education from local university. Former educator, head-teacher and superintendent in preschool. More than 30 years in teaching service.
4	Superintendent; initiative proponent and enforcer	Basic normal training in preschool education, Master's in Pedagogy, PhD in Critical Pedagogy, all from local universities. 30 years in-service.
5	Superintendent; initiative proponent and enforcer	Bachelor's in Preschool Education, Master's in Play Therapy, both from local universities. 10 years in-service.
6	Superintendent; initiative critic	Basic normal training in Preschool Education, Bachelor's in Education Sciences, Post-graduate degree in Personnel Management, all from local universities. 27 years in-service.
7	Head Teacher 1; initiative critic and enforcer	Bachelor's in Preschool Education, Master's in Pedagogy, both from local universities. 12 years in-service.
8	Head Teacher 2; initiative enforcer	Bachelor's in Preschool Education, Master's in Education, both from local universities. 21 years in-service.
9	Educator 1; initiative enforcer	Bachelor's in Preschool Education from local university. 12 years in-service.
10	Educator 2; initiative critic and enforcer	Bachelor's in Preschool Education, Master's in Basic Education, both from local universities. 7 years in-service.

(cont.)

TABLE 6.1   Participant characteristics (*cont.*)

No.	Participant	Background
11	Pedagogical Advisor at the Preschool Education Department; initiative critic	Bachelor's in Preschool Education, Master's in Teacher Development, both from local universities. 20 years in-service.
12	Head-Teacher Group Interview; initiative enforcers	Five head teachers, all of them have a Bachelor's in Preschool Education. Two have a Master's in Education, one has a PhD in Education. Their seniority varies from 11 to 21 years in-service.
13	Educator Group Interview; initiative enforcers	Seven educators, all of the have a Bachelor's in Preschool Education, one has a Master's in Special Education. Their seniority varies from 3 months to 11 years in-service.

this policy was developed and enforced in a sub-national setting. Considering that this research aims to explore LSAs at distinct scales (local, subnational and national), this initiative complied with the first criteria; being developed at a subnational scale with both state and municipal agents involved in its elaboration and enforcement. Second, the possible implications and repercussions of an initiative of the particular nature as the one being addressed in this unit makes it an interesting original case. For instance, historically, children from the preschool education level have not usually been subject to large-scale assessments. Student appraisal at this stage tends to be both descriptive and formative. Thus, the ways in which education agents at this level are making pedagogical use of the data produced by EXCALE is intriguing. A third reason for selecting this policy is its novelty. This initiative had recently been designed and enforced in schools (2016–2017) after its orchestration, just months prior to the data collection phase of this research.

In addition to the reasons outlined above, this policy was also chosen based on opportunistic criteria. Policy authors were interested in publicizing and promoting their initiative, and thus they were more than happy to participate and provide further access to other potential participants. It is widely known that many policies take time to make it all the way into classrooms. Indeed, some even remain in their initial "good intention" form for a considerable period. Studying this particular initiative granted me the opportunity to look into the design, decision-making processes and modes of enforcement of a sub-national initiative that was being employed in classrooms by ordinary teachers. By doing so, this research sought to go beyond the more abstract level of analysis of large-scale assessment aspirations; instead it set out to scrutinize a specific experience regarding the ways in which these aspirations are being materialized in a particular subnational setting *in vivo*.

2   EXCALE Large-scale Assessment

Currently there are three large-scale assessment programs operating in the Mexican setting. These are: PISA, at the global scale; ERCE-LLECE at the regional Latin-American scale; and PLANEA at the national site. The policy addressed in this chapter takes into account a former national assessment program namely, EXCALE. This assessment can be regarded as one of the predecessors of PLANEA (INEE, 2016). EXCALE operated from 2004 to 2014 (see Chapter 4). Even though it is not currently functioning, most of its aims and activities were absorbed and extended by PLANEA which will continue assessing students in preschool. It thus provides a useful moment to explore LSAs and the various actors involved in its implementation.

In early publications, EXCALE was originally advanced as a low-stakes test. Its results would not be used for making decisions that could directly affect students, teachers, or schools (Ruiz, Jornet, & Backhoff, 2006). Instead, EXCALE results were only intended to offer an overview of the state of learning amongst students in Mexico, and to provide pertinent and valid comparisons for decision-making concerning the education system as a whole.

The purpose of EXCALE for preschool was to "provide an account of what students have learned from the national curriculum regarding the learning fields of language-communication and mathematical reasoning at the completion of this educational level" (INEE, 2014a, p. 7). To this end, EXCALE for preschool was applied in two different rounds: the first of them in 2007, and again in 2011. The test was administered to different size samples of third graders at the preschool education level in all 32 subnational states in Mexico. Considering that children at this educational phase and age, roughly 6 years-old, are not expected to know how to read and write, the test format consists of a series of learning tasks supervised by test applicants (INEE, 2014a). Pre-schoolers carry out these activities, and test applicants write down the outcomes. EXCALE does not offer results per student, group, school, district, city, or state-level.

Rather it is only national, and by service type (General, Indigenous and Communitarian). Furthermore, its samples and outcomes are not representative per subnational entity.

There are two formal publications of EXCALE results derived from the preschool education cycles (INEE, 2008a, 2014a). In these documents, student outcomes are displayed in three formats: (a) proportion of students per proficiency level; (b) proportion of correct answers for each assessed learning standard; and (c) the percentage of proficiency levels, contrasted against different variables such as level of schooling of the mother, size of family, and socioeconomic features. Figure 6.1 illustrates EXCALE preschool results per proficiency levels in literacy and math, accordingly to the 2007 and 2011 rounds.

In both rounds of EXCALE for preschools, only two learning fields were assessed: mathematical reasoning and language-communication. The rationale for this decision was based on the belief that these fields are decisive for subsequent learning in the latter schooling levels. It is assumed that the learning standards achieved during this period and in these particular fields will determine learning outcomes in primary and secondary education (INEE, 2008a).

Even though EXCALE was not conceived as a high-stake test, it was nevertheless a public policy instrument, and as such, it was at least consequential (Ramirez, Schofer, & Meyer, 2012). In other words, despite the fact that EXCALE would not affect students' chances of being promoted or accepted to a further educational grade or level, it certainly generated consequences for students, teachers, and the education system. The initiative addressed in this unit of analysis and its offspring, which will be discussed in the following sections, can be read as consequential outcomes of the EXCALE program. It is interesting to note that in this particular case, the outcomes, test components, and effects of EXCALE, outlived the life-cycle of the EXCALE program. Notwithstanding EXCALE was

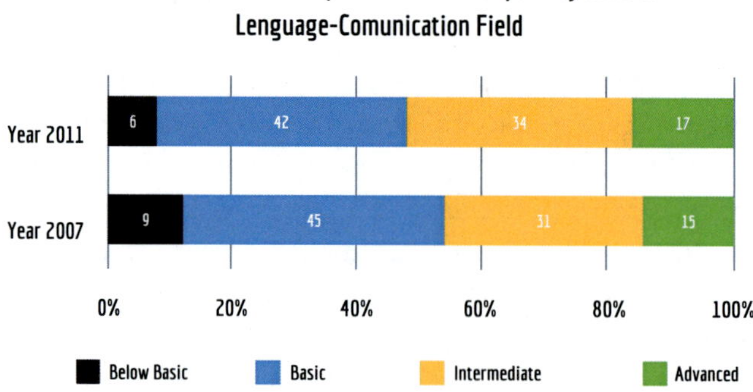

FIGURE 6.1   EXCALE 2007 and 2011 national preschool education student results
SOURCE: INEE (2014)

cancelled in 2014, policy proponents made use of it three years later. This should serve as an example of the long-lasting effects large-scale assessments can have on students, educators, and the education system in general.

3   Context of Preschool Education

The initiative addressed in this chapter takes place in the same geographical space where the local scale of this research was carried out. Hence, in this section I will not readdress the same contextual features as I did in Chapter 5. The reader can refer for more data regarding this subnational entity. Instead, in this chapter I will focus mainly on describing the general characteristics of the education level in which this policy has been advanced, emphasizing the nature of the municipality and sector in which it has been enforced.

3.1   *The Preschool Education Level*

Formal preschool education in Mexico dates back to the late XIX century. The first kindergarten or preschool accessible to the public was founded in 1881 in Mexico City, and operated under the pedagogical orientations, theories and principles advocated by Pestalozzi and Fröebel (Loyo & Staples, 2010). However, it was only until the first decade of the 21st century when this education level was made mandatory for all children and became part of the compulsory education cycle. Today, over 231,000 educators serve more than 4.8 million students in over 90,000 preschools nationwide (SEP, 2017). The preschool education service in Mexico is delivered to distinct publics through different modalities. These are operated by several branches of the Secretariat of Education and by private entities. Table 6.2 offers a brief account regarding preschool service type.

Preschool education in Mexico is comprised of three grades: 1st, 2nd and 3rd. Students are distributed among these grades accordingly to their age. Children enter first grade at roughly 3 years and 7 months of age, and graduate from third grade when they are approximately 6 years old. Commonly one educator is responsible for a single grade-age group. However, in multi-grade schools placed in rural areas, educators may have students from two or more different grades in the same class. Students enrolled in preschool education attend between 185 and 200 days of classes per schoolyear. During this period, they work from Monday to Friday in daily shifts of three hours, in either one of two school shifts: morning (9:00 to 12:00) or afternoon (13:00 to 16:00).

The purposes of preschool education are established and normed by the curriculum. Hence, whenever the curriculum shifts or is updated, the purposes

TABLE 6.2   Preschool service type

General	– Federal funded – Subnational funded – Private	Offered and regulated by the national and subnational Secretariats of Education. Provides service to students from urban and rural contexts in Mexico. Classes are conducted by college trained teachers in formal schools.
Indigenous		Offered and regulated by the national and subnational Secretariats of Education. Provides service to students from indigenous communities. Classes are conducted by college trained teachers in formal schools.
Communitarian groups		This modality is offered by the National Council for Educational Promotion (CONAFE for its acronym in Spanish). This service is provided in small localities with difficult geographical access. Classes are conducted by local members of the community that have finished primary or secondary education.

SOURCE: HTTPS://WWW.OEI.ES/HISTORICO/OBSERVATORIO2/ORGANIZACION.HTM

do too. The current purposes for this educational level are expressed in the following statements:

> It is expected that during the transition of students through preschool education in any modality – general, indigenous or community – children will live experiences that contribute to their development and learning processes, which will lead them to gradually: (a) Acquire confidence to express themselves, talk and converse in their mother tongue; (b) Use mathematical reasoning; (c) Be interested in observing living beings and discover characteristics they share; (d) Appropriate the values and principles necessary for life in society; (e) Develop a positive sense of themselves and learn to regulate their emotions, to work collaboratively; (f) Use imagination and fantasy, initiative and creativity to express themselves through artistic languages; (g) Become aware of the possibilities of expression, movement, control and balance of their body. (SEP, 2017, pp. 157–158)

The purposes outlined above inform and guide the learning standards within the curriculum for this education level. Regarding the learning standards, these are organized in six fields: (a) Language and Communication; (b) Mathematical

Reasoning; (c) Exploration and Understanding of the Natural and Social World; (d) Socioemotional Education; (e) Arts; (f) Physical Education. The first three fields are regarded as the 'Academic Training Fields', whereas the following three are labelled as 'Areas of Personal and Social Development' (SEP, 2017). In total there are 103 learning standards across the six learning fields which comprise the 2017 preschool education curriculum. Students are expected to meet all 103 learning standards during their passage throughout preschool education.

3.2   *Preschool in the Subnational Entity*

Tables 6.3, 6.4 and 6.5 show basic statistics regarding the preschool education level in the state where this research was developed, and in particular City 1, where the policy from this unit was deployed.

Table 6.3 shows that there are 1,474 preschools in this subnational entity. According to the interviewees, this entire cohort of schools is viewed as potential candidates for this policy in the near future.

Table 6.4 illustrates the distribution of preschools per service type in the city of City 1. During the data collection phase of this research, the policy had only been enforced in this city, and in the particular variant of Federal and Federal Transferred Schools.

Table 6.5 shows the distribution of students per grade and the total number of groups in the city of City 1. Currently, the EXCALE's use in kindergarten was only employed with students from the third grade. However, interviewees stated the intention of expanding it to the earlier grades in the following school years.

TABLE 6.3   Preschool enrolment per city

City	Students			Groups	Educators	Schools
	Total	Boys	Girls			
City 1	35,599	18,013	17,586	1,605	1,617	453
City 2	50,677	25,285	25,392	2,225	2,244	603
City 3	19,226	9,629	9,597	898	866	300
City 4	3,981	1,979	2,002	187	189	62
City 5	3,887	1,923	1,964	182	182	56
Total	113,370	56,829	56,541	5,097	5,098	1,474

SOURCE: OFFICIAL STATISTICS

TABLE 6.4   Preschool distribution per service type in City 1

City	Service type	Students			Groups	Educators	Schools
		Total	Boys	Girls			
City 1	State	10,162	5,074	5,088	427	432	88
	Federal	664	339	325	49	57	46
	Federal transferred	18,862	9,527	9,335	797	799	205
	Private	5,911	3,073	2,838	332	329	114
	Total	35,599	18,013	17,586	1,605	1,617	453

SOURCE: OFFICIAL STATISTICS

TABLE 6.5   Distribution of students per grade

City	Students per grade				Groups per grade				Multi grade
City 1	1st	2nd	3rd	Total	1st	2nd	3rd	Total	
	4,338	14,291	16,970	35,599	215	555	686	1,605	149

SOURCE: OFFICIAL STATISTICS

3.3   *Sector "Z" of Preschool Education in City 1*

In Mexico a school sector is the name assigned to a group, or set, of federal school districts from a particular region. In other words, it is a modality in which federal school districts are organized at the municipal level. The Preschool Education Department in the city of City 1 has three sectors which organize and provide assistance to all of 251 federal preschools.

A school sector is led by a Chief of Sector. This person is the immediate Superior of School Superintendents and answers directly to the Department Chief. Each school sector has a team of pedagogical advisors who help the Chief of Sector with regard to a diverse pedagogical and administrative activities. Sector "Z", where the current policy takes place, is comprised of nine different education districts; each of these has its own Superintendent responsible for a single district. Table 6.6 shows the total number of schools, groups, and students in Sector "Z".

TABLE 6.6　Number of schools, groups and students in Sector "Z"

Total number of schools in Sector "Z"	Total number of groups in Sector III	Total number of students in Sector III
64	209	3978

SOURCE: OFFICIAL STATISTICS

4　The EXCALE's Use in Kindergarten Initiative

4.1　*Development*

The EXCALE's use in kindergarten is an initiative that was designed during the 2016–2017 school year. Comments from interviews suggests that policy development involved five main actors: (1) State Director of INEE; (2) Chief of Sector "Z"; (3) Preschool Department Chief; (4) Superintendent One; and (5) Superintendent Two. The initiative emerged after the appointment of the Chief of Sector who was promoted from Superintendent in September of 2016. Following this event, she met the Preschool Department Chief who eventually introduced her to the INEE Director in October of that same year. The first formal meeting regarding this initiative was held in late October between the three agents outlined above, and the two Superintendents who formed part of Sector "Z". During this reunion, EXCALE related issues were discussed in more detail. This set of acquaintances and meetings laid out the early foundations and an overall blueprint for this initiative.

The agents involved in the phase of the development of this policy commented that they became acquainted with EXCALE through different means. For instance, participants mentioned that they either casually came upon information related to this program and consequently explored it further (Chief of Sector and Superintendents), or they were introduced to it by education authorities as part of their job functions (Director and Department Chief). In either case, participants shared a common interest to do 'something' with EXCALE, although driven by different reasons.

The motives which propelled initiative proponents to employ EXCALE were also mentioned during interviews. For instance, the Director of INEE claims that this is part of his job description: that is, "to put to use the outcomes of LSAs". This can be corroborated in Article 33, Clause 3, of the Organic Statute of the National Institute for Education Evaluation (INEE) which states that one of the main functions of the subnational directors of INEE, is to: "Contribute to fostering a culture of assessment through the dissemination and use of results of the different assessments carried out by the System" (DOF, 2017, p. 10).

Meanwhile, the Department Chief of Preschool claims to have been encouraged by the Director of INEE, her previous boss, to make use of EXCALE results. She comments: "we began to observe that educators were presenting difficulties with student assessments, and EXCALE clearly offered a solution". The Chief of Sector explained that since she had studied her Master's Degree: "assessment had always been an interesting and important topic for me, hence, after being introduced to the Director of INEE and getting to know EXCALE in more detail I became particularly interested in it". Lastly, Superintendent One claimed that:

When I was an educator, my Superintendent instructed us to only teach students minimum aspects of reading, writing and numeracy. I did not agree. By chance I found EXCALE on the internet and started using it because it bounded that students had to count up to 20. When I became a Superintendent, I started to employ it in all the district.

The comments outlined above indicate the different motives which encouraged participants to do something with EXCALE. This initiative could be interpreted as the result of a coincidence of education agents with similar interests in a common place and time, and who were mutually eager to put to work EXCALE outcomes. However, it could also be read as both an expression and crystallization of EXCALE's aims in combination with the setting into place of other initiatives and events linked to a widespread assessment culture. These issues will be discussed in more detail in the following sections of this chapter.

The policy design meetings for this initiative were held between October 2016 to March 2017. These sessions were presided over by the Director of INEE at his office in City 1, and they involved the main participations of the distinct agents outlined above, with occasional involvement of other members from the preschool education community. Interestingly, three initiative designers claimed that the original idea for this initiative was theirs. However, the formal credit is attributed to the Chief of Sector. Research evidence suggests some form of rivalry regarding authorship. This issue was not inquired into further to avoid early tensions or frictions that could affect the rest of the research process. However, it is important to notice that the INEE Director, Chief of Sector and one Superintendent, were all eager to claim credit for this policy.

Unlike the other units of analysis in this research, the subnational unit only entails one large-scale assessment program. When policy designers were questioned about the use, of other large-scale assessment programs in Mexico besides EXCALE for the advancement of this initiative, they responded:

No, in fact, the INEE director told us a bit about the other evaluation programs as a form of illustrating the work that was being conducted at other educational levels but, we focused on the assessment of our education level. (Policy designer A)

No, because they are not applied at the preschool level. Besides, we have more than enough with EXCALE. (Policy designer C)

Both of these comments suggest that evidence from other large-scale assessment programs were not consulted or used for the initiative addressed in this unit. The rationale for this decision can be linked to the fact that only EXCALE assessed children from preschool, *ergo*, only this is applicable, according to the logic of participants. The attitudes of interviewees towards other LSAs appeared to be one of indifference. This is a wake-up call for those assessments which claim to generate profiles of accumulated knowledge as to the full compulsory education cycle, such as PISA. At least this group of early childhood agents does not seem to care much for this program.

The EXCALE's use in kindergarten Initiative emerged as a response to a set of common problems identified by policy proponents. Some of these issues are expressed in the following comments:

Traditionally, since preschool education was made mandatory, the form of assessment carried out by educators is purely subjective and largely conducted through observation. I consider that this form of assessment is not sufficiently valid given that obviously, it is limited to educators' subjectivity and how they view student learning. This initiative – EXCALE's use in kindergarten – enforces a common evaluation framework in terms of the indicators regarding learning standards from the preschool education program. Because, although it is true the curriculum institutes the learning standards that students must acquire at the end of preschool education, each educator has their own theoretical reference on how these are achieved. Hence, currently, there are as much theoretical frameworks as there are educators. Endorsing EXCALE, which ultimately is carried out by INEE, is a reference I consider valid enough. It offers clear and precise information as to what does each learning standard refers to. And finally, these are the contents that will be assessed in our students. (Policy designer C)

At the beginning of the school year, I reviewed student diagnosis carried out by my educators. It was then when I realized that there were about ten student assessments that said the same things. It was as if they just had changed the student's name on the format. The language used in these assessments was not a professional one, they did not really talk about academic progress. Therefore, the methodological elements offered by the EXCALE program were very helpful. Specially in unifying the criteria for student assessment, which was very diverse before this. Finally, we're at a point where it's not about what this or that educator thinks learning standards mean, it's what EXCALE says. (Policy designer E)

The main problem is that preschool education program does not set a clear learning instruction, it does not tell us up to what or how much work must be done in each learning standard or grade. Some educators often said; (…) my students are fine because they can count up to ten", however, in no place did it say that students had to count up to ten. We now know, thanks to the proficiency levels in EXCALE, that by the end of preschool education, students must know how to count to 30. So, the main problem is the learning program, which does not offer details concerning how much, or up to what, students must learn. (Policy designer D)

According to these comments, there are two main problems this initiative sets out to address. First, the lack of an official measurement feature embedded in learning standards from the preschool education curriculum. Second, the subjective form of assessment historically carried out at the preschool education level. Unfortunately, there is no objective data that can confirm that the particular community of educators where this initiative was developed had a problem with assessing students. However, policy proponents agreed that this was a common problem in their setting and sought to address it with EXCALE through the advancement of the EXCALE's use in kindergarten initiative which proposes three shifts that will be discussed in the upcoming section.

4.2   *Purposes and Main Maneuvers*

According to interviews with the initiative proponents, the EXCALE's use in kindergarten has three main purposes, which also constitute three distinct maneuvers. The first of them seeks to replace learning standards from the curriculum with the assessment descriptors from the EXCALE test. The second aims to establish the set of proficiency levels employed by EXCALE test so as to determine and track students' progress during their preschool education cycle. The third, consists of administering – at the beginning, middle and end of the school-year – an "EXCALE like test" (created by policy designers) so as to diagnose and establish the base-line, and from there to trace students' advancement throughout the school-year. I will elaborate further on these maneuvers in the following paragraphs.

First and foremost, the preschool curriculum in Mexico is comprised of different elements. As outlined above one of its main, and also most important, components are the learning standards (SEP, 2017). Every knowledge field (e.g. Math, Science and Literacy) has its own set of learnings standards. Meanwhile, learning standards indicate what students should know and be able to do (SEP, 2011, 2017). They provide guidance as to the what and how to be learned of certain skills, knowledges and attitudes at the end of a time period (e.g. week, month or term).

EXCALE for preschool assesses how well and to what extent students are developing and acquiring the learning standards from the math and literacy fields from the compulsory curriculum at the end of preschool education. To this end, EXCALE employs a set of descriptors for assessing each particular learning standard. For each learning standard from the curriculum, there is an equivalent assessment descriptor from the EXCALE test that pertains to the assessment of that specific learning standard (INEE, 2014a). Table 6.7 shows two examples of this relationship: one from the literacy field, and the other from the math domain.

In the first column in Table 6.7, you can view two learning standards from the preschool curriculum. In the second column, you can view the assessment

TABLE 6.7   Contrast between learning standards from the preschool education program and assessment descriptors from the EXCALE test

Preschool education program learning standard	EXCALE test assessment descriptor for evaluating the learning standard
The student recognizes characteristics from the written system when employing own resources (such as: marks and letters) to express their ideas in writing (SEP, 2011, p. 47)	The student writes down his and other classmates names for different purposes (Identifying his belongings and schoolwork, to register his participation in some tasks, for loaning books from the class library) (INEE, 2014a, p. 98)
The student uses numbers in varied situations that implicate employing basic principles of counting (SEP, 2011, p. 57)	The student recognizes the value of coins and uses them in game-like situations (can compare with) (INEE, 2014a, p. 88)

SOURCES: PRESCHOOL LEARNING PROGRAM (2011) AND EXCALE REPORT (2014)

descriptors used by the EXCALE tests to assess those particular learning standards. The latter constitute the type of activities students are asked to carry out as part of the EXCALE assessment. What this initiative proposes is that instead of using learning standards to teach students, educators should use the assessment descriptors from the EXCALE test. Proponents of this initiative argue this shift is necessary because learning standards from the curriculum lack formal and precise indicators to assess them. Hence, the solution to this problem is to replace learning standards with assessment descriptors. This shift is not unproblematic, and some of its implications will be discussed shortly.

The second aim of the EXCALE's use in kindergarten initiative is to introduce the EXCALE proficiency levels and how to use them (Below Basic, Basic, Intermediate and Advanced), as a form of classifying and tracking students' progress during their preschool education cycle. Table 6.8 illustrates an example

TABLE 6.8   Example of EXCALE's use in kindergarten initiative proficiency levels and descriptors

Learning standard to be assessed	EXCALE proficiency levels			
	Level 1 below basic	Level 2 basic	Level 3 intermediate	Level 4 advanced
Writes down his and other classmates names for different purposes.	Does not understand the instructions, does not show interest in the activity.	Listens and understands the instructions, uses non-conventional letters or drawings to represent their name.	Identifies and writes the first letter of their name, either only the initial or accompanied by other undifferentiated spellings.	Writes their name establishing similarities with other names and words.
Student				
Emily		X		
Jimmy			X	
Betty	X			
Chris				X

of this shift. This table was provided by one of the heads who enforced this initiative at her school.

Traditionally, preschool educators assess students using descriptive report cards. This sort of instruments relay comments, thoughts and suggestions concerning students' progress with regard to learning standards or objectives. The EXCALE Results initiative substitutes this descriptive exercise with the enforcement of proficiency levels to indicate where students stand (Below Basic, Basic, Intermediate or Advanced) with respect to the realization of learning standards.

Lastly, the third aim of EXCALE Results seeks to employ an EXCALE like test developed by members of Sector III. Educators apply this test at the beginning of the school year to diagnose students' proficiency levels regarding learning standards from the literacy and mathematics reasoning fields. This is repeated again in the middle, and at the end, of the school-year. Educators are expected to aid students' transition from one proficiency level to the next, and so on, throughout the entire preschool education cycle. Educators are also expected to track and report the progress of their students through the terminology employed by this assessment.

Table 6.9 offers a summary of the purposes and maneuvers employed in the EXCALE's use in kindergarten initiative.

The purposes of the EXCALE's use in kindergarten initiative are varied and controversial. For instance, replacing a descriptive assessment with proficiency tables can be more manageable for educators and authorities. Ticking boxes instead of developing descriptive valuations also represents less work. However, the price to pay for this shift implies losing more detailed and specific assessments which are intended to respect and nurture the development of students so that they can achieve their maximum potential. Instituting proficiency tables as an outcome metric means that every child will be pressured to

TABLE 6.9   EXCALE's use in kindergarten maneuvers

1	Shift 1	(1) Replacement of learning standards with assessment descriptors.
2	Shift 2	(2) Replacement of the traditional descriptive report card for assessing students' progress in preschool with the EXCALE proficiency levels.
3	Shift 3	(3) Application of an EXCALE 'like' test to students at the beginning, middle and end of the school years. This emulation of EXCALE test is developed by the policy designers.

do the same irrespective of their interests and capabilities. Furthermore, this can bring about practices of "teaching to the rubric" (Jennings & Bearak, 2014).

After carefully studying the purposes proposed by the EXCALE's use in kindergarten initiative, there are two themes which caught my eye as the researcher. I kept asking: where and how are EXCALE results being employed here? And: why is there only interest in math and literacy? In the following two sections I will discuss of these recurring themes.

5   Use of Results?

In this section I ask questions about the use of EXCALE results by and for the initiative addressed in this unit of analysis – the EXCALE's use in kindergarten. Figure 6.2 illustrates two fundamental shifts advanced by this policy. First, it replaces learning standards from the curriculum with EXCALE test assessment descriptors. Second, it replaces the descriptive evaluation report card traditionally carried out at the preschool education stage with a proficiency level table for student appraisal.

Neither of the two shifts illustrated in Figure 6.2 indicate the use of assessment results. Policy designers were questioned about the use of assessment outcomes in or for this initiative. They shared the following thoughts:

> What we are using, regardless of the results by subnational entity, are the EXCALE proficiency levels as a metric to determine students' progress. (Policy designer C)

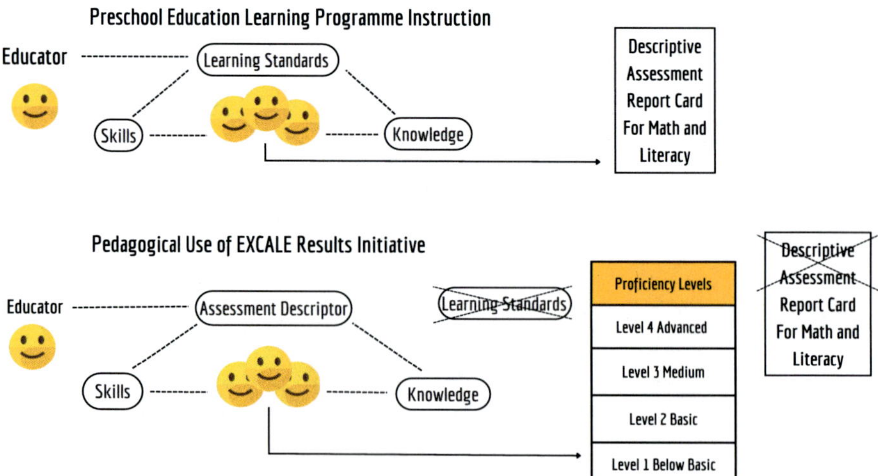

FIGURE 6.2   Shifts generated by the EXCALE's use in kindergarten initiative

> What happens is that we did not use hard data, like the results them-
> selves. They were only a reference. What we did use were the EXCALE
> proficiency levels. Each of these levels provides certain performance
> characteristics that are useful for placing children in advanced, interme-
> diate, basic or under basic levels. This part helped us a lot to unify criteria
> for student appraisal. (Policy designer D)

> The only elements we are going to use are the assessment descriptors and
> the proficiency levels as a form to measure, only these two elements for
> improving learning. (Policy designer A)

The logic of LSAs revolves around the idea that their outcomes could help make
"better" decisions regarding policies and practices. However, in this case, comments made by initiative proponents suggest that the outcomes were not used
in this sense. Following this train of thought, policy enforcers were questioned
about the use of EXCALE results, on the one hand, or their interaction with this
sort of data, on the other. Interviewees made the following comments:

> We just very quickly went through the results because time is limited, and
> it is not enough for everything. (Policy enforcer A)

> EXCALE results were shown to us at a workshop, however, educators did
> not find them so relevant. (Policy enforcer D)

> They only informed us in a general way what EXCALE was about, but
> never about the results themselves. (Policy enforcer C)

Policy enforcers emphasized that, in some cases, EXCALE results were barely
presented to them. In others, they were totally neglected. One would expect
that the results from this program are put to work to help improve education
practices. However, the evidence from this case suggests a different use of
EXCALE results. Here, it would seem that EXCALE results served as a driver
for enforcing the use of test features, such as assessment descriptors and proficiency levels for labelling students' progress. It is worth noting that these
developments raise two important concerns: (1) the amplification and reproduction of cardinal and nominal reasoning; and (2) teaching to the test practices in preschool. I will elaborate briefly on these two concerns and pick them
up again in Chapter 8.

First, in Chapter 3 I introduced the work of Fourcade (2016) around the principles of classificatory judgment. These principles are namely: nominal, cardinal, and ordinal, and are intended to help explain how comparisons have been

made possible throughout the history of humankind. In this research, these principles are seen in the context of measurement-based governing tools. Nominal and cardinal reasoning can be noted in the efforts outlined above that form part of the EXCALE's use in kindergarten initiative. For instance, nominal reasoning is at play when descriptive assessments are replaced with proficiency tables, and students are labelled as below basic, basic, intermediate or advanced. In this case, students' wide array of characteristics, their learning processes and progress, are all reduced to a single category (below basic, basic, intermediate, advanced), which now represents them. All students are branded and distributed across a horizontal map, namely, a proficiency table. For its part, cardinal reasoning is concerned with the dynamics of accumulation and collecting, we can note this reasoning is implicit in the educators' mission to focus on gaining or increasing the number of students in the intermediate and advanced categories of the proficiency table. These modalities of reasoning also matter because they are articulated with value judgments. For instance, in this case, a good student is one who is labelled as advanced, whereas a good teacher is one who helps students transition from the lower to the higher levels until they ultimately achieve an advanced level label.

Second, with regards to teaching to the test. If a certain learning standard from the curriculum states that the student; "Uses numbers in varied situations that implicate employing basic principles of counting" (SEP, 2011, p. 57), and the assessment descriptor from EXCALE as a mean for assessing the aforementioned learning standard states that the student "Recognizes the value of coins and uses them in game-like situations" (INEE, 2014a, p. 88), educators will teach students to recognize the value of coins and use them in game-like situations, instead of teaching the principles of counting *per se*. Replacing learning standards with test descriptors without a proper consideration and examination of the implications of this shift are likely to distort learning purposes, and reduce teaching and learning to less than what it could be (Eisner, 1985). Furthermore, inferences raised from the outcomes of this policy will have substantial limitations. For instance, even if policy proponents manage to raise test outcomes, they cannot claim that learning has improved because the outcomes will only be valid for the assessments descriptors that were assessed, not for the full learning standards or for broader learning claims (Jennings & Bearak, 2014).

In this regard, policy designers were questioned if replacing learning standards from the curriculum with EXCALE test assessment descriptors was in any way a form of teaching to the test, or cheating. Interviewees offered the following comments:

> That's an issue that has nothing to do with what we are discussing here. (Policy designer B)

> No, for me this a form to improve teaching practices. (Policy designer D)

> No, because we are not using the test items. In that instance, we could fall into teaching to the test. We only use assessment descriptors and proficiency levels. (Policy designer C)

Policy designers denied that this initiative constituted a teaching to the test practice. It is important to note that by replacing learning standards with assessment descriptors, educators are not teaching test questions or items. However, this practice means that instead of teaching the knowledge and skills of a particular learning standard, educators teach the specific ways in which that learning standard will be assessed by the EXCALE test. This dynamic can be interpreted as teaching the answer, which for some researchers is a form of cheating (see Nichols & Berliner, 2007).

It is not clear if policy designers genuinely do not know what they are doing, or if they do know, but do not care. Or perhaps they are so eager to do something that this has blurred their vision. Either way, there are serious ethical implications here, which involve different agents and institutional norms. Amongst them two in particular stand out. First, following the 2013 Education Reform in Mexico, education leaders are required, as part of their job description, to make use of external assessment results (SEP, 2014). This may boost or encourage the need for creating or employing initiatives such as the one being addressed in this unit of analysis. Second, INEE planned, developed, and applied EXCALE. Their publications were keen to emphasize that EXCALE results were only to be used for whole education system decision-making (INEE, 2014a). Nevertheless, the initiative studied in this case was designed and advocated in part by the State Director of INEE. Ironically, the initiative was published by the national INEE, as part of their catalogue of successful assessment practices. Here, INEE not only does not condemn the misuse of this sort of assessment but promotes and amplifies it.

My analysis indicates the omnipresence of Campbell's Law (the more any quantitative social indicator is used for social decision-making, the more subject it will be to corruption pressures and the more apt it will be to distort and corrupt the social processes it is intended to monitor, cited in Nichols & Berliner, 2007, pp. 26–27). This 'Law' can be found in the assessment processes that surround preschool education level in the subnational entity of this research.

6   Math and Literacy: A Myth?

There appears to be a consensus amongst policy designers at the subnational scale of this research, which revolves around the premise that literacy and mathematical reasoning fields are the most important for enabling learning in other knowledge domains. This discourse is encouraged by EXCALE assessments (INEE, 2014a). Nevertheless, more broadly, the theoretical underpinnings of this discourse can be linked to the economization of education and the insertion of Human Capital theory into the education spheres. In this section I discuss these two issues: that math and literacy are cornerstone for learning, and that this discourse is linked to the structuring political project, that of neoliberalism, and the economization of particular aspects of preschool education.

During interviews, policy designers were asked whether they considered assessing or making use of only two learning fields (literacy and mathematical reasoning), as EXCALE does, represented a limitation in any way. They shared the following comments:

> This is not a limitation because before this initiative there was nothing, now there is something. Moreover, as theorists, experts, educators, psychologists all say: literacy and mathematical reasoning are instrumental skills to access the other knowledge fields. If literacy and mathematical reasoning skills are not consolidated in a person, it will be difficult to consolidate other areas of knowledge. (Policy designer B)

> No. These two learning fields are definitely the basis for generating learning in any of the other fields. That is, language and communication (Literacy) are applicable in any of the other fields, in any of the other subjects, for any of the other learning standards. (Policy designer E)

> I don't see it as a limitation, because ultimately, these are cross-disciplinary learning fields. They are the basic ones, which enable students and equip them with the elements that will allow them to continue learning through life. (Policy designer C)

Literacy and math skills are presented as both natural and foundational for enabling learning in other knowledge domains. Yet there a several issues this rationale downplays. For instance: (1) not all aspects or elements of the literacy and mathematical reasoning fields are instrumental or enablers; (2) the expected enablement is not a cause-effect relationship; (3) it is not an exhausted nor straightforward science; and (4) this dominant view is linked to issues that go beyond learning. In the following paragraphs I will elaborate on these matters.

On the one hand, many issues regarding how students learn are highly contested, and on the other hand there is a lack of evidence as to which specific skills and content from the dominant learning fields enable what precise skills form the non-dominant fields and how? The literacy curriculum leader for the new 2017 curriculum in Mexico illustrates this problem in the following comment:

> There are many gaps in the field of research regarding how students learn. For example, we do not know for a fact, what is more difficult for a student, writing a description or writing a narrative? We intuit that narrating is easier than describing, and that arguing is even more difficult than both but, this assumption is intuition rather than a fact supported by data or references. Large-scale assessment programs don't always offer information regarding these matters. (2017 Curriculum literacy team leader)

Claiming that the full extent of the literacy and mathematical reasoning fields are instrumental for enabling learning in other knowledge fields is somewhat an overstatement. From a simplistic stance, this argument may sound rational. However, from a scientific point a view, there is still much to be understood about this relationship. The acknowledged limitations concerning current research outlined by the key policy developer, in addition to the issues highlighted above, indicate that this topic requires much more study. These types of claims and rationales form part of a governing tool which Robertson (2017) refers as to flattening (see Chapter 3). In this particular case, flattening is expressed by assuming, reproducing and amplifying the argument that the full extent of math and literacy domains are cornerstone for learning, without making any distinctions nor precisions. In the form of an analogy, it would be like arguing that everything we eat is nutritional, when in fact there are some foods that are more beneficial than others, and some that are not nutritional at all. The flattening argument will be elaborated and explored further in Chapter 8. For the moment, it is important to keep in mind how certain narratives, such as the one based on the idea that math and literacy are absolutely foundational, employ ontological flat arguments and views, such as: one size fits all, single solutions, universally valid, and so on (Robertson, 2012b).

In retrospect, preschool education in Mexico did not always conceive of math and literacy as the milestone for further enhancing learning, and nor were these fields regarded as more valuable than others. Table 6.10 shows key

TABLE 6.10   Preschool education learning programs-curriculum from 1979 to 2017

	Curriculum	Characteristics
1	Preschool Learning Program 1979	The curriculum was organized in six learning areas, namely: (a) cognitive; (b) social and emotional; (c) language; (d) gross motor skills; (e) fine motor skills (SEP, 1979).
2	Preschool Learning Program 1981	The curriculum was organized in three development axes, namely: (a) Social Affective development; (b) Cognitive development; (c) Psychomotor development. These axes were addressed using 10 Thematic Units: (1) Integrating the child to school; (2) Clothing; (3) Feeding; (4) Housing; (5) Health; (6) Work; (7) Forms of transport; (8) Means of communication; (9) Commerce; (10) National traditions and festivities (SEP, 1984).
3	Preschool Learning Program 1992	The curriculum was organized in four learning dimensions: (a) Affective Dimension; (b) Social Dimension; (c) Intellectual Dimension; (e) Physical Dimension (SEP, 1992).
4	Preschool Learning Program 2004	The curriculum was organized in six Formative or Learning Fields: (a) Personal and Social Development; (b) Language and Communication (Literacy); (c) Mathematical Reasoning; (d) Exploration and Knowledge of the World; (e) Art Appreciation and Expression; (f) Physical and Health Development. Theoretically, the program claims that it is competency based with some constructivism features, however, it does not make reference to particular authors of this theory (SEP, 2004).
5	Preschool Learning Program 2011	The curriculum was organized in six Formative or Learning Fields: (a) Language and Communication (Literacy); (b) Mathematical Reasoning; (c) Exploration and Knowledge of the World; (d) Physical and Health Development; (e) Personal and Social Development; (f) Art Appreciation and Expression (SEP, 2011).
6	Preschool Learning Program 2017	This curriculum is organized in three components namely: (a) Academic Training Fields; (b) Areas of Personal and Social development; (c) Ambits of Curricular Autonomy. These components are worked via six Formative or Learning Fields: (a) Language and Communication (Literacy); (b) Mathematical Reasoning; (c) Exploration and Knowledge of the World; (d) Socioemotional Education, (e) Arts; (f) Physical Education (SEP, 2017).

SOURCE: BASED ON PRESCHOOL EDUCATION PROGRAMS FROM 1979 TO 2017

characteristics of the different preschool education curriculum programs over the past 40 years.

Table 6.10 presents important insights regarding the structure of preschool education learning programs from 1979 to 2017. These features help illustrate that, contrary to today's beliefs, mathematical reasoning and literacy have not always been viewed as key enablers for further learning in other knowledge domains. For instance, curriculum programs from 1979 to 1981 have a strong theoretical foundation and focus on achieving students' personal and social development. One of the superintendents interviewed for this case made it clear that the most important feature linked to enabling learning in the 1979 program was students' self-esteem and self-confidence. On this matter, she stated:

> When I started working in preschool, it was forbidden to teach numbers and letters. During the federal administration of Salinas (1988–1994) there was a great boom, due to the release of pedagogical orientations to work oral and written language at this educational level. This was ground-breaking because it had been forbidden. I believe these were ideas of the authority of that time. If you ask me personally, which was the most important learning field in preschool? My answer would be the "Personal and Social Development Field". Language is important, but prior to acquiring language, students need to develop the confidence and self-esteem to stand in front of challenging situations and address them. This program sought necessary to nourish love and security in preschool children, as a form of preparing them for further life challenges. (Preschool superintendent)

According to this excerpt by an education superintendent, the dominant rationale for enhancing student learning at the preschool educational level during the 1979 program period was linked to students' self-esteem, rather than to mathematical reasoning and literacy, which was actually forbidden at that time.

Table 6.10 suggests a gradual reconfiguring of the focus of preschool education programs from 1979 to 2017. This reconfiguration can even be viewed in physical terms. For instance, in the 1979 program, mathematical reasoning did not figure as part of the learning areas, language (literacy) did; however, it did not occupy a protagonist role. In the 2004 program, the first learning field to be listed is Personal and Social Development. When the 2011 program was published, although it ensures many of the structural features of the 2004 version, this same field was sent to the bottom of the list and replaced by the Language and Communication Field (Literacy), followed by the Mathematical Reasoning Field. This reordering of learning fields may seem harmless. However, it should not be taken for granted because what counts as knowledge, the way it is introduced, presented and ordered, are all forms of symbolic and theoretical positioning and fundamentally what counts as power and control (Apple, 2000, 2016).

Further analysis suggests that if the timeline embedded in Table 6.10 is contrasted against the rolling out of neoliberalism as a political project in Mexico, we can observe a thread which suggest that the more Mexico approached organizations linked to the expansion of neoliberalism around the globe (i.e. IMF, OECD, WB), and embraced structural reforms, preschool education programs began shifting in particular directions. These directions can be linked to neoliberalism, the economization of education, and Sahlberg's characterization of the global education reform movement (GERM). In the following paragraphs I will elaborate on these relationships. Before continuing to this point, it is important to note that this is relevant because shifts in these programs can result in practices such as the ones studied in this chapter, where education agents at this distinct schooling level see and approach assessment issues in particular ways, that of proficiency reporting. This matters because of the omission or displacement of other forms of assessment that can be more useful and meaningful to the overall process of learning.

The onset of neoliberalism as a political project in Mexico dates back to between 1988 and 1994 (Ornelas, 2018). During this period, Mexico tightened relations with the International Monetary Fund (IMF), resulting in a series of policy papers (IMF, 1992) which recommended employing structural reforms such as: opening the public sectors to private participation, privatization of state-owned companies, and economic deregulation, amongst other initiatives (Salas-Porras, 2014). Also, during this period, the North American Free Trade Agreement (NAFTA) was under negotiation. This agreement sought to reduced trade barriers between North American nations, and to open national markets to foreign participations from Canada and the United States of America. Furthermore, one must also consider the fact that in 1994, Mexico also joined the OECD. This enrolment signified amongst other things that Mexico would now be expected to embrace similar policies to other nation-members of this club. Altogether, this set of events represented an important part of the genesis of neoliberalism as political project in Mexico.

Interestingly, the 1992 preschool education program in Mexico reflects the outcomes of the new formed relationships outlined above. One can note the subtle shifts in program discourse, and their underpinning and structures between the 1979 and the 1992 versions. For instance, the latter introduces discursive elements linked to the economization of education, particularly human capital. Bits of these components can be inferred from the following text:

> Within the framework of economic, political, and social transforma-
> tions that Mexico has set in motion, education should be conceived as
> a pillar of the integral development of the country; therefore, it is neces-
> sary to make a transformation of the national education system to raise
> the quality of education. For this purpose, the National Agreement for
> Educational Modernization has been signed. (SEP, 1992, p. 5)

The previous text constitutes the opening paragraph of the 1992 preschool education program. As one can note, the text invokes economic concerns. In this respect, education is portrayed as a means for bringing about a desired state of affairs in economic, political and social terms. Consequently, the government makes a call to raise education quality levels, linking means to ends.

Aside from incorporating discursive elements from the economization of education, the 1992 preschool education program also integrates three ground-breaking empirical mechanisms. First, this program employs constructivism as its main pedagogical orientation theory. For Robertson (2012a), constructivism fits perfectly with the ontology of neoliberalism and pushes forward its values, particularly its concern for the individual. This pedagogical view is particularly challenging for a fragmented society, like that of the Mexican, which needs its people to work together in order to achieve a more equitable progress. Meanwhile, Sahlberg (2014) argues that constructivism is one of the main inspirations for the GERM, in that this paradigm shifts the focus away from teaching to learning, with particular emphasis on problem solving and conceptual understanding. Consequently, it redirects attention to the math and literacy fields. Spring (2017) explains that in the context of human capital, hard skills such as numeracy and literacy are viewed as a priority in that they help prepare students for the needs of the market. Sahlberg (2014) claims both of these fields became a target of education reform around the globe in countries with a GERM spread. By doing this, it begins to comply a bit more formally with the needs of the market and the human capital view of education (Spring, 2017). Here it is important to mention that Sahlberg (2014) notes that this is one of the main characteristics of GERM countries; their emphasis on core subjects, which, in turn jeopardizes the acquisition and development of other important knowledges and skills. The third and last mechanism introduced in the 1992 program consists of orientations to educators for teaching literacy at this particular educational stage.

Following the 1992 program, the 2004, 2011 and 2017 preschool education programs, increased their emphasis on the dominating learning fields (Mathematical Reasoning and Literacy), as outlined above received preferential treatment as enhancers, enablers and predictors of further learning. This move is encouraged and legitimized by discourses that link these fields and student performance to economic development (OECD, 1999, 2001a, 2016a).

What I have discussed in the previous paragraphs is that following the setting in place of neoliberalism as a political project in Mexico, the preschool education curriculum began to develop and incorporate practices and theories which pushed forward the values of this economic doctrine. In the case of the particular initiative studied in this chapter, the outcome between the interaction of these values, theories and context can be observed in move to proficiency reporting based on a standardized table.

Given that curriculum issues in Mexico are highly complex (see Pinar, 2011), the rhetoric concerning foundational knowledge for enhancing further learning requires a more measured approach. In this regard it is important to: (a) recognize the current research limitations to this narrative; (b) cease the spread of misinformation regarding this enterprise; (c) acknowledge the links between this discourse and the economic agendas tied to it; and (d) recognize the cases that challenge the assumptions between dominant learning fields and economic growth. A good example of this is Cuba; a country that happens to have one of the best education systems in Latin America (Carnoy, 2016) based on learning outcomes, yet its economy is quite limited. This case shows that in some instances, economic growth does not entirely depend on domestic factors. In another case, Chang (2012) explains that the economic growth of a nation does not (for the most part) depend on the proportion of literate people that a country has but, rather, on the natural resources that a nation has in combination with its capacity to organize themselves to produce services and goods.

7   Conclusions

In this chapter I have focused attention on early years learning at a subnational setting in Mexico. The findings here suggest that EXCALE has been used to resolve problems of initial teacher training, continuous professional development, and alleged curricular faults, in turn neglecting the roots of the problems it intends to solve. I have argued that this policy embraces the belief amongst policy designers that math and literacy are cornerstones for further learning. However, the short review of preschool learning programs in Mexico from the late 70s to the current time suggests that this has not always been the case. Moreover, findings indicate that as Mexico continued to embrace structural reforms linked to neoliberalism, preschool education programs shifted away from their early principles founded on children's self-esteem and confidence as an enhancer for enabling further learning, to the current dominant under-standing of math and literacy as cornerstone. I have also discussed that by replacing learning standards with EXCALE test assessment descriptors, edu-cators are tending in the direction of a form of teaching the test answers. As a result of this, Campbell's law is extended into the education level of preschool education in Mexico and can be conceived of as an institutionalized form of cheating. Large-scale assessments and their sponsor bodies are supposed to prevent this type of misuse of assessments. However, in this particular case, they presume and amplify the practice, posing an important ethical issue.

National Scale

Legislators and Secretariat Officials

So far, we can see a pervasive influence of LSAs in Mexican education at the local and subnational levels. So, what of the national? In Chapter 7 I focus on two distinct national (federal) policies; the first, The General Law for the Professional Teaching Service, looks into the deliberations and decisions surrounding this policy by a group of Senators from the Honorable Congress of the Union of Mexico (2012–2018 Legislation). The LGSPD regulates the new mechanisms for entering the public teaching service and a system for universal teacher appraisal in Mexico. The second policy is Key Learnings for an Integral Education; the 2018–2022 national curriculum for compulsory education. In this case I address policy decisions amongst a group of high-ranked federal officials and specialized collaborators from the Secretariat of Education in relation to the advancement of the most recent national curriculum. In this respect, Chapter 7 entails the study of two distinct policies involving significantly different groups of participants with particular needs yet potentially dependent on the same sort of data produced by PISA, PLANEA and ERCE. This chapter will focus on the relationships and outcomes between these policy decision-makers and their use or not of LSA data.

1 Policy I: The General Law for the Professional Teaching Service

The General Law for the Professional Teaching Service was approved by the Honorable Congress of the Union of Mexico in September of 2013. My focus is on policy decisions amongst Senators regarding this initiative. To this end, this section is divided into: (a) sources of data; (b) Honorable Congress of the Union context; (c) the General Law for the Professional Teaching Service development; and (d) main findings.

1.1 *Source of Data*

The study of this case draws upon an original data set comprised of two main sources: (1) policy and large-scale assessment-related documents; (2) six individual semi-structured interviews with Senators from the Honorable Congress of the Union of Mexico from the 2012–2018 legislation. Table 7.1 is a summary

TABLE 7.1   Senator participants

No.	Participant	Background
1	Senator 1	Left-wing liberal Senator, former National Secretary of State, former National Secretary of Education, previous Senator, and Congress Deputy. Non-member of the Education Commission. Voted against this initiative.
2	Senator 2	Left-wing liberal Senator, former Mayor of Mexico City, former Congress Deputy. Non-member of the Education Commission. Voted against this initiative.
3	Senator 3	Left-wing liberal Senator, former Education Union Leader, former Congress Deputy. Member of the Education Commission at the Senate. Voted against this initiative.
4	Senator 4	Right-wing conservative Senator, former Chair of the National Council for Science and Technology, former Governor of the State of Guanajuato, former Rector of the University of Guanajuato, Chairman of the Education Commission at the Senate. Voted in favor of this initiative.
5	Senator 5	Right-wing conservative Senator, former Senator, and Congress Deputy. Member of the Education Commission at the Senate. Voted in favor of this initiative.
6	Senator 6	Right-wing conservative Senator, former Mayor, Congress Deputy, and businessman. Member of the Education Commission at the Senate. Voted in favor of this initiative.

of the professional backgrounds and previous political experiences of the Senators that were interviewed for this research.

Initially, I had contemplated purposive sampling which envisaged interviewing only those Senators who formed part of the Education Commission at the Senate. However, since not all of them showed interest in participating in this study, other Senators were invited based on their previous experiences with the education sector. Finally, the sample was comprised of four Senators from the Education Commission, and two non-members. It is important to note that all participants possess substantial experiences working in public office.

Access to these participants was nothing less than challenging. I began by sending formal email invitations attached with: (a) a research outline of this unit; (b) confidentiality forms; and (c) my personal curriculum vitae, to all members from the Education Commission at the Senate. This was followed up by constant emails and telephone calls to their offices so as to secure their interest in participating. Finally, face-to-face meetings were arranged and scheduled. I personally met with each individual Senator who granted me an interview. Meetings were held in their offices at the Senate between January and March of 2018. The cohort of participants from this unit is comprised by Senators from six different sub-national states. My intention was to balance participation by political ideology. Thus, three participants are from two right-wing political parties, whereas the other three are from three left-wing parties.

Selecting this particular policy as one of the units of analysis to be addressed at the national scale of this research is based on the following criteria: (1) this initiative was advanced at the national scale, and considering that this book aims to study LSAs at distinct scales within Mexico, this policy complied with the first requisite; (2) preliminary readings of this policy indicated connections of some sort with large-scale assessments; (3) this policy affected all teachers nation-wide, thus looking into it through a critical lens seemed necessary; (4) considering its novelty, there is scarce research which addresses this policy, and no indications were found of research from a governance point of view that looked into this matter; and (5) the group of policy decision-makers involved in this policy (Senators) represent one of the audiences targeted by LSAs.

1.2 *Honorable Congress of the Union Context*

Before discussing the Honorable Congress of the Union context, it is important to note that Mexico holds a presidential republic form of government, which is bound by a federal system mandated in the 1917 Constitution of the United Mexican States. The political structure is comprised by three levels of rule: (a) Federal; (b) State; and (c) Municipal. In territorial terms, the nation is divided into 32 states, which in turn are distributed in 2,458 municipalities. Table 7.2 offers more details regarding this arrangement.

Although the territorial organization of Mexico has three levels of rule, many matters are federally centralized. For instance, in the field of education, the curriculum is designed and mandated at the federal level. The state level is responsible for its enforcement, and education authorities, either funded by state of federal resources, overview its application at the municipal level. In terms of funding, Scott et al. (2018) note that "finance is really controlled by the federal government, which must give its approval to local programs before the funds are released; and state governments have little if any funds of their own to use" (p. 10).

With regards to the topic of education policy, most initiatives are designed and mandated either by the Congress or by the Secretariat of Education at the national level. State governments have some discretion over state policies.

TABLE 7.2   Mexican political structure

	Level/ branch	Executive figure	Legislative figures	Judicial figures
1	Federal	President	Congress: two chambers	Supreme court, federal courts.
2	State	Governor	State Congress	State courts
3	Municipal	Mayor	City Council	Local courts

However, as noted before, these are largely restrained by the lack of resources. Local initiatives at the municipal level arise from time to time, however, in addition to monetary resources, education authorities at these levels lack of the normative power to make them mandatory. By way of contrast, federal initiatives have the normative power to do so. For instance, municipal superintendents can propose initiatives to their schools and persuade schools to carry them out, however, they cannot mandate them.

The Honorable Congress of the Union of Mexico is the major legislative entity in the country. It is comprised of two chambers, houses, or cameras. The upper chamber, also known as the Senate, is constituted by 128 members, of which, 64 are directly elected in pairs by universal vote from the electorates from each of 32 subnational states in Mexico. Another 32 senators are elected for being the first runner-up from each subnational entity, and the remaining 32 are assigned via plurinominal votes (Camacho, 2013). This last variant – plurinominal – grants a number of chairs or Senate seats to each political party based on the total percentage of votes acquired in the elections in turn. The lower chamber, most commonly known as the Camera of Deputies, is comprised of 500 members, of which 300 are directly elected by universal vote from the electorates of each individual federal district or constituency in Mexico. The remaining 200 seats are assigned via plurinominal (Camacho, 2013).

Senators have a tenure of six years, the same period of the Federal Administration. By way of contrast, Deputies terms only last three years. Hence, each Federal Administration has two different Deputy Cameras during its single term. This was one of the main reasons why only Senators were targeted to participate in this study. The Deputies who participated in the General Law for the Professional Teaching Service legislative process in 2013 had already left office at the time of this research's data collection phase, hence, obtaining access to them was not possible. Each of the Congress chambers is led by a Board of Chairs in which all political parties are represented. This board and its members

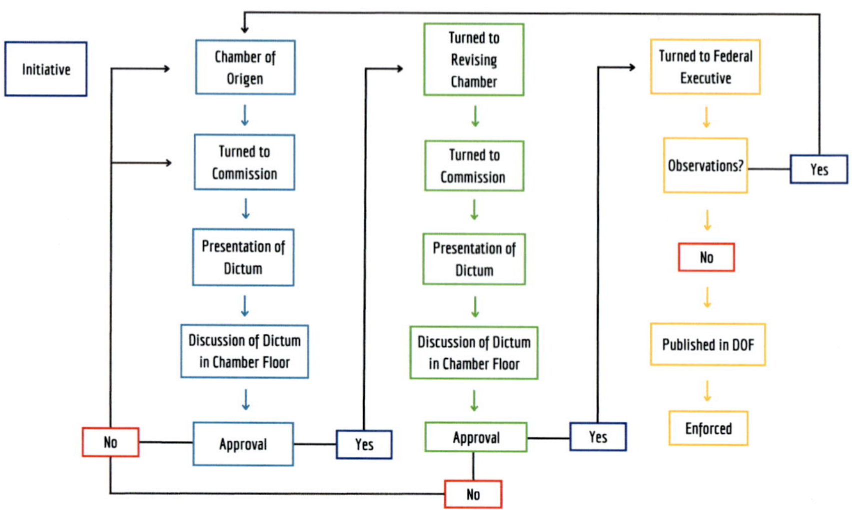

FIGURE 7.1   Diagram for creating or amending a law at the congress in Mexico
SOURCE: CAMACHO (2013, P. 112)

are renewed each year. Once instituted, each chamber organizes commissions by strategic subject (i.e. Education, Health, Science, etc.). These commissions overview particular issues related to that area. Furthermore, they are the first parliamentary groups to analyze new initiatives, and to decide whether or not to pass them to the chamber floor to be discussed and ruled upon. The number of members per commission varies in each case, from a minimum of three to a maximum of fifteen. The Congress carries out varied processes, mandates, and tasks. The three main activities of Congress are to: "a) represent the nation and its subnational states; b) to fiscally and politically overview and control the public administration in turn; c) to create, review or amend laws, acts and institutions of federal domain" (Camacho, 2013, p. 116). The process for creating or amending a law by Congress is illustrated in Figure 7.1.

1.3   *The General Law for the Professional Teaching Service Development*
On December 1st, 2012, Enrique Peña Nieto assumed office as the 57th President of The United States of Mexico. One of his first, and undoubtedly crucial, political moves was the establishment of an alliance, The Pact for Mexico (Ornelas, 2018). The pact consisted of a formal accord between the three major political parties in Mexico at that time: PRI, PAN, and PRD (Ramirez, 2016; OECD, 2018b). This maneuver granted President Peña Nieto an overall majority in Congress that was in turn translated into a virtual fast-pass lane for conveying and approving a great deal of his agenda of structural reforms.

Later that same month, on December 21st, three weeks after assuming the Presidency, Peña Nieto achieved a historical constitutional reform in education matters approved by the Honorable Congress of the Union and formally decreed on February 26, 2013. This reform, later known as the 2013 Education Reform, introduced the term "quality" into the Third Article of the Constitution – as a key issue and policy goal for education – and laid the foundations for: (a) universal and mandatory teacher appraisal; (b) a new mechanism for entering the public teaching service and tenure; and (c) a new mechanism for teacher promotion, both vertically and horizontally.

In order to regulate the new goals mandated in his 2013 Education Reform, on August 13th, 2013, President Peña remitted an initiative to the Honorable Congress of the Union, the General Law for the Professional Teaching Service. In this initiative, he proposed an array of details based on notions of "Teacher Performance Evaluation" which would eventually determine the rules and conditions for operating the modifications to the constitution made eight months earlier. This initiative mandated the bases for regulating all the three forms of assessment for teachers outlined above. Within the rationale of this bill, teachers were held 100 per cent responsible for their personal performance and those of their students. It should be pointed out, however, that this new law neglected the state's historical responsibility for their role in poor initial teacher training, in particular the insufficient and inadequate continuous professional development of teachers over the decades. In a broader sense, this bill transformed a systemic problem into a personal one.

The General Law for the Professional Teaching Service generated much criticism due to its punitive bias (Bartlett & Benavides, 2016). It sent the message that if teachers did not achieve ideal results in their personal evaluations they would be restricted, if not prohibited, from entering the public teaching service, whilst those already in-service could be fired from their current employment with no liability or responsibility around performance attributed to the state. An outcome of this nature was unlikely to occur before this law due to teachers civil-servant status. It is important to note that in Mexico, the education union, namely SNTE (its acronym in Spanish), holds a collective contract with the federation and subnational governments. This labor arrangement grants all education workers civil servant status, including teachers, leaders, administrative and classified staff (ILO, 1991; Santiago et al., 2012). Before the approval of the General Law for the Professional Teaching Service, job tenure was automatically granted after six months and one day of worker's initial appointment. Figure 7.2 provides a legislative chronogram of the processes and stages that brought about the General Law for the Professional Teaching Service.

Figure 7.2 shows that the initiative was sent to Congress and approved in less than one month. According to official records from Congress, and to commentary by Bartlett and Benavides (2016) (Bartlett was a Senator at that time), the law was discussed and approved on the same day it reached the floor in

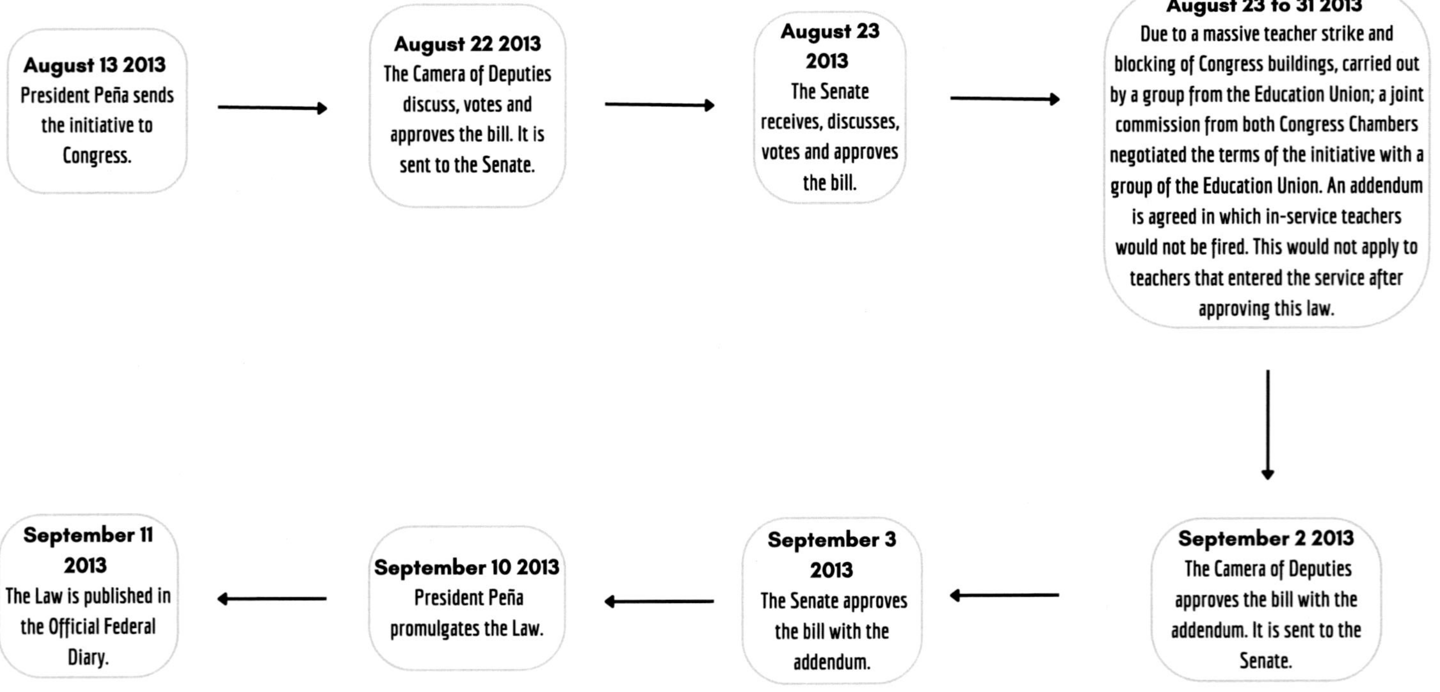

FIGURE 7.2   Legislative processes and stages of the general law for the professional teaching service
SOURCE: BARTLETT & BENAVIDES (2016, P. 298)

both of the chambers, leaving scarce time for robust discussion or debate. The initiative was approved at the Senate with 102 votes in favor, 22 against and 2 nulls. By way of contrast, at the Deputies Chamber, it was approved with 357 votes in favor, 73 against and 1 abstention.

In merely eight days, the General Law for the Professional Teaching Service was presented, studied, debated, and approved. Naturally, with only a few days prior to reaching the Congress floor and only one day on them for discussion, many doubts arise concerning the extent and depth of the debate that took place. In this respect I am particularly interested in analyzing and discussing whether, how and in what ways large-scale assessment data was used in the decision-making processes leading to the approval of this policy.

1.4   *LGSPD Main Findings*

1.4.1   Legislators and LSA Data

The relationship between LSA data and the General Law for the Professional Teaching Service lies in the broader linkages between this data and the main agents involved in the approval of this initiative. Thus, it is fundamental to first reflect upon the ways in which legislators become acquainted and engaged with LSA data. First and foremost, all legislators interviewed for this study were aware of the existence of PISA, PLANEA and its predecessors. Similar to the survey outcomes reported in Chapter 5 of this book, these legislators would seem to disregard ERCE-LLECE assessments. Senators stated that none of the international LSAs which operate in Mexico today send their reports or data to them. This stands in contrast to the domestic assessment (PLANEA) where the Secretariat of Education, in alliance with the National Institute for Education Evaluation (INEE), send information. However, these bodies do not distribute LSA data to all Legislators. According to the interviewees, this was mainly for those Senators who formed part of the Education Commission or those that had some link to government branches. The following statements elaborate on this:

> There is a mix chamber (Senate and Deputy) commission meeting in which the Secretary of Education is present, each of us receive the results, however, I cannot say if all other Senators receive them, but the members from the Education Commission do. (Right-wing politician, Education Commission member)

> INEE delivers an annual report to the Congress, it is made public, there is a session with at least the Education Commission and courtesy is given to other legislators to assist. The level of reading of these documents varies

> because each legislator is at least in four or five different commissions.
> Thus, not all of them find the time to get into this matter. (Right-wing
> politician, Education Commission member)

With regard to the issue of acquaintance, Legislators explained that any
engagement with large-scale assessment data was prior to the legislative processes leading to the approval of the General Law for the Professional Teaching
Service. These interactions were the outcome of former professional experience and other channels and not the result of the initiative of the assessment
programs or their sponsor bodies to inform these particular agents or aid the
policy decisions. The following comments are instructive:

> Let me tell you about the PISA topic and those programs. I knew a lit-
> tle bit about them, for instance, why they were administered and their
> aim, but that was before becoming a Senator. When we recently occupied
> office at the Senate, the Secretary of Education, back then, who was a
> member of our political party, came to talk to us about the usability of
> these programs and their importance, but only to the Senators from our
> party. (Right-wing politician, Education Commission Member)

> I had previous contact with this data because I worked as an academic,
> but also as a public servant. (Left-wing politician, Non-member of Edu-
> cation Commission)

> Many issues are brought up by the newspapers and in the news but, these
> are mainly related to statements made by this or that person, many from
> INEE itself. (Right-wing politician, Education Commission Member)

Participants clarified during interview that throughout the 21 days which comprised the period that accounted for the reception and voting of the General
Law for the Professional Teaching Service, no data was provided by any of the
LSA bodies. Drawing upon the comments outlined above by Senators, there
are several important issues to note. For instance: (a) legislators know PISA,
PLANEA and its predecessors; (b) International large-scale assessments do not
send their data to Senators; (c) national assessments do send their data to legislators, but not to all of them; (d) legislators are very busy, thus it is uncertain
to what extent this data is consulted; (e) legislators get acquainted and interact
with LSA data as a result of previous professional experiences and informal
channels; and (f) the LSA data most noted by legislators are: results and assessment aims. Consequently, one fundamental question arises from this complex

combination of characteristics and experiences: what sort of governing effects does this arrangement provoke in relation to the LGSPD and more broadly? I will come back to this question at the end of this section.

1.4.2   The LGSPD and LSA Data, What Happened?

The previous sections suggest it is unlikely that legislators will have engaged in any systematic way with large-scale assessment data prior to or during the legislative process leading to the approval of the General Law for the Professional Teaching Service. In this section, I shall explore furthermore: (a) Senators' opinions regarding large-scale assessment data in this legislative process; and (b) the factors that influenced their decision on this matter. I start by sharing comments that could help to answer a fundamental question regarding national-level policy making: do Senators feel that large-scale assessment data influenced their voting decision concerning the General Law for the Professional Teaching Service?

> Assessment programs were not instruments that were considered in the debates and in the legislative processes. I believe that large-scale assessment programs do generate information. However, their objective is not to support legislators, since we only have access to this data when we ask for it, or when we look for it ourselves. They offer information, but decisions are not made based on these indicators. In education, decisions are made based on a political nature. (Left-wing politician, non-member of Education Commission)

> No, this data did not influence me. In other words, I have a broader diagnosis because I have all my life in the education sector. I have been a teacher from high school to graduate school, I worked in a university and had the privilege of being Rector of that university. Much of my life has been developed around the education theme. (Right-wing politician, Education Commission member)

> Well, they influence, but not in my decision. I know the education system, these programs are technical inputs that do help, but do not determine a decision. (Left-wing politician, Education Commission member)

According to the statements above, it is unlikely for large-scale assessment data to have shaped legislators' decisions concerning the General Law for the Professional Teaching Service. The following statements offer key insights as to what may have.

The majority voted by instruction of their political parties, including the members of the Education Commission, some of which are teachers, they understand these things, they have been union leaders. They argued that; it is a political decision. (Left-wing politician, Education Commission member)

Using a mechanism of electoral falsification, the pact for Mexico unifies the political parties namely: PRI, PRD and PAN. These political parties betrayed their electorate and joined the Neoliberal agenda advocated by President Peña Nieto. This initiative was not discussed, it arrived one night at the respective commission and when the commission turned it to the floor, the final version of it was already made. A Senator in that commission presented the document, it was never discussed on the Senate floor, and it was approved by a political machinery subject to the interests of the OECD. The PRI blindly obeys President Peña Nieto, who proposed the structural reform agenda, and who instructed the senators from the PRI party to vote without even knowing the initiative. Senators from PAN and PRD followed, all of this was carried out by direct instruction. (Left-wing politician, non-member of the Education Commission)

The legislative process has another orientation, that is, the Education Commission is comprised by 15 members, I think it is one of the most numerous. There are some members who just come and sign, why? Because their party tells them to; 'Vote this or that way' Things are usually done in consultation, because they come from the executive through the office of the president or based on consultations with education authorities. (Right-wing politician, Education Commission member)

Voting is very vertical and disciplined here. Hence, there was alignment of a lot of Senators who, wanting to vote against, voted in favor, so their decision was of a political nature. (Left-wing politician, non-member of the Education Commission)

Comments shared by legislators illustrate relevant issues concerning policy decisions in Mexico, and in relation to governance more broadly. These comments can be seen as querying the extent of the vertical and horizontal move of power in the classic definition of governance (as a move away from government) advanced by Rhodes (1996). In essence, whilst it is evident that a range of organizations and actors including state, private and NGOs are at play, there is still a very strong sense of hierarchical government and governing here. Rhodes

(1996) argues that policy decisions in these new governance settings are likely to be the outcome of network relationships, as opposed to government, where they are more hierarchical. If this were the case, the policy approved (LGSPD) would be linked to external agencies, such as the OECD (Cuevas & Moreno, 2016; OECD, 2010b, 2011b). However, public decision-making, such as legislators casting a vote, was carried out in a hierarchical manner. This governing maneuver is interesting because to the public eye, it is legislators who are running the political agenda; it is they who ought to be blamed. Meanwhile, those who are determining education policies appear to be invisible. This, of course, limits further discussions as to the nature of the initiatives at hand, who will benefit from them, and what is actually going on regarding education policies in Mexico.

There are two important moments concerning the advancement and approval of the General Law for the Professional Teaching Service outlined above. The first one of them is where networks of agents and organizations both exogenous and endogenous decide on the enforcement of this legislation and its substance. Cuevas and Moreno (2016) published a paper contrasting the content of the General Law for the Professional Teaching Service against the content of a public policy recommendation document advanced by the OECD (2010b). They suggest that the presence of the OECD as an agent of governance with regards to the development of the LGSPD is quite clear. The second big moment is where political machineries are put to work. In this particular case, they are known as: The Pact for Mexico, the Congress, and the legislation process. These help to legitimize what has been previously decided in the upper end. Drawing upon these two moments, governance in this case is comprised of both networks and hierarchical relationships and decision-making, with the latter being more perceptible to the common person. This means that the shift from government to governance in this case in Mexico is not just a matter of flipping a page. What we can see here is both network and hierarchy work together alongside each other.

1.4.3   Governing Relationships, How Did LSA Aid?

LSAs in Mexico claim that they generate data so as to aid policy decisions. According to the evidence outlined in the previous section, Senators believe that LSA data did not determine the ways in which politicians voted in this policy. Thus, the question remains: was there any way in which LSAs data was used to contribute to the General Law for the Professional Teaching Service, and if so what were the mechanisms? Both of these queries will be addressed in the following paragraphs.

To understand the relationship between LSA data and the General Law for the Professional Teaching Service, one must take into consideration several issues. First, it is essential to acknowledge this law as an offspring of the 2013

Education Reform. Second, the rationale used to support the case for approval of the 2013 Education Reform, is an important antecedent for the General Law for the Professional Teaching Service. Third, although some Legislators acknowledge that the voting process was strongly constrained by the will of their political party and their commitment to the Pact for Mexico, Legislators nevertheless justify their vote by referencing LSA data. It is therefore crucial to pose the question: what problem does the General Law for the Professional Teaching Service seek to resolve? This, because an important part of policy-making is that of framing or defining the problem to which policies are than drawn. In the following paragraphs I elaborate on these issues and explain their connections.

The General Law for the Professional Teaching Service is an offspring of the 2013 Education Reform. Without the approval and enforcement of the broader Education Reform first, this secondary law would never have come to be. That said, the main initiative document for the 2013 Education Reform made reference to both PISA and ENLACE within its text (Senado de la Republica, 2012). References to these programs focus upon the following issues:

a.   The Bill argues that according to the OECD and PISA, the level of education quality in Mexico is below national and international standards in comparison with their peers.

b.   The initiative states that Mexico achieved 425 points in PISA (although it does not mention in which round) which placed the country in the 47th position amongst 65 participating nations/economies.

c.   The document draws attention to the fact that the United States of America and Canada, Mexico's main trading partners, achieved 500 and 524 points respectively.

d.   In relation to the national assessment, the Bill notes that 58% of students obtained insufficient and elemental proficiency levels in Spanish (literacy) and math.

e.   The initiative argues that it is urgent and essential to adopt and employ measures to reduce the high proportion of students who show a low level of proficiency in literacy, math and science.

f.   The document argues that evidence suggests that a person who is not proficient in reading and math will not be successful in a specialized work, and thus be constrained to low-level productivity employments with low pay.

The arguments advanced in the 2013 Education Reform Bill which draw upon LSA data flag and pursue the need for change, argue the case for urgent reform, emphasize Mexico's low performance in relation to others, and raise a warning as to what is likely to happen to those who are not proficient in math and literacy. It is important to note that these arguments seek to make the case for pushing forward the 2013 Education Reform aimed at imposing a universal system for teacher appraisal.

As outlined above, after the 2013 Education Reform was approved, the Federal Government proposed the General Law for the Professional Teaching Service initiative as a measure to regulate and overview the dispositions mandated in the first. This initiative sought to manage the ways in which teachers entered the public service and obtained tenure, the mechanisms for teacher and leadership promotion, both vertically and horizontally, and the introduction of a universal appraisal system for all teachers and educational leaders, which ultimately would determine permanency in the workplace.

Prior to the 2013 Education Reform and the General Law for the Professional Teaching Service, permanent teaching positions were mainly allocated by the Education Union (SNTE for its acronym in Spanish) based on seniority. Leadership promotion was determined by a ladder-based system which was overviewed by the sub-national Secretariats of Education in alliance with the Education Syndicate (Navarro, Cordero, & Torres, 2011). Although publicly these processes were jointly regulated, to an important extent both of these procedures were dominated and operated by the Education Union (Ornelas, 2006). It is important to highlight that the Education Union was able to bargain regarding these benefits though often through highly questionable political practices and customs (Ornelas, 2018). For instance, during electoral campaigns, education workers were commonly deployed by union leaders as political fronts so as to campaign for or vote in favor of a particular candidate who had reached a previous agreement with either the subnational or national union leader. These political favors were returned once the candidate assumed office by granting the union power over many education affairs.

The Senators interviewed conceived the situation outlined above as one of the main problems in the education sector in Mexico with undoubted effects upon the quality of education. Removing the competence from the Education Union and applying different mechanisms to regulate the entrance and tenure of teachers and leaders in the public teaching service seems to be a proper response. The following comments illustrate participants' opinions regarding education quality in Mexico, whilst a second set of statements make reference to the reasons for supporting the General Law for the Professional Teaching Service.

> PISA and PLANEA suggest a critical situation, and there is one. (Left-wing Senator, non-member of the Education Commission)

Well, I do believe education is low quality compared to other countries with which we compete like South Korea and Vietnam, I consider that our academic capacity is very low. We had evidence from the OECD and prior tests that were telling us that education in our country it quite behind, followed by the other tests that we introduced, which also showed that students were doing badly. This is a sign that education in our country is of low quality, right? (Right-wing politician, Education Commission member)

I believe it is a troubling situation, my opinion is based on test results that are promoted by international and national assessments such as ENLACE, PLANEA among others, and obviously, they make a lot of sense, because there has been an abandonment of the public education in Mexico. In theory these statistics and the exams that are applied around the world that tell us how we are doing internationally are very important. All Senators have seen the difficulties that the National Educational System faces. (Left-wing politician, Education Commission member)

Education problems were made visible through many sources, for example OECD observations, World Bank reports, assessments such as: The PISA test and the PLANEA antecedent. Domestic assessments were suggesting that stellar actors in all of this are the teachers. (Right-wing politician, Education Commission member)

The poor state of education quality seems to be mutually agreed upon by both sides of the ideological divide, the left- and right-wing legislators. These ideas appear to be informed by LSA data. Senators who voted in favor of the General Law for the Professional Teaching Service link low education quality to teachers and argue that implementing a policy for universal teacher appraisal is the right decision. This line of thought can be appreciated in the following comments.

First, it was something that had already been functioning. Evaluation was an instrument that helped students improve in math and literacy, so, that's when you say; this is worth putting into the constitution. (Right-wing politician, Education Commission member)

I thought in the country's situation. This law modified a series of issues; a more democratic hiring system, teaching posts were not going to be inherited. The Union would go back to carry out other functions. Before, education was dominated by the Education Union, who did and undid internally for political reasons. Education had been neglected at the

> expense of agreements and other interests. One of the things that this law wanted was to rescue the control of the teaching profession. (Right-wing politician, Education Commission member)

> I voted in favor of this law because for the first time in Mexican history it regulated teacher entrance, permanence, recognition, and promotion. Second, because they proposed open public competitions. Third, in the future not only graduates of normal universities, but graduates of universities could also be included at compete for teaching positions. Fourth, because we were removing an attribution from the Education Union that was not legally recognized. This is supposed to have resonance in students learning, although it will take many years. (Right-wing, Education Commission member)

According to the statements outlined above, the central problem according to the Senators is the role of the Education Union in contributing to the poor quality of learning in Mexico. It was seen to be a priority for the federal administration and legislation to take competences away from the Education Union and give them to the government. Here we can argue that large-scale assessment data introduces and reinforces notions regarding the poor state of the education system in Mexico, and the role of the teachers' union in this. This in turn amplifies the view that change is required. Hence, proposals like the General Law for the Professional Teaching Service, which more or less may seem reasonable (simplistic), are then easily accepted. And although legislators voted as instructed by their political parties, LSA data helps aid the justification for their decisions.

Lastly, what we can see at play in comments made by legislators outlined above, are features associated with competitive comparison (Robertson, 2012a), an issue I pick up in Chapter 8. For instance, we can observe how participants pitch Mexico against other countries in relation to performance. They also explain that it is large-scale assessment data and its regular cycles which help make these issues visible.

2   Policy II: Key Learnings for an Integral Education

The second national policy to be addressed in Chapter 7 is called Key Learnings for an Integral Education, which was the national curriculum for compulsory education in Mexico, between the years 2018 and 2022. Unlike some Federal systems of education, such as the United States of America who have a decentralized system of governance, in Mexico the curriculum for compulsory education is national, and its design is centralized by the Secretariat of Education. In this section, I focus on whether, how and with what outcomes large-scale assessment programs influence the Key Learnings for an Integral Education policy. To this end, the analysis in this section is presented in the following way: (a) Sources of Data; (b) Secretariat of Education Context; (c) Key Learning for an Integral Education Development; and (d) Main Findings.

2.1   *Sources of Data*

This case draws upon an original data set comprised of two main sources: (1) policy and large-scale assessment-related documents; and (2) six individual semi-structured interviews with officials and collaborators from the Secretariat of Education who participated in the advancement of the new national curriculum. Interviews were conducted face-to-face in Mexico City during the months of February and March 2018. Table 7.3 details the cohort of interviewees who participated in this unit.

The participants outlined in Table 7.3 were targeted based on purposive and opportunistic sampling criteria. A previous professor of mine put me in contact with high-ranking secretariat official 3. We met during February 2018 in Mexico City. The second interviewee was high-ranking official 2. This individual is responsible for making many of the big and significant decisions concerning the policy addressed in this section. Given my previous experience working as a Secretariat official from a subnational entity, I was aware that the person who held this chair was responsible for coordinating all the activities and teams for the advancement of the new curriculum. I initiated contact with this person via email. I also sent a formal invitation to participate in this study, attached with a research outline of this unit, confidentiality forms, and my personal curriculum vitae. This was followed up by emails to gauge their interest in participating, and then to arrange and schedule the interview.

After meeting and interviewing this person in Mexico City, I requested their help in approaching other potential interviewees. A couple of days later, this individual kindly put me in contact (through an email) with three of the team leaders who participated in the development of the curriculum sections of Mathematical Reasoning, Language and Communication and Socio-Emotional Education. It is important to note that neither of these three participants works directly at the Secretariat of Education. Their relationship with the Secretariat regarding the development of the new curriculum was in terms of external remunerated specialized collaborators. Interviews with these individuals were carried out face-to-face during March 2018 in Mexico City.

TABLE 7.3   Secretariat of education participants

No.	Participant	Background
1	High-ranking secretariat official 1	Prior Secretary of State of a subnational entity and congressmen. Public Policy Master's from Ive league University
2	High-ranking secretariat official 2	Former chair of the General Directorate for Curricular Development. University Lecturer, Educational Researcher. MPhil and PhD Candidate in Education, from Russel Group University
3	High-ranking secretariat official 3	Teacher Educator, University Lecturer, Former Subdirector of Arts Education at the Curriculum Design and Development Department of the National Secretariat of Education
4	Secretariat Collaborator 1	Professor at UNAM. External consult at INEE for the design of the national standardized tests. MA and PhD at CINVESTAV
5	Secretariat Collaborator 2	Professor of Mathematics Education. Emerita Researcher. External consultant at the Secretariat of Education for over 20 years. External consult at INEE for the design of the national standardized tests. MA and PhD at CINVESTAV
6	Secretariat Collaborator 3	Independent consult of Socioemotional Education. External consult at INEE, for the design of the national standardized tests. Master's from Ive league University

Through the Chairman of the Education Commission at the National Senate I was able to obtain an interview with the high-ranking secretariat official 1. The logistics for setting up the interview with this person were also coordinated via email, and the interview was conducted face-to-face at the Secretary of Education in March 2018. It is important to note that the identities of participants have been reserved for ethical reasons.

Selecting this particular policy as a policy area to analyze is based on the following criteria: (1) this initiative was advanced at the national scale, considering that this book aims to study LSAs at distinct scales within Mexico, it met the first criteria; (2) preliminary readings of this policy indicated connections of some sort with large-scale assessments; (3) this policy affected all teachers and students nation-wide, thus looking into it using a critical lens seemed necessary; (4) considering its novelty, there is little research which addresses this policy, and no indications were found of research from a governance stance that looked into this matter; and (5) the group of policy decision-makers involved in this policy (Secretariat officials) represented a different and distinct sector from the area of analysis reported in the first half of this chapter.

2.2   *Secretariat of Education Context*

The Secretariat of Education, or Secretariat for Public Education (SEP for its acronym in Spanish), is the supreme executive branch of the Federal Government responsible for education matters in Mexico. Its main goal is to carry out the mandate conferred in the Third Article of the Mexican Constitution and the General Law of Education. It is also responsible for implementing the programs and objectives embodied in the National Development Plan and National Plan for Education of each Federal Administration. The SEP was founded in 1921, and is currently organized in four broad Sub-Secretariats namely:

a.   Sub-Secretariat for Basic Education
b.   Sub-Secretariat for Upper Secondary Education
c.   Sub-Secretariat for Higher Education
d.   Sub-Secretariat for Planning, Evaluation and Coordination

Each of the Sub-Secretariats outlined above are divided into multiple directorates, sub-directorates and departments. The policy addressed here, Key Learnings for an Integral Education, was developed at the Sub-Secretariat for Basic Education. This Sub-Secretariat is divided into five different directorates namely, (a) General Directorate for Curricular Development; (b) General Directorate for Educational Materials; (c) General Directorate for Educational Management Development; (d) General Directorate for Indigenous Education; and (e) General Directorate for Continuous Development.

The General Directorate for Curricular Development is led by one Director and one Adjunct Director. The main attributions of this Directorate are to elaborate proposals of learning plans and programs for basic education, and to propose pedagogical methods, processes and approaches that promote the achievement of relevant learnings in students of various levels and modalities of basic education (DOF, 2016). The Directorate for Curricular Development is divided into approximately 20 sub-directorates (i.e., preschool education, primary education, lower secondary education, etc.), these in turn entail 28 departments (i.e., math in preschool, math in primary, math in secondary, etc.).

2.3   *Key Learnings for an Integral Education Development*

Key Learnings for an Integral Education forms part of a larger package of policies which came into effect by the 2012–2018 Federal Administration namely, 2016

Education Model. This policy plan sought to reform issues such as the curriculum, school management, a system of loans and bonds for school infrastructure development, amongst other issues (Pla, 2018). The 2016 Education Model was formally introduced to the public on July 20th, 2016. From that date onwards the General Directorate for Curricular Development was tasked with designing the new national curriculum for compulsory education. Due to the timeframe shaping of this book, it was only possible to address a single policy from the 2016 Education Model. The new curriculum was chosen based on its national reach, that it involves all teachers and students, and the potential relationships and linkages assumed between this particular policy and large-scale assessment data.

The published version of Key Learnings for an Integral Education was released in March 2018. During its formal presentation, the Secretary of Education announced that it would be employed in schools nationwide starting August 2018. Key Learnings is a 676 page-long document addressed to educators, school-principals, superintendents and other pedagogical leaders from preschool, primary and lower secondary schools.

Given that Key Learnings for an Integral Education is a vastly extended publication, here I focus on issues concerning two chapters of the document. These are (a) Chapter 4, The Curriculum of Basic Education; and (b) Chapter 5, Study Programs of Basic Education. The analysis and discussion of this unit will focus on the relationships between large-scale assessment data and decision-making regarding these two chapters mainly.

According to the published version of this document, roughly more than 150 secretariat collaborators and external specialist or consultants contributed both directly and indirectly to its development. Through this research I was able to interview some of the main officials and collaborators involved in the design processes.

2.4   *Main Findings*

2.4.1   Secretariat Officials, Collaborators and LSA Data

Secretariat officials and collaborators stated that they were aware of the existence of PISA, PLANEA, its predecessors, and surprisingly ERCE-LLECE assessments. However, similar to the case with legislators from this study, officials and collaborators commented that international large-scale assessment programs (PISA and ERCE) fail to provide their data or publications to them directly. Also, similar to the case with legislators, the Sub-Secretariat for Planning, Evaluation and Coordination at the Secretariat of Education, in alliance with the National Institute for Education Evaluation, invite high-ranked Secretariat officials and collaborators to the public presentations of PLANEA outcomes. However, only general results and issues are raised and presented in these meetings. Additional LSA data must be searched for. Here it is important to note that many middle and low ranked officials are not invited to these meetings so they must obtain this data by other means. Participants experiences with LSA data are revealed in the following comments:

> We consult what is available on the internet. I do not know if they have mechanisms of diffusion beyond public presentations and uploading this data onto the internet, but look, this happens with everything. (Secretariat Collaborator 1)

> I searched for this information when I carried out a comparative study for INEE. (Secretariat Collaborator 2)

> We were the ones that were looking for the publications and results. (Secretariat Collaborator 3)

> In the case of PISA, the OECD makes them public, and we get the information from there .... In the case of PLANEA we participate in the application and well, we are very attentive waiting for the results to know how the different subnational entities performed. (Secretariat Official 1)

> Well, when I arrived in 2016, I consulted what was online (PLANEA) on my own initiative and now in 2017, the Secretary and the Sub-Secretary received them, and we got it from them. (Secretariat Official 2)

Comments outlined above indicate that officials and collaborators tend to search for LSA data on a personal basis. Here we must note that anyone with some motivation and access to the internet could potentially access some of the data or publications generated by large-scale assessment programs. However, in the case of the OECD, much of the more technical or specialized literature that one would expect policy decision-makers would require comes at a cost, meaning that even though they are public they are certainly not free or accessible to all. PLANEA and ERCE don't have this problem, however, compared to PISA not as many secondary analysis and specialized publications are produced.

In contrast to legislators, one can note that Secretariat Officials and Collaborators appear more engaged with LSAs and their data. For instance, we can observe that: (a) these particular policy-agents know all assessments currently operating in Mexico, including the much less regarded ERCE-LLECE assessments; (b) these agents have the initiative to search for LSA data themselves;

and (c) they are on the lookout or awaiting LSA results. If we were to compare these particularities against that of legislators, the first question that comes to mind is: to what extent are the needs of curriculum designers and legislators similar? In the words of Mortimore (1999), each of these independent groups operates and interacts in different currencies, which makes it difficult for a generic form of evidence as large-scale assessment data to function properly for both of them in terms of decision making.

By offering curriculum designers and legislators the same data, what is at play here is a flattening maneuver that denies differences – in effect seeing the world as ontologically flat. In Chapter 3 I have argued that this process flattens or erases particularities in order to create equivalences to meet the criteria of comparability on the one hand, and interpret, mediate or enforce indistinctively outcomes derived from this enterprise, on the other. In this instance, assessment programs supply their outcomes to both groups of policy decision-makers; despite their unique particularities and the singularities of their work, they are assumed to be the same, when in fact they can vary significantly. For instance, to become a legislator in Mexico there are no minimum schooling requirements. Currently, only 56% of the Deputies from Congress have a full undergraduate degree (Alemán & Rosas, 2018). Yet LSAs offer the same data to all of them.

2.4.2   Key Learnings and Decision Making: What Happened?
Research findings indicate that decisions in at least four parts of Key Learnings for an Integral Education were influenced by large-scale assessment data. These are: (a) Outline of Math and Literacy learning fields; (b) Math and Literacy subject structure and learning standard design; (c) allocation of teaching hours per subject; and (e) the newly introduced component of curricular autonomy. I will illustrate and discuss these relationships in the following paragraphs.

Key learnings for an Integral Education groups together learning subjects into three big domains namely: (1) Academic Development Fields – include literacy, mathematical reasoning and exploration and understanding of the social and natural world; (2) Areas of Personal and Social Development – to include arts, physical education and socioemotional education; and (3) Areas of Curricular Autonomy – comprised of an array of different elective courses and clubs. Secretariat Officials and Collaborators suggested that the outline of the literacy and mathematical reasoning fields were influenced by LSA data. The following comments elaborate on this matter:

> I believe that the entire proposal of Literacy and Mathematics academic fields are closely linked to the information we have from these assessments.

> The teams that developed these fields are experts, pedagogues, practitioners that took into account the results of these assessments. (Secretariat Official 2)

> Especially the Literacy and Mathematics teams made use of this data. Teams from the other subjects were not prompted to revise this data. (Secretariat Official 1)

> Probably in Math this can be identified. Maybe in other areas the relationships are blurrier. Here for example, If I see that in PLANEA the part of basic arithmetic operations presents serious deficiencies, then probably in the curriculum I have to put some emphasis on this. (Secretariat Collaborator 2)

These comments acknowledge that LSA data influenced at least the literacy and math learning fields. The way in which this was likely to occur, besides "putting emphasis" on topics which showed deficiencies on PLANEA, is explained in more detail in the following paragraphs. Considering that math and literacy are the common knowledge domains assessed in all three LSAs in Mexico, it can be expected that policy decisions concerning the outline of these fields in the new curriculum would be more related to LSA data. It is important to note that this is not the first curriculum that was influenced by LSAs. According to Martinez-Rizo and Silva-Guerrero (2016), the 2011 curriculum put forward a competence base approach to learning in Mexico as the result of LSA mediating.

Two secretariat officials suggest that, in principle, the development of other knowledge fields (e.g. Socioemotional Education and Social Sciences) and its links to large-scale assessment data are less clear. However, comments made by one of the participants offers a slightly different account. This is reflected in the following statement:

> In the case of Arts Education, I can say yes, LSAs were consulted but in general terms. Assessment results gave me many elements to continue advocating why it is important to promote quality teaching in the arts. Mainly because these contribute to the development of intellectual skills, attitudes and knowledge that subscribe to mathematical reasoning, the structure of language, and the resolution of problems in the sciences. (Secretariat Official 3)

This individual suggests that in the case of Arts Education, there was a predetermined intention to promote and enhance the relevance of the arts, not in terms of their inherent value but rather in terms of what they can contribute to performance in Math, Science and Literacy. This can be interpreted as the advancement of a new sort of economy regarding the curriculum. Here, the value of a certain subject, competence or objective is determined based on what it can do, or how much it can contribute towards the development of competencies from the dominant learning fields. There are two important issues to note here. First, in Key Learnings, the number of teaching hours allocated to Arts Education was in fact increased, in some cases up to five more hours per week (SEP, 2017). Second, in 2014 the OECD published in Mexico the Spanish version of the report, Art for Art's Sake? The Impact of Arts Education. This report was developed by Winner, Goldstein and Vincent-Lancrin (2013) and was released one year earlier in French and English. Interestingly, this document looks into an array of correlational, quasi-experimental and experimental studies with regard to the effects of the arts on dominant subjects (Math, Literacy, Science and General IQ). The main argument of this publication is that the Arts can act as boosters for raising performance in Math, Science and Literacy.

A potential risk here is that art education curriculum and educators may well start focusing mostly on the aspects or contents of arts education, such as design or certain areas of music, which could contribute to the dominant learning fields, whereas those that do not (fine art) would be in danger of being neglected. A major problem with justifying the relevance of arts education in terms of what it can do for the economic domain, is that it downplays the inherent value of arts and its contributions to the overall development of students. For instance, critically selecting the music we consume, learning how it affects us and others, and understanding who benefits from this enterprise, is valuable *per se* regardless of its contributions or not to dominant learning fields and the economy.

The second component of Key Learnings assumed to have been influenced by large-scale assessment data is closely linked to the first (outlined above) and involves Math and Literacy subject structure and learning standard design. Learning standards indicate what and how students ought to learn regarding particular knowledge fields (SEP, 2017). The following comment elaborates on this matter:

> The spectrum of contents and skills that PLANEA evaluates is very much in accordance with the type of learning standards that we put into the curriculum that will be enforced in August. I can provide some examples, especially in terms of reading comprehension as well as writing, which have been greatly strengthened in the learning standards inside the new curriculum. Regarding the subject of mother tongue – Literacy Spanish – this

was structured into three major domains: (1) language for study; (2) language for literature and recreational spaces; (3) language for social participation. Each of them is divided into social practices. There is a very intense work in all education levels, including preschool, but very specifically from the first year of primary school to the third year of secondary school. This was decided to provide students with multiple learning opportunities in terms of reading comprehension and writing, which is directly associated with what PLANEA and PISA measure. (Secretariat Official 2)

According to this Secretariat Official, literacy learning standards from Key Learnings have been aligned with the skills and knowledges assessed by PLANEA. Furthermore, this subject has been structured into similar domains as those assessed by PLANEA: (1) language for study; (2) language for literature and recreational spaces; and (3) language for social participation. This move can be corroborated in PLANEA's main document (INEE, 2016) and Key learnings (SEP, 2017).

Looking further into this matter, Table 7.4 shows a contrast between the Math learning field structure advanced in Key Learnings, and the domains, topics, processes, capabilities, and contents assessed by PLANEA and PISA.

Table 7.4 indicates that the mathematical reasoning learning field of Key Learnings was configured much alike the structure put forward by the PLANEA assessment. Furthermore, we can observe that both of these meet the category content assessed by PISA. Here it is important to note that although since 2011 LSAs had influenced curriculum design in Mexico (Martinez-Rizo & Silva-Guerrero, 2016), what seems to be different is this straightforward configuration. Aligning learning standards and subject structure with the test can be considered a teaching to the test practice (Jennings & Bearak, 2014). Yet this shift does not seem to raise major concerns amongst policy decision makers. This move has also been carried out in countries such as the United States, Chile and Japan (Baker & O'Neil, 2016; Cox & Meckes, 2016; Sellar, Lingard, Rukowski, & Takayama, 2018). What should be highlighted here is that we have not only reduced having conversations about the implications of teaching to the test, but also that this practice has become normalized through being made compulsory nationwide. It is now more difficult to see whether teachers are teaching to the test because this feature has been embedded into the curriculum.

The third issue which was argued to have been influenced by LSA data involves the distribution of teaching hours per subject. In the Mexican context, each subject has a fixed number of teaching hours allocated to it by the curriculum. Decisions over how many classes of math are taught per week comes

TABLE 7.4   Key learnings, PLANEA and PISA domains

Key learnings		PLANEA		PISA		
Math		Math		Math		
Domain	Topic/theme	Domain	Topic/theme	Math processes	Math capabilities	Category content
Number algebra and variation	– Number – Addition and subtraction – Multiplication and division – Proportionality – Equations – Functions – Patterns, geometric figures, and equivalent expressions	Numerical sense and algebraic thinking	– Numbers and numbering systems – Problem additives – Multiplying problems – Patterns and equations	a. Formulating situations mathematically b. Employing mathematical concepts, facts, procedures, and reasoning c. Interpreting applying and evaluating mathematical outcomes	1. Communication 2. Mathematising 3. Representation 4. Reasoning and argument 5. Devising strategies for solving problems 6. Using symbolic, formal, and technical language and operations 7. Using mathematical tools	Quantity change and relationships
Shape, space and measure	– Spatial location – Geometric figures and bodies – Magnitudes and Measures	Shape, space and measure	– Figures and bodies – Measure – Spatial location			Space and shape
Data analysis	– Statistics – Probability	Data management	– Proportionality and functions – Analysis and data representation – Notations of probability			Uncertainty and data

SOURCE: SEP (2017, P. 303); INEE (2016, P. 82); OECD (2019A, PP. 84–86)

from the national Secretariat of Education. With regard to this, one Secretariat official commented:

> Large-scale assessment data specially influenced the allocation of teaching hours in the case of Literacy and Mathematics. I still believe that Spanish (literacy) is the core of the curriculum. Language is key for learning other subjects, as well as math. If you don't know how to write, then you don't understand what you read. In that sense, the allocation of teaching hours does have relation with large-scale assessments. These programs focus on certain parts of the curriculum because these areas are what society requires, hence it is what students need to learn. (Secretariat Official 2)

The allocation of teaching hours across the different subjects of the curriculum is a complex task. The decision over granting more time to math and literacy can be linked to the tendencies that have emerged in many OECD countries; the economization of education in large part through the use of human capital theory to justify education policies (Spring, 2015). By these means, allocating more teaching time to math and literacy is justified by claims that these subjects will contribute to learning in other areas, and that the skills advanced in these areas will contribute to the broader society through economic development and enhanced productivity.

This simplistic rationale is problematic. For instance, granting more teaching hours to these subjects is no guarantee that students will learn more or perform better. In Singapore, students in secondary schools are in fact taught five hours of math per week (Low, Goodwin, & Snyder, 2017), which is equivalent to the allocation of teaching time in the new curriculum in Mexico. However, one of the big differences between these two education systems is the number of paid hours (24) that teachers are granted a week for class planning, preparations, and student assessment. Such a scheme neither exists in Mexico, and nor is it contemplated in this curriculum. Class preparation, student assessment and lesson planning in Mexico must be carried out during teachers' personal time. Here we must note that in the past 15 years, the curriculum in Mexico have shifted three times, yet assessments such as PISA indicate only minor variations amongst performance in Mexican students. As Fullan (2011) points out, fragmented or isolated shifts (e.g., only reforming the curriculum and redistribution of teaching hours) like the ones we can observe in Mexico over the past 18 years will hardly bring about substantial change. Education requires more systemic, integrated, and holistic measures.

Lastly, the fourth part of Key Learnings for an Integral Education to be influenced by LSA data refers to the newly introduced component of Curricular Autonomy. The following comment elaborates on this:

> I could mention the various studies that the OECD has published regarding different PISA aspects. We rescued many things from these studies. For example, the Curricular Autonomy component. I can recall that according to these publications, students that have good results in PISA also have the possibility to practice a sport, play a musical instrument or develop a series of other activities regarded as extracurricular. These insights gave us more impetus for our component of Curricular Autonomy. (Secretariat Official 2)

The new component of Curricular Autonomy instituted in Key Learnings mandated that a minor space within the curriculum be dedicated to activities, courses or clubs selected or designed by schools according to their interests, resources and needs (SEP, 2017). This shift was legitimated using PISA evidence. Key Learnings refers to a particular publication from the OECD (2016d) which asserts that students who participate in extracurricular activities outperform on PISA in comparison to their peers who don't do extra-curricular activities.

Introducing this measure into Mexican schools based on PISA evidence from the United States can be regarded as reducing complexity and offering a flat view of social activity. In this particular case, flattening functions as a condition that enables Mexico and the United States of America to be 'viewed' as equivalents, in which the particularities of each nation are erased so that they can exchange and share practices. As I mentioned in Chapter 1, such processes form part of a double flattening of space and solution: both of these nations are projected as ontologically flat, and in turn offered a flat solution with the result that Mexico can apply these practices without a hint of blush. Furthermore, important characteristics of the Mexican context such as resources, culture and needs are erased so that it could employ practices from US schools. This shift, however, ignores that school funding in the US functions quite differently. Schools in Mexico lack of formal long-term governmental funding beyond teachers' salaries or special funding for particular initiatives. In Mexico, schools generate their own recourses through fundraisers and charity activities. At the beginning of each schoolyear, schools request parents' cooperation in buying or bringing personal hygiene supplies for their children, including basic products such as toilet paper and hand soap. Without the participation of parents, schools would lack of these resources.

A second issue to note here is that since 2010 (OECD, 2010b), the OECD has recommended granting more autonomy to schools in Mexico. The OECD, however, refer especially to autonomy with regard to teacher hiring. This is a major challenge in Mexico because teachers are civil servants. Teacher hiring decisions are made outside schools. It is the subnational Secretariats of Education who develop recruitment and employment processes and who coordinate the distribution of teachers to different workplaces. Thus, due to lack of funding as outlined above so as to design and operate the clubs or elective courses for pupils proposed by the newly introduced Curricular Autonomy component in Key Learnings; this move can be read as an approximation strategy (implementing changes through gradual steps). Here, it would appear that the term "autonomy" is strategically included in the new curriculum (official discourse), which in turn is put into circulation and introduced to educators, parents, students and the public as a way of paving the way, or preparing the terrain, so as to in the near future propose additional forms of autonomy, such as those linked to teacher hiring, parent choice, school governing and so on.

2.4.3   Looking into Other Curriculums

One of the purposes of large-scale assessments programs, such as PISA, is to develop data so that low performing nations can learn from high performing countries' experiences and adapt it to their particular settings (OECD, 2014). Here the use of LSAs seems to misrecognize that not all practices and policies from successful countries should be adopted. Furthermore, there is a lack of consideration of the mechanisms for overviewing and assessing the appropriateness of the policies and practices that are being employed and their respective adaptations. Although this concern applies to all countries, it is particularly troubling for those nations, such as Mexico, in which policies and practices derived from these instruments seem to be employed with very low consideration or discretion from the domestic community.

During the development of the policy studied in this unit, participants affirm that they looked into the curriculums of other countries. The following comments elaborate on this:

> If you analyze a document namely the Ends of Education in the 21st Century published by the Secretariat of Education, you will find inside a table which addresses the learning standards. This document was inspired by a similar publication made in Singapore, it was used as a guide to figure out and define which learning standards could be helpful for us. (Secretariat Official 1)

> Not only did we review the curriculum of Singapore and Finland, but curriculums from countries regarded as high performers, such as Canada and Japan. (Secretariat Official 1)

> There was an invitation to revise the curriculum from Singapore and from other countries that had improved rapidly in PISA. (Secretariat Official 2)

The evidence here is that Mexican curriculum designers were guided by Singaporean guidelines, as mentioned by the Secretariat official outlined above. Nevertheless, these two nations are very different. For instance, their political systems, how they came into being, and how they currently operate, differ substantially. However, it is implied that Mexico could learn from the Singaporean way, regardless of their distinct backgrounds and particularities. The number of students enrolled in the Mexican education system (30 million) itself is five times larger than the entire population of Singapore, not to mention other indicators that differ substantially between these nations, such as GDP per capita and expenditure on students. Table 7.5 provides some indicators to illustrate how different Singapore and Mexico are.

Issues concerning violence, corruption, poverty, and social justice are erased in the creation of equivalences between both Mexico and Singapore. In other words, they are portrayed and projected as commensurate with each other when in fact they are not. The risks that many students face in Mexico are by no means equivalent to the risks Singaporean students face. Furthermore, a fundamental historical feature is neglected in this enterprise. This refers to the fact that Singapore first achieved political and social stability via a benevolent dictatorship (Friedman, 1990; Meadow, 1988), which in return developed an education system that reproduces its values (Sim, 2011), not vice versa, as it is promoted in Mexico. In Singapore, education quality is the result of a political, economic, and social development process, not the starting point of it. Lastly, it is important to note that according to statistics from the Singapore government website,[1] since the 1980s, the budget for education has consistently increased year by year. In 1994 this country invested around 3.4 billion in the education sector. By the year 2018 this area received around 13 billion in funds. This heavy and steady increase is reflected in World Bank indicators, particularly the Human Capital Index (HCI), where Singapore has a score of 0.88 HCI, that in turn places them in first place amongst 157 nations. It is important to stress that Singapore lacks other non-human-capital resources. Advocates of education quality in Mexico (OECD), contend the opposite of the Singapore case. It is argued that if Mexico is to become capable of raising education

TABLE 7.5   Indicators amongst some PISA participants

No.	Country	Population	GDP US dollars	GDP per capita US dollars	Population below poverty line	Child labor ages 5–14	Education expenditure GDP	Student expenditure per year US dollars	PISA 2018 positions		
									M	Sc.	Lit
1	Finland	5,476,922	224.7B	41,200	NA	NA	6.8%	$ 9,507	16	6	6
2	Singapore	5,674,472	468.9B	85,700	NA	NA	2.9%	$ 9,304	2	2	2
3	USA	321,368,864	17.97T	56,300	15.1%	NA	5.2%	$ 12,263	37	18	13
4	UK	64,088,222	2.66 T	41,200	15%	NA	6.0%	$ 10,085	17	14	14
5	Mexico	121,736,809	2.22 T	18,500	52.3%	1,105,617	5.1%	$ 2,863	61	57	53
6	Argentina	43,431,886	964.3B	22,400	30%	435,252	5.1%	$ 2,757	59	71	63

SOURCE: THE WORLD FACT BOOK, CENTRAL INTELLIGENCE AGENCY HTTPS://WWW.CIA.GOV/LIBRARY/PUBLICATIONS/THE-WORLD-FACTBOOK; OECD, EDUCATION AT A GLANCE 2015 HTTP://WWW.OECD.ORG/EDU/EDUCATION-AT-A-GLANCE-19991487.HTM

quality (test scores), it will in turn lead to political, social, personal, and economic development. However, there is no clear explanations on how this will actually come about.

2.4.4   Aiding Beliefs and Views

A common finding between participants from studies of policy initiatives at the national scale and LSAs lies in the beliefs and views regarding the state of learning in Mexico, and how these are fueled. The following comments are illustrative:

> Yes, of course, there is a low level of education quality, we have a great challenge. The great educational challenge of the twentieth century in Mexico was universal coverage. We made a national effort in the second half of the twentieth century to bring schools to all the corners of the country and achieve a 100 per cent coverage rate in basic education. The big challenge today is that of education quality, coverage is no longer the challenge, it is quality and equity. The approach of the 2016 Educational Model is the strategy for achieving education quality. (Secretariat Official 1)

> It seems terrible to me that people are finishing basic education with such unfortunate levels of language knowledge, because that is going to block their access to many, many things. (Secretariat Collaborator 1)

> Of course, both from the results of international exams and from national evaluations. (Secretariat Collaborator 2)

> From these sources (large-scale assessments) but also from many of the research my graduate and students develop. (Secretariat Collaborator 2)

> From the studies, surveys, large-scale studies, PISA, and UNESCO. (Secretariat Official 3)

> It's made evident through the different evaluations that have taken place in the country. I think that it is very clear that the results are very unfortunate, when one sees the results of PLANEA and the percentage of children or youngsters who can really dominate the different fields of literacy and mathematical reasoning, it is very limited! (Secretariat Official 2)

We can note several issues here. First, participants agree that the state of affairs concerning learning in Mexico is challenging. Second, the main source which informs these opinions are large-scale assessments. This narrative does not highlight degrees of variation in terms of levels of achievement across the system; rather what is implied is that all education in Mexico is of low quality. Normalizing this view might be seen to be politically expedient in that it supports certain political projects. However, the landscape of learning in Mexico is highly complex and varied. For instance, each year Mexico sends more than 5000 students to undertake postgraduate studies at elite universities around the world. These students are the result of the "faulty" or "dodgy" Mexican education system, the same system that appears amongst the last positions in PISA rankings.

By spreading the narrative that learning is awful in Mexico, and that this is for the most part the fault of bad teachers, we are avoiding other conversations regarding social justice such as unequal levels of resources which are distributed, underrepresentation of historically oppressed groups, and uneven participation of different agents, and how this plays out in the learning landscape (Fraser, 2008). Furthermore, the reproduction of this sort of narrative fuels certain political projects and agendas. For instance, as Kohn (2000) argues, "if your goal was to serve up our schools to the marketplace, where the point of reference is what maximizes profit rather than what benefits children, it would be perfectly logical for you to administer a test that many students would fail in order to create the impression that public schools were worthless" (p. 2).

3   Conclusions

LSAs claim that they generate data regarding student learning so as to aid policy decisions. Findings from this chapter illustrate that there are, in fact, distinct groups of policy-decision makers who are provided with a single source and narrative regarding large-scale assessment programs. Although there is important variation regarding how LSA outcomes are employed amongst the two distinct groups addressed in this chapter, an important commonality is that the data feeds into a general narrative that sees and projects learning in Mexico as poor or deficient.

Findings from the first policy under scrutiny in this chapter indicate that LSA data did not determine legislators' votes in relation to the approval of the General Law for the Professional Teaching. In this case, what is at play is a complex governing setting in which network governing is present at the upper end, whereas at the bottom end, one can note a very linear and hierarchical dynamic regarding decision making. I have argued that this setting is interesting, because who appear to be governing education as a sector are legislators, however, those who are setting agendas remain in the shadows; the OECD is a good example here. Furthermore, we can note that whilst LSA data did not aid policy decisions per se, it nevertheless aids arguments and justification regarding the decisions made by politicians.

Findings from research on the second policy and its use of LSAs show that unlike in the first case, LSA data did in fact aid decisions regarding the new national curriculum for compulsory education in Mexico. We can note relevant influence in: (a) outlining the learning fields of Math and Literacy; (b) subject structure and learning standard design; (c) allocation of teaching periods; and (d) the component of Curricular Autonomy. Like the first policy in this chapter, we can note that certain features of large-scale assessments fuel particular views about learning in Mexico. These views can in some cases be regarded as misleading, unprecise, an exaggeration or even a distraction.

Note

1   See https://data.gov.sg

Governing Tools

How Large-scale Assessments Shape Visions?

There is what amounts to a vast industry of researchers focused on large-scale assessments, like the OECD's PISA tool, with much of this work particularly attentive to the OECD's influence in the global governance landscape on national education systems. Chapters 2 and 3 of this book are dedicated to introducing this literature. Many of these studies also point out that education agents and policy decision-makers around the globe have been moved to enforce or justify a range of shifts in their education systems because of PISA outcomes. Yet the question that I am particularly interested in asking is about whether and how the scripts for improving education practices and policy decisions are taken up in local, subnational, and national settings so as to make a positive difference to the quality of student learning.

Indeed, in the literature there is an assumption that LSA data has effects on education practices and policy decisions, however, many of this work rarely moves beyond a discursive and top-down analysis, rather than undertaking a closer look at the multiple scales that constitute an education system like Mexico. Furthermore, this enterprise is subject to a strong focus on individual LSAs, and in many recent cases this has tended to be the OECD's PISA survey. Here, it is worth noting that few studies have addressed combinations of LSAs and how these might work with or against each other in particular education systems, depending upon the distinctive program ontology that shapes the form and content of the assessment tool and in turn its governing capacity. Over Chapters 5–7, I have advanced an analysis of the content of three LSAs in Mexico, and presented empirical data collected at three scales: the local, subnational and national.

It should be recalled that in Chapter 3 I introduced the work of Sorensen and Robertson (2020) who argue that whilst much of the research related to the field of large-scale assessments and governance draws upon arguments linked to governing through numbers and the comparative turn (Grek, 2009; Martens, 2007), governing through statistical reasoning, large numbers and comparisons has been around for at least a couple centuries (see Desrosiéres 1998; Lingard, 2013). If this is the case, what is it about the current scale and scope of LSAs that have enabled them to capture the imagination of education policymakers and program implementers? Do these large-scale assessments really lead to improvement, and if so, how? Do teachers make use of the data?

© KONINKLIJKE BRILL NV, LEIDEN, 2023 | DOI:10.1163/9789004682849_008

How do policymakers make use of the test results? What is really happening on the ground, how are these assessments used and by whom, and what are their (intended and unintended) effects? There are two key issues of concern to this book. One is theoretical, and the other is related to evidence. Theoretically, Sorensen and Robertson (2020) call for more finessed and nuanced explanations regarding the ontology of comparisons as a mode of governance. Others, such as Komatsu and Rappleye (2021) clamor for PISA discussions to move beyond a dichotomic frame of "for or against". I agree with them, and this book should be read as an empirically driven effort to explore their concepts, claims and concerns in light of the empirical data presented so far. The second issue is with evidence regarding how assessments are being used, and by whom?

So, what is that evidence? Research findings on the governing tools and processes regarding the Mexican case suggest that the "how" of governing is indeed more complex than simply the presence of a number. Evidence shows traces of a complex arrangement of modalities of power at play at these different scales, which produce varied effects, yet in rare instances they are those envisaged by the test makers. Indeed Robertson's (2012a) work on principles and practices of competitive comparison, and Sorensen and Robertson's more recent research (2020) on principles of classificatory judgment and flattening, have provided me with the necessary conceptual grammar to offer a nuanced exploration of how PISA and PLANEA work as governing instruments in the context of Mexico. Deploying these emerging conceptual resources is in line with this book's theorical stance, that of critical theory, where Cox (1981) argues: "as reality changes, old concepts have to be adjusted or rejected and new concepts forged in an initial dialogue between the theorist and the particular world he tries to comprehend" (p. 128).

In this chapter, I will be discussing how these governing tools mediate education governance in that they help frame, put into circulation, enhance, reproduce, and reinforce assumptions, beliefs, feelings (affect) and justifications amongst educators, education leaders and policy decision-makers. Although the capacity, activity and trajectory of these tools varies in each scale and case, they are nevertheless commonplace in the governing relationships studied in this book. This chapter will thus focus on how and so what of LSA governing tools and processes in Mexico, with what kinds of effects, and for whom.

1   Scales, Bits and Tools

Research findings suggest that the main commonality amongst the different scales of this research consist of an array of governing tools and processes

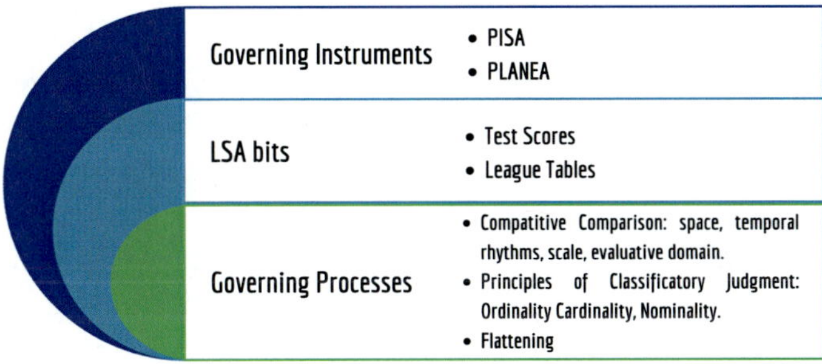

FIGURE 8.1   LSAs, bits and tools

which are dependent on, and mobilize competitive comparison, principles of classificatory judgment, and flattening, that underlie those bits of LSA which are referenced or employed by participants and policy initiatives. By LSA bits I refer to a variety of LSA elements which include, but are not limited to test scores, league tables, outcomes, categories, and test parts. Figure 8.1 illustrates this enterprise.

Figure 8.1 indicates the relationship between the governing instruments, LSA bits such as test scores and tables, and the nature of the processes that are at work. In this section, I shall focus on the relationship between these aspects. The purpose of doing so is twofold. Firstly, to explain the dynamics of these relationships, and secondly to illustrate which elements or bits of LSAs are more popular. The latter is particularly relevant for the second section of this chapter.

1.1   *Which Bits at the Local Scale and How They Matter*

At the local scale (in this case, schools) of this research I conducted a survey of educators to explore their knowledge, reading practices, and views on the usefulness of large-scale assessment programs and the data they produce. This was followed up by a series of semi-structured interviews to explore the main outcomes from the survey. When analyzing participants' responses from the interviews, one can notice an emphasis on particular large-scale assessments bits, for example: (a) the score average; (b) the ranking itself; and (c) comparing themselves against their peers (see Chapter 5). In the following paragraphs I elaborate on each one of these features and explicate how they are key aspects in governing through LSAs.

First, participants at the local scale attach a great deal of importance to the score average. Here, the need to, or a sense of obligation towards, attain higher score averages in every test round can be noted. Employing Fourcade's (2016) concepts to this situation, this need is underpinned and boosted by cardinal reasoning which is oriented to the dynamics of accumulating and collecting, in this case increasing or decreasing, adding, or subtracting. In cardinal judgments, numerical values become meaningful in their own right (Fourcade, 2016, p. 177). In this case, cardinal judgments encourage education agents to focus on increasing the general score average of students, groups, and schools and to guard against subtracting or decreasing scores. These relationships are most likely encouraged and boosted because of three particular situations: (a) in many cases, test scores represent the only 'external objective indicator' of learning progress, decline or stagnation, and as a result this grants them a degree of scientific value (Martens, 2007); (b) oversimplified and commonly spread claims which assert marvelous and multiple uses for LSA data which, as argued in Chapter 5, tends to be unprecise and ambiguous but nevertheless effective for inflating the relevance of assessment outcomes; and (c) formal norms or mandates which obligate education agents to look at and make use of test scores (DOF, 2017). At a more informal level, through public exhibitions of shaming or praising, test scores also speak to some of the most basic of human instincts; that of survival, competition, and recognition. Together, these situations trigger and propel the relevance of this cardinal product.

Second, participants at the local scale focus their attention on league tables. This particular offspring of LSAs can be linked to ordinal judgments. According to Fourcade (2016), these judgments are concerned with the ranking and ordering of people and things, from the lowest to the highest, and particularly with the downplaying of the magnitude or the nature of the differences between the ranks. What we can note amongst participants at the local scale is a concern with their position on the league table, and their perceived need to climb as many positions as possible, or at a minimum maintain their current position. This issue matters, because it is linked to interpretations of how schools value themselves and others, mediated by their location on league tables.

Third, we can note that participants at the local scale focus on comparing their performance against their peers. This particular practice or effect of LSAs is enhanced by the modalities of power inherent in competitive comparison (Hierarchical Space, Temporal Rhythms, Evaluative Trajectories, and Scale). For instance, the first modality of power is hierarchical space, or vertical vision. The advancement of a multi-scalar LSA landscape with distinct and multiple assessments in Mexico enables and lays out a terrain in which comparison practices are made possible. Furthermore, thanks to the multiplicity and overlapping of assessment programs (PISA, ERCE and PLANEA) in this context, comparisons are nested and encouraged. In this respect, the dynamics of this space enable the framing of multiple-parallel rankings (at least one for each assessment program at play), and consequently the advancement of a ranking based culture in schools and education more broadly. This is a culture of performers and underperformers giving rise to vertically-organized social relations which I will discuss in the following section. A second modality of power that can be identified is the notion of temporal rhythms. Again, given the multiplicity of assessment programs in Mexico, there are several assessment cycles in action at any one time. Consequently, education agents are not only able to obtain test results periodically (each year in the case of PLANEA), but as the product of the current assessment regime, multiple results are produced and fed to them continually.

1.2 *Which Bits at the Subnational Scale and How They Matter*

At the subnational scale of this research, I explored policy decisions regarding the design and enforcement of an initiative namely, the EXCALE's use in kindergarten. To this end, I carried out a series of semi-structured interviews with policy makers from a subnational setting. Following the analysis of the interview data and a thorough review of the aims, structure, and content of the initiative, one can note that policy developers focused on particular LSA bits for the advancement of their policy. This was specifically noticeable in one of the main aspects of the initiative which consisted of replacing the traditional report card with a proficiency table for assessing students and tracking their progress (see Chapter 6).

This maneuver is underpinned and driven by nominal and cardinal judgments. Nominal judgments involve two main processes: (1) the design of categories; and (2) category recognition, which refers to the assessment of objects or people to determine the category they belong to (Fourcade, 2016). In essence, replacing descriptive assessments with a proficiency table is a nominal move. Here, proponents 'design' (copied from the EXCALE test) the categories for the proficiency table, and educators are expected to 'fit' their students according to their performance into these classifications. Cardinal reasoning can be seen in that educators are encouraged to prioritize that dynamic which shifts students from one level to the next. This represents a risk, because it can lead to the narrowing of education practices because educators center their efforts on moving as many students as possible from the lower to the upper levels with the consequence that they overlook or undermine other aspects of learning.

1.3 *Which Bits at the National Scale and How They Matter*

At the national scale of this research, I studied two distinct policies. First, I addressed policy decisions regarding the voting process for the General Law for the Professional Teaching Service. Second, I looked into policy decisions in relation to the development of the new national curriculum namely, Key

Learnings for an Integral Education. In both cases, I carried out a series of semi-structured interviews; the first with Senators, the latter with Secretariat of Education Officials and Collaborators.

As discussed in the first section of Chapter 7 with regard to the approval process of the General Law for the Professional Teaching Service, Senators voted in a particular direction, mainly instructed by their political parties. In spite of this overarching dynamic which determined voting decisions, legislators still invoked and referenced certain parts of LSA assessments when they provided justifications for their actions. This behavior is similar to that of federal authorities in the United States of America where PISA results from 2012 and onwards were used to legitimize reform paths post-hoc (Niemann et al., 2018). Another case of employing LSA to post-hoc legitimize reform pathways can be seen in England during the period Michael Gove was Secretary of Education (Thomas et al., 2016). Going back to the Mexican context, we can note special emphasis being placed on test scores. These indicators are a cardinal product, which in this case enriches a widespread narrative amongst legislators which sustains the view that learning in Mexico is poor. Fourcade (2016) argues that in real life, nominal, cardinal, and ordinal judgments overlap and intersect all the time. The intersection entailed in this case is problematic because as we can note, it pushes legislators to uncritically justify simplified solutions to problems that are actually highly complex. Furthermore, the justifications based on test scores prevent Senators from taking any further action because these indicators help confirm that they did the "right thing".

The second case addressed at the national scale differs substantially from the first, especially because Secretariat of Education Officials and Collaborators confirmed that LSA data was employed directly for the development of different sections of the new national curriculum. For instance: the (a) structure of dominant subjects (Literacy and Math); (b) design of learning standards; (c) distribution of teaching time; and (d) advancement of new curricular components. Martinez-Rizo and Silva-Guerrero (2016) argue that LSAs in Mexico have influenced curriculum in the past; however, it should be noted that in the current curriculum, the structure of Literacy and Math have been designed to meet the evaluative dimensions of PLANEA. Other countries, such as Chile, have also undergone similar shifts as the result of LSAs. For instance, since the early PISA rounds, Chile adapted lower secondary Science and Math subjects to fit PISA dimensions (Cox & Meckes, 2016).

Furthermore, in this Mexican case, we can note that the design of math and literacy learning standards were also influenced by LSAs. In relation to this, Takayama (2008) argues that "international league tables have become a significant source of influence in the design of national education policies.

Countries ranking high on the league tables instantly become the symbol of educational excellence" (p. 387). In Mexico, ranking tables offered data to Secretariat Officials, which made visible the "best" performing education systems around the world. This, in turn, triggered an urge for policy borrowing, which, was materialized in the design of the learning standards that drew upon the work advanced by Singapore, who is amongst the first places in the PISA league tables. Whilst on the one hand this is a matter of policy borrowing, what precedes it involves flattening practices. For instance, the particularities of each of these countries were erased in order to see and treat them as equivalents. By erasing the differences, Mexico could then apply, indiscriminately, policies and practice that are being enforced in Singapore. In theory, this dynamic may seem rather straightforward and simple. However, in real life it is complex and charged with cultural, political, and economic obstacles.

The explications outlined above indicate a range of distinct ways in which the governing tools/processes introduced in this study are evident. Occasionally, these tools/processes overlap or reinforce themselves. In some instances, only a few are at work, yet in other cases we can see them working more fully. To this moment, this research has identified where and how these tools underlie bits of LSAs that are at work in different scales and cases. However, further data and research is needed in order to identify and explicate additional issues. For instance, to what extent do these tools/processes follow patterns? Do these tools/processes enable or enhance others, and if so, how? What are their relational dynamics? These issues will be a matter of further research.

2　Shaping Vertical Vision

In the previous section I addressed the relevant findings from the empirical part of this book, in which, bits of LSA are invoked or deployed. There are two peculiar LSA elements that constantly surface across this investigation: test scores and leagues tables. In this section I shall discuss how visual representations of league tables and the configuration of nominal categories based on test scores contribute towards the shaping of vertical vision.

Taking a cue from Slobodian (2018), Robertson (2018, 2022) puts forward what she has theorized as "vertical vision". This entails both a way of seeing and advancing ways to see the world; in this case in a vertical stratified manner in which people, countries, things, places and so on, are not just reduced to numerical commensuration but which constantly and concurrently are ranked ordered top to bottom using an ordinal scale. Robertson (2018) argues that vertical vision sets in motion "an endless race to the top, kept in place by annual cycles of representing and presenting the winners and would-be winners, the mobilization of affect, and an economy of worth and value" (p. 13). In education, vertical vision aims to impose a rationality for seeing and thinking about education, its problems and possible solutions, which inevitably invites us to act in certain directions, and pushes education governance to support the realization of particular wider social projects and values (e.g., neoliberalism and political liberalism). In the following subsections I will discuss how league tables and test scores, underpinned by the governing tools advanced in this book, contribute towards vertical vision.

2.1   *Test Scores and Nominal Categories*

Test scores are one of the most common LSA features that are mentioned in policy documents and the participants from this research. As it was discussed in the previous section, test scores constitute a cardinal product, which is meaningful in itself. However, as this research shows, assessment programs, such as PISA and PLANEA, tend to: (a) convert test scores into nominal outputs; and (b) bring much emphasis to, and prioritize, discussions around these categories. This move advances a vertical organization of space, of top and bottom, winners, and losers (Robertson, 2019), which can be appreciated in different ways across large-scale assessment publications (OECD, 2007, 2010a, 2013, 2016a). An early example of this can be noted in one of the initial PISA publications. Here, Finland is feted as the "top-performing country" in the 2000 PISA round, whereas Mexico is labelled the "lowest performing OECD nation" (OECD, 2004). Through this categorization, these nations are ordered, labelled and judged solely on their tests scores. Consequently, this outcome leads to stigmatization. According to Starr (1992, cited in Fourcade 2016, p. 182), "these categories matter because once institutionalized, classifications have consequences. Some cause damage: some advantage, nominality matters so much here because it is articulated with claims of identity, authenticity, and value". Drawing upon the work of Prunty (1984), what follows from the advancement and enforcement of this arrangement is a selective allocation of resources, opportunities, obligations, and commitments, such that decision makers in Mexico feel obligated to act in response to this turn of events, which means undertaking structural reforms.

There are different ways in which LSAs convert test scores into nominal outputs, and in turn contribute towards the advancement of seeing the world through global competition. I will briefly discuss two. The first of them consists of proficiency label fitting. Recalling the work of Fourcade (2016), nominal judgments entail two basic processes: (a) category building (e.g. Level 6, Level 5, Level 4, etc.); and (b) assessing and fitting students or nations into these categories. Drawing upon the results of PISA 2015, Figure 8.2 shows a good example of this.

	Proficiency level	Lowest score point in the level		
		Mathematics	Reading	Science
Students who score above the baseline proficiency level	Level 6	669	698	708
	Level 5	607	626	633
	Level 4	545	553	559
	Level 3	482	480	484
	Level 2 (baseline)	420	407	410
Low-performing students (below baseline)	Level 1	358	Level 1a 335 Level 1b 262	335
	Below Level 1	.	.	.

FIGURE 8.2   Proficiency levels in PISA
SOURCE: OECD (2016D, P. 37)

Figure 8.2 indicates that based on their test scores, students are located into one of eight different proficiency levels. In turn, these levels are lumped together into two big nominal categories: (a) above the base line and (b) below the base line (low performing students). According to the OECD (2016a), "the baseline of proficiency defines the level of achievement on the PISA scale at which students begin to demonstrate the science competencies that will enable them to participate effectively and productively in life situations related to science and technology" (p. 72). The final product here is a vertically dichotomous space which, on the one hand, "predicts" the future participation and productivity of students, whilst on the other hand, it aligns itself with contemporary language and experiences, such as those displayed more commonly by digital platforms such as YouTube or Netflix, in which assessing (fitting) a service or a product is either a matter of "thumbs up or thumbs down", with no intermediate option.

A second form in which test scores are converted into nominal outputs is the articulation of two main categories: that of (1) high-performers and (b) low-performers, in terms of students and nations. For instance, with regard to the first and drawing upon the OECD (2016a), low-performing students are those whose scores locate them at level 1 and below level 1, whereas high-performing students are those whose scores situate them at level 5 or level 6. Despite the fact that PISA manages a wide range of proficiency levels which can give rise to many different categorizations, the OECD tends to over-emphasize and organize their arguments and discussions around this dichotomy of high and low performers. Another example of this can be noted in the 2015 PISA Results Volume 1. Here, the OECD (2016a), in its opening arguments, refers to Singapore and Macao (China) as high-performing education systems. By way of contrast, it refers to Peru and Colombia as low performing countries. The deployment of these nominal categories are an invitation and a reminder to see the world as vertically organized and globally stratified, of those who are great and those who wish to be great (Robertson, 2019).

Overall, this enterprise – the conversion of test scores into nominal categories – contributes to vertical vision in that it sets up, reproduces and 'normalizes' the nominal categories that are put forward, and the values and beliefs which accompany them. As outlined above, this dynamic sustains the polarized idea that there are winners and losers. Furthermore, as noted by Robertson (2019) this advances a new kind of economy of worth and value tied not to education *per se* but winning and losing. Whilst the high-performers are elevated as the status to follow, those regarded as low-performers become clients or victims of the markets, services and products that assure their escalation to the high-performing class.

2.2 *League Tables*

League tables are a popular feature of LSAs and mentioned by participants as well as in policy documents in this research. In essence, these representations are a combination of cardinal products (test scores) and ordinal processes (ranking). A league table consists of a representation based on numerical commensuration, most commonly emerging out of test scores in which schools, subnational entities and nations are hierarchically-ordered – from best to worst; from first to last. It is important to note there are different variants of league tables amongst and between assessments programs. Focusing on two distinct variants from PISA and PLANEA, in this section I will discuss their particularities and how they emphasize certain issues and views. It is worth mentioning that Takayama (2008) has drawn upon the theory of externalization to address the politics of league tables in his study of the broad dynamics of these instruments on national shifts. By way of contrast, in this section I focus on explicating the tools through which league tables are built, and how they contribute to vertical vision.

First, with regard to the PISA, there is a variant of league tables (Figure 8.3) which ranks countries based on the proportion or accumulation of students in each proficiency level. This variant is particularly interesting because it goes beyond the normal scope of league tables in which countries or sub-national states are hierarchically ordered according to their mean test scores. Figure 8.3 illustrates a representation that integrates cardinal, nominal and ordinal judgments. Here, test scores (cardinal) are fitted into proficiency levels (nominal), followed by the ordering (ordinal) of nations based on the accumulation or quantity of students at the upper proficiency levels. In the following paragraphs I will discuss some of the implications that emerge from the complexity of the governing tools and dynamics at play in this sort of representations.

As it can be noted from Figure 8.3, these devices are becoming more sophisticated. Robertson (2019) notes that "representations of this sort have their own distinct politics so that what is projected also shapes ways of seeing" (p. 12). There are important issues to note from Robertson's claims and the

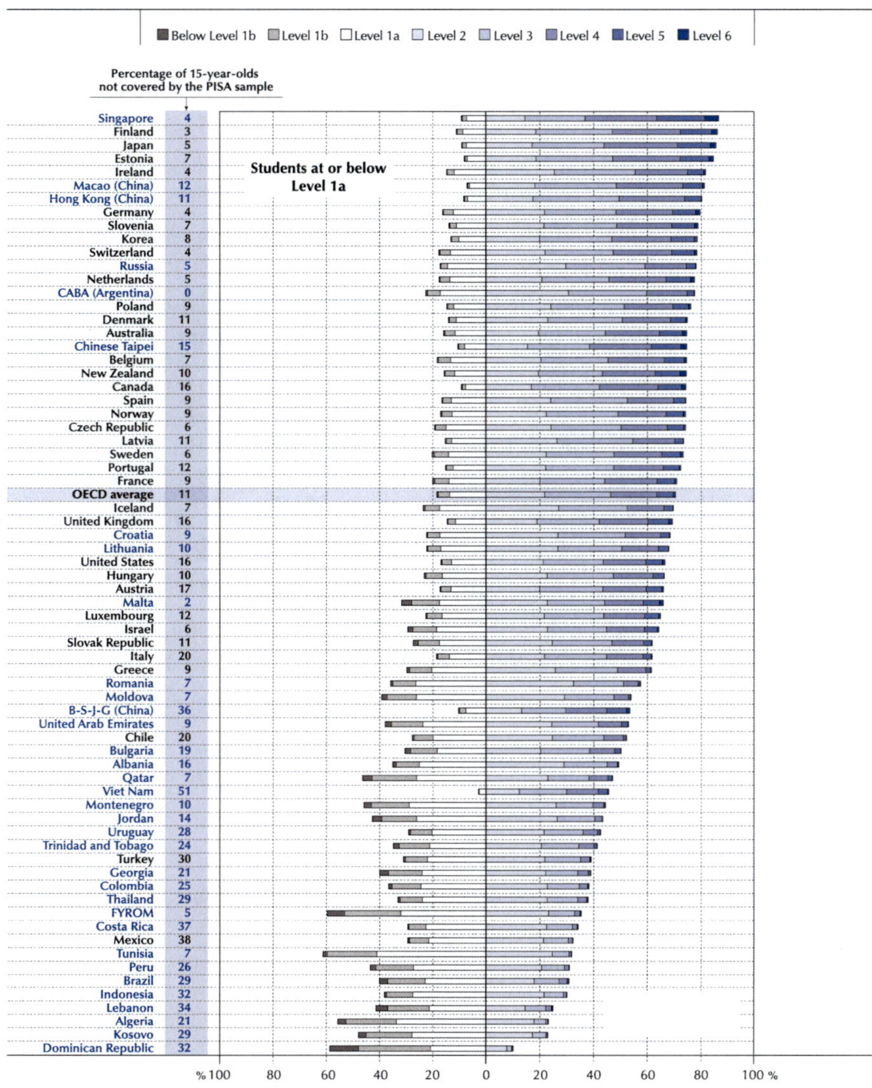

Note: The length of each bar is proportional to the percentage of 15-year-olds covered by the PISA sample (Coverage index 3; see Annex A2).
Countries and economies are ranked in descending order of the number of students who perform at or above Level 2, expressed as a percentage of the total population of 15-year-olds in the country.
Source: OECD, PISA 2015 Database, Table I.2.1b.

FIGURE 8.3   PISA 2015 proficiency levels in science per country
SOURCE: PISA OECD (2016, P. 73)

league table outlined above (Figure 8.3). For instance, the first column to the right constitutes a vertical space; an ordinal list where nations are organized from first to last, or from the best to the worst. Here, we can observe that Singapore occupies the first position, yet the chart on the left indicates that in spite of this, Singapore still has a considerable proportion of students in levels

1a, 2, and some below 1b. Here it is important to acknowledge research from the field of psychology which sustains that the human condition tends to focus on negative aspects rather than the positive. For example, Baumeister et al. (2001) argue that "negative information receives more processing and contributes more strongly to the final impression than positive information" (p. 323). Hence, whilst the list to the right in Figure 8.3 awards 1st place to Singapore, the graph to the left is a reminder that although you may be first, you nevertheless still have an accumulation of students who perform poorly. This situation is likely to garner more attention than the first. Here we can see a cardinal-nominal output feeding into an ordinal dynamic. This in turn contributes to vertical vision by not only making it a matter of a race to the top, but also a parallel endless internal struggle to pass as many students as possible from the lower levels to the higher levels. Furthermore, this becomes a restless battle because of the unlikeliness of having all students from one nation in proficiency levels five or six. A second variant of league tables is put forward by the Mexican national assessment, namely PLANEA. Figure 8.4 illustrates an example of this.

Figure 8.4 illustrates a less common variant of league tables. This representation combines a vertical and horizontal approach. At the bottom part of the projection, we can see the names of all sub-national entities, organized by

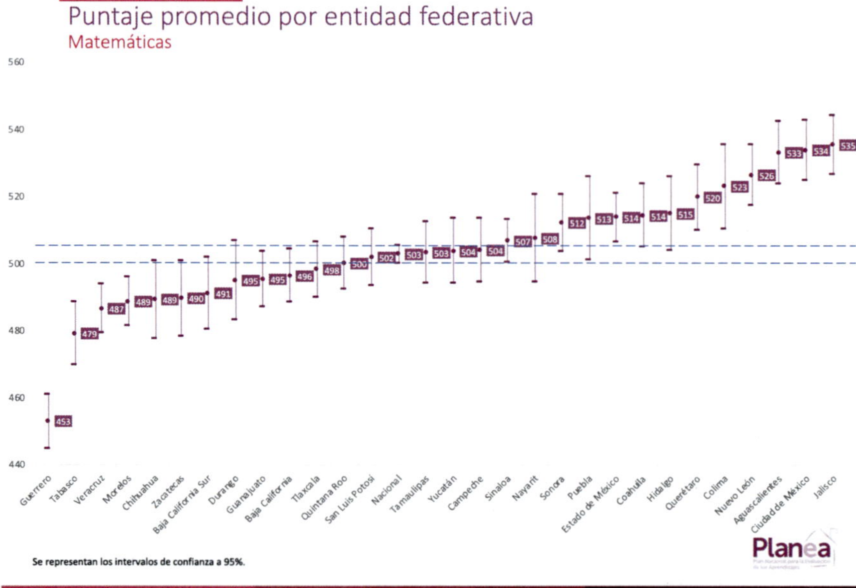

FIGURE 8.4   PLANEA 2018 six grade median scores in mathematics per state
SOURCE: PLANEA NATIONAL RESULTS (2018); INEE (2018, P. 14)

their test scores, from the lowest (Guerrero) to the highest (Jalisco). Interestingly, participants are set at the same horizontal level, what fluctuates and is organized in a vertical space are their mean scores. This organization of space is interesting, because sub-national states are projected as: (a) equivalents; and (b) participants share as even ground. This in turn creates the impression that they share the same conditions and positions required to compete, when in fact there is virtually very little that is similar between these states. As Fourcade (2016) puts it: "Horizontal difference functions most of the time as a social fiction, which helps sustain all kinds of unequal social orders" (p. 177). The PLANEA representation outlined above is underpinned by a flattening rationale, in which the particularities of each state are erased in order for them to be comparable. For example, cultural characteristics, geographic qualities, and economic features, amongst other aspects, are entirely neglected. The numerical commensuration of these states based on test outcomes, is the only thing that stands.

Unequivocally, the league table displayed in Figure 8.4 puts forward open-high-low-close figures (reminiscent of a stock exchange and not common in the field of education) for each participant (entity), ordered from the lowest to the highest. These particular figures show the range from the lowest to the highest scores for each sub-national state. Interestingly, this move establishes vertically organized social relations, where what matters is one's location on the league table, and the variance or spread between the lowest and highest scores, given that this is an indicator for inequality: the smaller the spread, the more homogeneous; the larger the spread, the more unequal. Yet again, like Figure 8.3, this feature is tricky because it triggers an endless internal struggle because there will always be variance and a spread in human behaviors and performance.

In the case of the PISA league table (Figure 8.3), what seems to be at the heart of this dynamic is accumulating as many students as possible at the top-performing proficiency levels so as to guarantee first place in the league table. In the case of the PLANEA league table (Figure 8.4), two issues are important: (1) achieving high mean scores; and (2) reducing the spread or variation amongst participants. In both instances, what can be noted is that the race to the top will be accompanied by "an internal endless struggle", which will be bound to perpetuate this enterprise.

It is important to note that participants were not questioned about the league tables they were familiar with; however, both of the examples analyzed in this section are commonplace amongst PISA and PLANEA pamphlets, presentations and reports. Hence, it is assumed that this is what they are subject to.

In the previous sections I have discussed two of the most popular LSA features that were brought up, mentioned, or referenced by participants and policy documents in this research. I have explained how these LSA features are underpinned by the governing tools introduced in this research, and how they feed into the shaping of vertical vision. In the following section I will question their performance under particular challenging circumstances posed by the ERCE-LLECE assessment.

3   Governing Tools and the ERCE-LLECE Case

The preceding sections of this chapter have been drafted around two broad arguments. First, that the governing tools put forward in this book are ubiquitous amongst scales. Second, that through distinctive LSA bits, these governing tools seemingly contribute towards the reinforcement of what Robertson (2019) has conceptualized as vertical vision. Both of these arguments accentuate the relevance and strength of these governing tools and their effects. In this final section, I draw upon ERCE-LLECE so as to look at them from an alternative angle and give thought to their performance in light of the particularities of this distinctive assessment program.

For the sake of the discussion, it is worth reminding the reader of the broad facts of the ERCE-LLECE assessment which have been elaborated in more detail in Chapter 4. First, the Latin American Laboratory for Assessment of the Quality of Education (LLECE) emerged as the result of initial meetings in 1994 by UNESCO's Regional Office for Latin America and the Caribbean (OREALC) based in Santiago Chile (OREALC-UNESCO, 1998). This consortium envisioned new forms of cooperation between Latin-American countries so as to achieve many of UNESCO's core aspirations linked to the realization of fundamental human rights (UN General Assembly, 1948) and the expansion of well-being in the region.

LLECE oversees the Regional Comparative and Explicative Study (ERCE for its acronym in Spanish); one of the three large-scale assessment programs currently operating in Mexico. This regional bureau has administered three individual assessments in Latin America since 1997 namely: First Regional Comparative and Explanatory Study (PERCE), Second Regional Comparative and Explanatory study (SERCE) and the Third Regional Comparative and Explanatory Study (TERCE). A fourth evaluation round of LLECE took place between 2018 and 2019. The consortium decided that from this round onwards, the name of the assessment would remain the same; that is, Regional Comparative and Explicative Study (ERCE).

The ERCE-LLECE assessment distinguishes itself from its peers PISA and PLANEA in the following way. The most relevant, seen through the lens of this research, lies in its distinctive human rights program ontology which seeks to promote the advancement of statistical data amongst countries for the purpose of cooperation and lesson learning between blocks of countries with similar cultural, social, and economic backgrounds, in line with the advancement of statistics at UNESCO's (Cussó & D'Amico, 2005).

The survey applied in the local scale of this book (See Chapter 5) showed that only 5 out of 319 survey participants from the sub-national state claim to know LLECE assessments (PERCE, SERCE and TERCE).

This odd situation was reinforced through comments made by participants from the sub-national and national levels which indicate that ERCE was also largely disregarded amongst these populations, with the exception of the authorities and collaborators from the Secretariat of Education. This finding raised many questions, such as why PISA and PLANEA are more popular than ERCE-LLECE? and what factors might help explain this course of events? Additionally, this also involved questioning the governing tools that underlie LSAs, and asking how it is that they function so well in some cases, but in other occasions and under particular circumstances not so well? Drawing upon the wider literature, and interviews with members from the National Institute for Education Evaluation Governing Board, I shall discuss how irregular cycles, inefficient pitching, scarce scale and inconvenient convergence contribute to the downplaying of ERCE-LLECE.

3.1   *Irregular Cycles*

Robertson (2012a) argues that temporal rhythms constitute one of the main modalities of power shaping the dynamics of competitive comparisons. Through the enforcement and operation of regular data collection cycles, a space for improvement and learning is enabled. In the case of PISA, since the year 2000 the OECD has set in motion a 3-year assessment cycle. For its part, PLANEA has three variants of its assessment, each collecting data at different rhythms (see Chapter 4). For instance, the main variant PLANEA ELSEN is conducted every three-years; PLANEA ELCE each year; and PLANEA EDC also every year. By way of contrast, the LLECE assessments have followed no temporal rhythm either for the test application nor for the publication of outcomes. For example, PERCE was carried out in 1997; SERCE was conducted in 2006; TERCE took place in 2013; and ERCE 2019. Here appears to be no temporal rhythm.

Members from the National Institute for Education Evaluation Governing Board expressed the following thoughts related to this matter:

> It (LLECE) does not have consistency, that is, it is not applied every "x" number of years so that people are waiting for it. It also takes a long time

> to provide results, it is the longest exercise, and then there is a lack of relationship between when it is applied and when results are published.

> LLECE has no regularity and that has been very problematic. Partly because our countries do not see LLECE as something of our own that we have to take care of and that can bear fruits.

> LLECE takes longer, let's say, the cycles are less regular in this sense.

From these comments it can be noted that assessment and publication cycles are identified as a pivotal issue. The evidence here indicates that the ERCE assessment lacks one of the main features on which competitive comparison thrives (Robertson, 2012a). Without this key element, ERCE is at a disadvantage in relation to its peers, PISA and PLANEA.

Temporal rhythms matter because different sorts of organizations take advantage of them to generate controversy, create expectations, establish benchmarks, and develop and reinforce arguments. Interestingly, these practices seem to produce an acquired need for this sort of data.

3.2 *Inefficient Pitching*

For Robertson (2012a), hierarchical space is another modality of power entailed in competitive comparison. This modality frames a space for classifying students, schools and education systems accordingly to their performance into categories of high and low performers. Consequently, this gives way to participants pitching against each other as means to raise performance. Extending Robertson's (2012a) argument, I would suggest that hierarchical space enables additional forms of pitching; for instance, (a) pitching a country against itself, (b) pitching a country against external threats, and (c) pitching a country against or in favor of particular reforms. Mexico's current state of affairs in ERCE prompts us to question the dynamics of these pitching relationships, especially when a participant (country) is amongst the top performers. In the following section I shall elaborate on this matter.

First, Tables 8.1, 8.2 and 8.3 display participants' mean scores per domain (Mathematics, Language and Science) regarding the TERCE testing round. These outcomes indicate that Mexico and the Mexican sub-national state Nuevo Leon who participated in this assessment as an independent economy, both achieved scores amongst the highest performers in Latin America.

TERCE outcomes show that amongst the most populated and diverse countries in Latin America (Brazil, Colombia, Argentina, and Peru), Mexico and/or the Mexican State of Nuevo Leon lead the way in all assessed domains. In this sense, a large-scale assessment program that places Mexico amongst high performers

TABLE 8.1   TERCE mathematics general league table

Third grade mathematics			Sixth grade mathematics		
No.	Country	Mean	No.	Country	Mean
1	Chile	787	1	Chile	793
2	Nuevo Leon	755	2	Nuevo Leon	793
3	Costa Rica	750	3	Mexico	768
4	Uruguay	742	4	Uruguay	765
5	Mexico	741	5	Costa Rica	730
6	Brazil	727	6	Argentina	722
7	Argentina	717	7	Peru	721
8	Peru	716	8	Brazil	709
9	Ecuador	703	9	Colombia	705
10	Colombia	694	10	Ecuador	702
11	Honduras	680	11	Guatemala	672
12	Guatemala	672	12	Honduras	661
13	Panama	664	13	Panama	644
14	Nicaragua	653	14	Nicaragua	643
15	Paraguay	652	15	Paraguay	641
16	Dominican Rep.	602	16	Dominican Rep.	622

SOURCE: THIRD INTERNATIONAL COMPARATIVE STUDY LLECE
(OREALC-UNESCO, 2015, PP. 58 & 68)

is not a useful instrument for pitching this nation in favor of projects which constantly call the need for reform. Drawing upon the example of the United States of America and its participation in early IEA studies (1960s), Baker and O'Neil (2016) argue that the IEA received little support from the US because policy makers felt that a comparative exercise which showed US students amongst the top performers would undermine the demand for educational funding. In this respect, the tail offered by LLECE to Mexico does not favor the advancement of a neoliberal project which requires the population of Mexico to think that learning is awful, and thus needs urgent and drastic structural reforms.

Following the line of thought of the US case, we can see how assessments can favor or oppose certain projects. During the early 80s, the Reagan administration made use of the report "A Nation at Risk" to enforce a strategy based on public exhibition, propagation and inflation of assessment outcomes, and a politics of fear in order to gain sympathy and support from the public so as to push forward education reforms (Scott, 2011). In this respect, over the past

TABLE 8.2   TERCE language general league table

Third grade language			Sixth grade language		
No.	Country	Mean	No.	Country	Mean
1	Chile	802	1	Chile	776
2	Costa Rica	754	2	Nuevo Leon	761
3	Nuevo Leon	733	3	Costa Rica	755
4	Uruguay	728	4	Uruguay	736
5	Peru	719	5	Mexico	735
6	Mexico	718	6	Colombia	726
7	Colombia	714	7	Brazil	721
8	Brazil	712	8	Argentina	707
9	Argentina	703	9	Peru	703
10	Ecuador	698	10	Ecuador	683
11	Honduras	681	11	Guatemala	678
12	Guatemala	678	12	Panama	671
13	Panama	670	13	Honduras	662
14	Nicaragua	654	14	Nicaragua	662
15	Paraguay	653	15	Paraguay	652
16	Dominican Rep.	614	16	Dominican Rep.	633

SOURCE: THIRD INTERNATIONAL COMPARATIVE STUDY LLECE
(OREALC-UNESCO, 2015, PP. 31 & 42)

15 years, the Mexican Government has adopted a similar approach with PISA, PLANEA, and its predecessors. The National Institute for Education Evaluation develops and publishes an extensive national report for each PISA round. In the case of PLANEA, there is a whole mediatization effort in which test scores are publicized on radio, on open television broadcast and through different digital platforms. Whereas ERCE-LLECE assessments have never received similar treatment.

3.3   *Scarce Scale*

Fourcade (2016) and Sorensen and Robertson (2020) argue that numerical reasoning works best with the inclusion of the largest population possible; the more comprehensive the scale, the less contestable, and the more significant and thus more legitimate in terms of objectivity, rational judgement, so as to be deployed as a policy tool for management and control. A member of the

TABLE 8.3   TERCE science general league table

TERCE sixth grade science		
No.	Country	Mean
1	Chile	768
2	Costa Rica	756
3	Nuevo Leon	746
4	Colombia	733
5	Mexico	732
6	Uruguay	725
7	Ecuador	711
8	Peru	701
9	Argentina	700
10	Brazil	700
11	Guatemala	684
12	Panama	675
13	Honduras	668
14	Nicaragua	668
15	Paraguay	646
16	Dominican Rep.	632

SOURCES: OREALC-UNESCO (2008, P. 19);
OREALC-UNESCO (2015, P. 84)

National Institute for Education Evaluation Governing Board made the following comment with regard to this matter:

> We can argue that an assessment with 70 or 72 of the world's countries is much more appealing. The OECD puts a lot of money, a lot of resources to position PISA globally. While LLECE has a lower profile and does not intend to position itself as if it were PISA. Remember the case of the IEA. PISA displaces the IEA's TIMSS and PIRLS which had led this field for more than 50 years, Andreas himself came from the IEA. Remember that the IEA is a civil association with very few resources, nothing else besides what it gathers from these assessments. On the other hand, the OECD has an impact on the economic and on the political, the OECD apparatus is 100 times larger than that of the IEA and it is well positioned in all domains.

According to this comment, ERCE is at a disadvantage in relation to other assessment programs, both in terms of the largest population country-wise, but also with regards to the domestic landscape. This is especially so, given that ERCE only assesses students from primary schools, whereas PLANEA assesses all compulsory education levels. The total number of participants in a large-scale assessment program is fundamental for its legitimacy. However, as it can be noted from the comment outlined above, there are also other issues at play; for example, the qualities or particularities amongst participants. A member of the INEE Governing Board elaborated on this issue:

> Have you heard about social stratification? In this world you have *the rich* and you have *the poor*, well, that's why. This program (LLECE) does not shine because we're not first world countries. In a sense, Latin America does not matter, we are not interested in comparing ourselves with Venezuela, Costa Rica or Cuba. (Emphasis added)

In this respect, we can note that scale it not only a matter of quantity but also an issue of quality. As pointed out above; it is not the same to compare Mexico with poor countries than with wealthy nations. In a nutshell, with regard to LLECE, whilst quantity is a fundamental scale issue, it is also the case that prestige and status amongst participants also matters.

3.4   *Inconvenient Convergence*

Governing by comparisons operates on the premise that participants regarded as high performers become the model to follow. As Martens (2007) puts it: "the parties evaluated are implicitly pressured to converge towards those practices, forms of organization, or behaviors, that are regarded as best (either most effective or most appropriate)" (p. 42). However, converging to the best practice is slightly problematic when the entity regarded as the best has features which make it an inconvenient example, or when it goes against certain interests.

In the first two rounds of the LLECE assessment (PERCE and SERCE), Cuba excelled in all assessed domains. This was a surprising outcome such that, according to one of the interviewees from the INEE Governing Board, "In PERCE, CUBA was asked to retake the tests, based on suspicions of cheating. Cuba was indignant but complied". After the second round of testing for PERCE, Cuba surprisingly exceeded its initial outcomes, scoring even higher than the first time. Years later, SERCE came along, and the Cubans did it once again: they outperformed their Latin-American peers. This proved that according to LLECE indicators, socialist Cuba had the best education system in Latin America (Carnoy, 2016). Tables 8.4, 8.5, 8.6 and 8.7 show that in the PERCE

TABLE 8.4   PERCE mathematics general league table

Third grade mathematics			Fourth grade mathematics		
No.	Country	Mean	No.	Country	Mean
1	Cuba	351	1	Cuba	353
2	Argentina	251	2	Argentina	269
3	Brazil	247	3	Brazil	269
4	Chile	242	4	Chile	265
5	Colombia	240	5	Colombia	258
6	Bolivia	240	6	Mexico	256
7	Mexico	236	7	Paraguay	248
8	Paraguay	232	8	Bolivia	245
9	Dominican Rep.	225	9	Dominican Rep.	234
10	Venezuela	220	10	Honduras	231
11	Honduras	218	11	Venezuela	226

SOURCE: FIRST INTERNATIONAL COMPARATIVE STUDY LLECE (OREALC-UNESCO, 1998, P. 51)

TABLE 8.5   PERCE language general league table

Third grade language			Fourth grade language		
No.	Country	Mean	No.	Country	Mean
1	Cuba	343	1	Cuba	349
2	Argentina	263	2	Chile	286
3	Chile	259	3	Argentina	282
4	Brazil	256	4	Brazil	277
5	Venezuela	242	5	Colombia	265
6	Colombia	238	6	Mexico	252
7	Bolivia	232	7	Paraguay	251
8	Paraguay	229	8	Venezuela	249
9	Mexico	224	9	Honduras	238
10	Dominican Rep.	220	10	Bolivia	233
11	Honduras	216	11	Dominican Rep.	232

SOURCE: FIRST INTERNATIONAL COMPARATIVE STUDY LLECE (OREALC-UNESCO, 1998, P. 50)

TABLE 8.6   SERCE mathematics general league table

Third grade mathematics			Sixth grade mathematics		
No.	Country	Mean	No.	Country	Mean
1	Cuba	647,93	1	Cuba	637,47
2	Nuevo Leon	562,80	2	Uruguay	578,42
3	Uruguay	538,53	3	Nuevo Leon	553,95
4	Costa Rica	538,32	4	Costa Rica	549,33
5	Mexico	532,10	5	Mexico	541,61
6	Chile	529,46	6	Chile	517,31
7	Argentina	505,36	7	Argentina	513,03
8	Brazil	505,03	8	Brazil	499,42
9	Colombia	499,35	9	Colombia	492,71
10	Paraguay	485,60	10	Perú	489,98
11	El Salvador	482,75	11	El Salvador	471,94
12	Perú	473,94	12	Paraguay	468,31
13	Ecuador	473,07	13	Ecuador	459,50
14	Nicaragua	472,78	14	Nicaragua	457,93
15	Panamá	463,04	15	Guatemala	455,81
16	Guatemala	457,10	16	Panamá	451,60
17	Dominican Rep.	395,65	17	R. Dominican	415,64

SOURCE: SECOND INTERNATIONAL COMPARATIVE STUDY LLECE (OREALC-UNESCO, 2008, PP. 191–192)

and SERCE rounds of LLECE, Cuba outperformed all other Latin-American countries.

Cuba's achievements in LLECE assessments were astonishing. After their 1959 revolution, this small Caribbean Island enforced a socialist political project embedded with Marxist-Leninist ideologies. This project led the Cuban nation to achieve a collectivist society which in turn produced students with high levels of attainment of schooling and provided high levels of healthcare for all of its people (Lopez, 2011). Similarly, Finland was the poster country for PISA, except that Finland harbored an inconvenient truth; that it did not follow the prescription promoted by the OECD regarding how to be a top performing country (Sahlberg, 2012, 2014). It did not have high stakes testing, employ new public management tools, or have a devolved system as a way of coordinating its education activity.

TABLE 8.7   SERCE language general league table

Third grade language			Sixth grade language		
No.	Country	Mean	No.	Country	Mean
1	Cuba	626,89	1	Cuba	595,92
2	Costa Rica	562,69	2	Costa Rica	563,19
3	Chile	562,03	3	Chile	546,07
4	Nuevo Leon	557,80	4	Nuevo Leon	542,35
5	Mexico	530,44	5	Uruguay	542,15
6	Uruguay	522,65	6	Mexico	529,92
7	Colombia	510,58	7	Brazil	520,32
8	Argentina	510,04	8	Colombia	514,94
9	Brazil	503,57	9	Argentina	506,45
10	El Salvador	496,23	10	El Salvador	484,16
11	Perú	473,98	11	Perú	476,29
12	Nicaragua	469,80	12	Nicaragua	472,92
13	Paraguay	469,09	13	Panamá	472,05
14	Panamá	467,21	14	Paraguay	455,24
15	Ecuador	452,41	15	Guatemala	451,46
16	Guatemala	446,95	16	Ecuador	447,44
17	Dominican Rep.	395,44	17	Dominican Rep.	421,47

SOURCE: SECOND INTERNATIONAL COMPARATIVE STUDY LLECE (OREALC-UNESCO, 2008, PP. 193–194)

Following the premises of governing by comparison (Martens, 2007), and in the view of policy lessons sketched by ERCE, Mexico should feel pressured to converge towards Cuba's policy route, which is inevitably tied to its political project; that of socialism. Needless to say, this is not occurring at all. Furthermore, the idea of lesson learning from CUBA is highly inconvenient and contradictory with the dominant political and economic agenda in Mexico today. By way of contrast, PISA, the current global hegemonic LSA which carries out benchmarking exercises and ascertains which countries should serve as the world's educational examples (Rautalin et al., 2018), pushes forward, more recently, the view that countries such as Mexico, ought to follow the Singaporean way, which is much more in harmony to the undergoing neoliberal project in Mexico (IMF, 1992; Ornelas, 2018). In this respect, governing by comparisons seems to be more fruitful when countries are prompt to converge to policies and practices from educational systems that are aligned with dominant political views and agendas.

Cuba did not participate in the third ERCE survey (TERCE). In this round, Chile achieved the highest scores amongst Latin-American countries. If this were to continue in the upcoming ERCE rounds, Chile may displace Cuba as the best education system in Latin America, and in turn be positioned in terms of Martens (2007) as a model to converge towards. Given Chile's historical ties to neoliberalism, this may boost LLECE's popularity. Similar to the case of IEA assessments which emerged from UNESCO's principles, it might boost practices linked to assessments with human capital or public accountability program ontologies, such as the case of the United States of America where the TIMSS assessment has paved the way for the implementation of value-added models (Schmidt & Burroughs, 2016).

4 Conclusions

In Chapter 8 I have argued that the governing tools introduced in this book are commonplace amongst the different scales and cases in Mexico. I have explained how modalities, principles and practices of competitive comparisons, principles of classificatory judgment and flattening underlie particular bits of large-scale assessments, which are picked-up and referenced by participants and policy documents. Moreover, I have explained how two of the most popular LSA offspring employed by participants and policy documents (underpinned by these governing tools) contribute towards the advancement of vertical vision. This theoretical conception advanced by Robertson (2019) helps us to see how some LSAs mediate in framing problems and solutions. Finally, making use of the ERCE-LLECE assessment I have brought into question these governing tools. Findings suggest that: (a) irregular cycles of data collection matter; (b) when a nation is situated amongst high performers, it is more complex to pitch it against its peers; (c) scale size is relevant, but qualities are also important as they appeal to issues that are important to participants; and (d) when converging means going against dominant interests, it becomes inconvenient.

Conclusions

In this book I set out to explore large-scale assessment programs and governance in Mexico; a setting that holds a complex multi-layered centralized-decentralized education system in which various LSAs have coexisted over the past 18-years. I was particularly interested in studying this enterprise from: (a) a critical theory stance, which according to Cox (1981): "is directed to the social and political complex as a whole rather than to the separate parts" (p. 129); and (b) in the light of two overarching and overlapping aspirations which seem to characterize LSAs. These consist of producing data for the purposes of (i) contributing to education practice improvement, and (ii) aiding policy decisions. The existing body of literature in the field of LSAs and governance tends to focus on the outcomes of these governing relationships with an overemphasis on one or two assessments from one scale and in a single setting: for example, PISA and TIMSS and their influence on national policies (Wagemaker, 2014).

By way of contrast, this book offers a multi-scalar approach which involves studying a group of distinct large-scale assessment programs which function concurrently (PISA at the global; ERCE at the regional Latin-American; and PLANEA at the National), and their governing processes, practices, and outcomes at three layers of the Mexican education context: national, subnational and local. In order to achieve such a task, I employed critical theory as a meta-theory. This allowed me to approach, question and problematize LSAs both as a mode of assessment and also as a political instrument aimed at social control (Scott, 2011). In addition to this paradigmatic underpinning, I embraced a range of different disciplines and theories to help me study and explain these phenomena in Mexico.

This final chapter aims to: (a) outline a series of main research concluding thoughts; (b) shed light onto methodological, theorical and empirical contributions of the study; and (c) inform what has happened in Mexico since the time of the research. Additionally, it offers some options for future research concerning the theme of this book.

1   **Main Research Concluding Thoughts**

1.1   *The Histories, Politics, and Governance Arrangements of the Current*
        LSA Regimen in Mexico

The current large-scale assessment program regimen in Mexico can be read as an offspring of a broader set of global measures focused on the: (a) reconstruction of nations devastated during the World War II period; (b) peacekeeping; and (c) struggle over a new world order in a polarized post-war context. These situations unleashed efforts to improve education systems based on two antagonistic projects: (a) the advancement of statistics for sharing and cooperation amongst nations lead by UNESCO; and (b) the advancement of an indicator-based culture grounded on competition, ordinal reasoning, and lesson learning, led by OEEC-OECD. These opposing projects based either on cooperation or competition as drivers for improving education systems is at the heart of the current assessment arrangement in Mexico. Central to this is the advancement of the IEA, which is linked to meetings at UNESCO (Wagemaker, 2014). This Association believed that education statistics should not merely focus on the quantity of people that were being educated, but also on the extent to which they were learning.

Taking this premise further, in the new millennium PISA emerged with a strong rhetoric which claimed that competence levels in Math, Literacy and Science were foundational for economic growth and thus the future of nations. Hence, if countries were interested in their development, they had to pay attention to these particular aspects of their education systems. In this respect, through PISA, the OECD simultaneously framed a problem and offered a solution (Meyer & Benavot, 2013), based on generating and providing data for aiding policy decisions and contributing to education practice improvement. The narrowing of the discourse around improving education systems is also relevant to the proliferation of the current assessment arrangement in Mexico. The evolution of this discourse can be broadly understood in the following phases: (a) first the concern was on the number of people that had access to schooling; (b) second, the emphasis was on the extent to which people in schools were learning: (c) third, the concern lied in the competence levels (quality) of students in three particular knowledge areas (Math, Literacy and Science); (d) fourth, the attention prevails strongly on quality, but with growing concerns on equity in terms of student outcomes (test scores).

Today, the assessment arrangement in Mexico is comprised of three LSAs which can be linked to distinct historical events, projects, and organizations, such as the OECD, UNESCO, and INEE-SEP. I argue that the core values, principles and overall missions of these institutions permeate their respective LSAs and shape their program ontology. For instance:

a.   The Program for International Student Assessment (PISA) which oper-
     ates at the global scale emerged out of the OECD, which consequently
     came about from the transition of the OEEC. Since its inception, the
     OECD has been concerned with the economic development of nations
     based on market-driven competition, indicator production and lesson
     learning. PISA reflects these principles in that it functions with a particu-
     lar orientation towards the improving of education based on them. This
     has been supported by the insertion and promotion of human capital
     theory in education, which fundamentally views students as investment
     assets which can provide returns based on their performance levels in
     Math, Literacy and Science.

b.   The Regional Comparative and Explanatory Study (ERCE) emerged
     as a collaborative effort put forward by UNESCO's Regional Bureau for
     Education in Latin America and the Caribbean. This program is currently
     operated by the Latin American Laboratory for Assessment of the Quality
     of Education. Since their inception both the Bureau and the Laboratory
     have focused on planning, advancing and fostering education initiatives
     that can, on the one hand, ensure rights to, in and through education, and
     on the other, contribute to the development of this region. ERCE reflects
     these values in that it shares a similar mission; that of reducing levels of
     inequality in learning and by increasing overall learning to then contrib-
     ute to the expansion of wellbeing in the region.

c.   The National Plan to Evaluate Learning (PLANEA) came about as the result
     of the cancellation of two prior national large-scale assessments in Mexico,
     namely ENLACE and EXCALE. This program absorbed and 'improved' the
     functions of its predecessors. PLANEA is jointly managed and operated by
     the Secretariat of Education and the National Institute for Education Eval-
     uation in Mexico. In this respect, it echoes their particular values linked to
     contemporary approaches to public accountability, which starts from the
     premise that if education and policy agents are given proper, orderly and
     periodic accounts, they can consequently improve their processes and
     practices, and in turn raise performance levels.

Together, these large-scale assessment programs, with their distinct program
ontologies contribute to a highly complex, at times contradictory, multi-scalar,
multi-purpose assessment regime in Mexico.

1.2   *Aiding Education Practice Improvement and Policy Decisions at Different Political Scales*

If aiding is understood as an act of "helping", then claiming that LSAs "aid" policy decisions and education practice improvement is questionable. However,

this research views the act of aiding as assisting, intervening, or mediating. In this respect, LSAs in Mexico claim that they generate data to aid policy decisions and contribute to education practice improvement. Research findings indicate that aiding relationships between LSAs and policy decisions or education practice improvements are complex and varied. In the following paragraphs I elaborate on this matter accordingly to each scale of this research.

At the local scale, findings show that LSAs fail to provide clear and straightforward guidelines or suggestions as to how their data is to contribute to education practice improvement. LSAs recommend that low-performers should see what high-performers are doing, learn from them, and then adapt it to their contexts. This is highly problematic because it overlooks the needs and particularities of countries and their respective systems, and it offers a single solution to all of them. Further findings from this scale show significant variations regarding LSA awareness amongst educators, especially: (a) when PISA and PLANEA are contrasted against their peer ERCE-LLECE; and (b) awareness amongst early primary school educators regarding PISA. Evidence also suggests that participants engage lightly with LSA publications, and that roughly only one third of educators or less consider that LSA data is useful for improving education skills linked to lesson planning and student assessment. Nonetheless, participants from the local scale express concern for and stress the importance of particular forms of LSA data and issues, such as: test scores, league table positions, improving test outcomes and comparing themselves against their peers. These indicators suggest that LSA data is at work mediating and invoking feelings (affect), shaping views, influencing thoughts, raising concerns, and pressuring softly.

At the subnational scale, findings suggest that despite the multiplicity of assessment programs in Mexico, in some cases initiative proponents or education agents merely look at or make use of those LSAs which assess students from the education level in which they work. For instance, only the EXCALE assessment is employed. Findings show that a group of subnational and municipal education agents developed an initiative namely, the EXCALE's use in kindergarten. This policy put forward three important shifts in a set of preschools in one subnational state: (a) the replacement of learning standards with EXCALE test descriptors; (b) replacement of descriptive assessments with proficiency tables; and (c) employing an EXCALE 'like' test to track students' progress during their preschool education cycle. LSA data is at work in two distinctive ways in this case: (a) first, it offers an apparent solution to problems associated with faults regarding initial teacher education and curricular limitations; and (b) EXCALE outcomes functioned as boosters for employing test features such as assessment descriptors and proficiency levels for tracking and marking students. Evidence from this scale indicates that not only LSA data aids policy decisions and education practice improvement, but also fragments of the assessment itself can be at play in these dynamics.

Lastly, evidence from the two cases addressed at the national scale suggest important variances as to how LSA data aids policy decisions. With regard to the first case, the approval of the General Law for the Professional Teaching Service, findings indicate that Senators voted here in a particular direction (in favor or against), instructed by their political parties. Nonetheless, particular forms of LSA data constitute one of the main references used by Senators for justifying their actions in this turn of events, and LSA data was employed in the rationale that put forward the 2013 Education Reform which in turn opened the pathway for the advancement of General Law for the Professional Teaching Service.

Overall, large-scale assessment data presents and reinforces views concerning the health of the state of learning in Mexico. This in turn fuels the idea that change is essential. Consequently, propositions such as the General Law for the Professional Teaching Service appear rational and therefore are uncritically and easily justified. In a distinctive dynamic, Secretariat of Education Officials and Collaborators confirm that LSAs directly influence decisions with regard to the advancement of the new national curriculum, namely Key Learnings for an Integral Education. Participants commented that LSA data broadly influenced the whole design by inviting curriculum designers to look at the curriculum of successful countries (e.g., Singapore). However, it can be noted in that it: (a) shed light onto learning standards that require more emphasis; (b) helped put forward a new curricular component by illustrating how it functioned in other contexts; (c) is central to the distribution of teaching hours across the curriculum, based on the relevance of these for enabling further learning; and (d) figures as a sort of blueprint for structuring the domains of the Math and Literacy learning fields.

1.3   *Unintended Consequences of the Assessment Regime*

Teaching to the test can be seen as the most common unintended consequence of the evaluation regime in Mexico. Evidence from the three distinct scales show traces of this phenomenon. Teaching to the test is carried out in four main variants: (a) test preparation; (b) emphasizing test subjects and standards; (c) teaching previous test and look-alike items; and (d) aligning instruction with test. Evidence from the local scale shows that educators focus on employing test like items and previous test items during class. Furthermore, research findings reveal that a sub-system of upper secondary schools from the local scale, which provide schooling for around 40,000 students, have institutionalized teaching to the PLANEA test by: (i) formally incorporating this activity into their structure; (ii) overviewing and regulating it; (iii) mandating all schools from the subsystem (n = 50) to instrument this initiative; and (iv) obligating all Math and Literacy educators to carry out this policy.

At the subnational scale, teaching to the test is advanced mainly by aligning instruction with the test. In this respect, through an initiative namely the EXCALE's use in kindergarten initiative, a group of schools at the preschool education level (n = 64) have replaced learning standards (from the official curriculum) with test descriptors from the EXCALE test. This shift implies that instead of teaching towards the achievement of the learning standards that are mandated in the official curriculum, educators focus on teaching the assessment descriptors from the test. Lastly, regarding the advancement of the new national curriculum at the national scale, findings revealed a predetermined intention of curriculum designers to align Literacy and Math learning standards and subject structure with PLANEA and PISA domains.

Drawing upon the work of Lascoumes and Le Gales (2007), it can be argued that LSAs produce effects independently of the objectives and aspirations they claim and pursue. In this research, these effects are viewed as unintended consequences. These matter because they shape our judgments around what is to be valued, which in turn leads people and institutions to see and act in certain ways. For example, (a) they position some subjects as more valuable than others, (b) prioritize some teaching activities over others, and (c) prevent or avoid conversations that contest dominant views and finally overlook flaws and problems with the existing order of things.

1.4 *Frictions, Tensions and Contradictions*

The most distinctive tension or friction between assessments programs in Mexico surrounds differences in their program ontology. Whilst PISA's human capital and PLANEA's public accountability are broadly compatible, ERCE's human rights ontology is essentially in constant tension with human capital theory. The evidence from this book suggests that this particular friction is handled by downplaying, neglecting or marginalizing ERCE. For instance, at the national scale of this research I discussed that the rationale employed for approving the 2013 Education Reform made use of PISA and ENLACE scores (the antecedent of PLANEA). The data was incorporated through a confirmatory approach; that is, they used one set of data to confirm the other. One more example of this can be noted in the second case addressed at the national scale. Secretariat of Education Officials and Collaborators often anchored particular parts of the curriculum to PISA and PLANEA, whereas ERCE is ignored. Unlike the three other units of analysis of this book, participants from the Secretariat do know ERCE assessments. However, they are not included in decision-making.

In this research I have argued that ERCE offers a slightly different account to the state of learning in Mexico and avoids putting to work the governing tools that PLANEA and PISA employ. Hence, the outcome of this enterprise is that ERCE is systemically marginalized, and consequently disregarded by education and policy agents.

1.5 *LSA Governing Tools*

I have also argued that the intention of aiding education changes through the use of LSA data is mediated through modalities of governing that include competitive comparison, flattening, and principles of classificatory judgments. Although the depth and extent to which these tools function vary in each scale and case, they underpin the policy decision and education practice improvement relationship dynamics in this research. Competitive comparison enables spaces for carrying out comparisons, testing cycles, pitching dynamics and value judgments. Flattening practices compress or erase differences amongst people, groups, schools, and education systems in order to create equivalences for comparing, and for applying outcomes. In other words, what is produced here is a double flattening of space-agents and solutions. The principles of classificatory judgment enable comparisons: nominality, creates categories out of resemblance and fits people, things and cases into them; cardinality generates collections, groups or accumulations; and ordinality enables rankings, from 'best to worst' based on numerical commensuration. As it can be noted, these tools enable and boost comparison. Taken together, this analysis has offered a more nuanced explication of comparison as a mode of governance. Lastly, these tools matter because they contribute to what Robertson (2019) has coined as vertical vision, which in turn strengthens broader stratification projects and allied values (e.g. neoliberalism and political liberalism).

2 Contributions of This Study

In the broadest sense, this book should be understood as a contribution to the debates in the field of large-scale assessments and governance. It puts forward an original multi-scalar approach to researching this enterprise, which combines a focus on assessment programs – PISA, ERCE and PLANEA – which operate concurrently at distinct scales, with focus on their governing practices, processes and outcomes in three layers or scales – local, subnational and national – of one setting. This research constitutes an effort to study not just this or that assessment but an entire arrangement of programs. In doing so, it surpasses an individual approach and aims to offer understandings of the whole enterprise and its complexities, especially what such an arrangement represents for the landscape of education governance.

Methodologically and theoretically, the research the underpinned this book aims to make a modest but relevant set of contributions. In terms of methodology, it incorporates a multi-scalar approach into the traditional Embedded Case Study design advanced by Yin (2014). In this respect, it surpasses the uncritical and apolitical limitations of Yin's design and enables an approach for critical policy analysis of education within and across scales (Dale, 2003; Robertson, 2012a). Regarding theoretical contributions, drawing upon the work of Fourcade (2016), Robertson (2012a, 2017) and Sorensen and Robertson (2020), this book draws upon a set of concepts aimed at understanding how LSAs work though modalities such as competitive comparisons, flattening and the principles of classificatory judgment to help explain the governing dynamics in large-scale assessments in Mexico and how these tools enable certain beliefs, views and judgments. Additionally, by extending our understanding of the how of LSAs, this book speaks to literatures that are asking for a more nuanced understanding of comparisons as a mode of governance.

3 The Large-scale Assessment Landscape in Mexico Since the Study

Following the 2018 presidential elections, the large-scale assessment landscape in Mexico shifted to a certain extent. In this section, I shall broadly shed light on critical events and issues that frame the present state of these programs. Considering that some of these matters are currently unfolding, this is not an exhaustive account but rather a brief overview that invites readers to look further into these issues.

In 2018, the presidential candidate for the National Regeneration Movement party (MORENA for its acronym in Spanish), Andres Manual Lopez Obrador (AMLO), won the presidential election. AMLO's campaign rhetoric pivoted around controversial ideas that included putting the poor first, anti-neoliberalism, anti-corruption, and anti-establishment, among others. As a result of this political platform, his critics describe him as a left-wing populist (Castro, 2022).

Regarding the education sector, one of AMLO's campaign promises was to cancel the 2012 education reform; this included revoking the universal teacher appraisal system and putting an end to the National Institute for Education Evaluation. AMLO kept his word, and twelve days after assuming office in December 2018, he sent a bill to congress that would eventually terminate the 2012 education reform on May 15, 2019.

Ending the INEE had severe implications for the large-scale assessment landscape in Mexico, mainly because this institute was co-responsible for administering PISA, ERCE and PLANEA. Furthermore, part of INEE's mission was to consolidate an assessment culture by gathering, processing, and disseminating large-scale assessment data. Consequent to the fall of INEE, their activities were distributed and transferred to the Secretariat for Public Education, the National Commission for the Continuous Improvement of Education (MEJOREDU), tendered to third parties or disregarded. It is important to note that all three large-scale assessment programs continue to operate in Mexico. However, subtle changes have taken place with PISA and PLANEA.

Regarding PISA, the 2021 testing round was delayed worldwide due to COVID-19. During that period, rumors emerged that Mexico would opt out of the PISA consortium (IMCO, 2021); nevertheless, these were later denied by the Secretariat for Public Education. In previous PISA rounds, INEE overviewed the application of surveys. Notably, for the 2022 round, this was tendered to the National Center for Education Evaluation (CENEVAL for its acronym). We have yet to see the implications of this shift, especially regarding the dissemination of student outcomes.

Concerning PLANEA, two shifts stand out. Firstly, INEE published a calendar establishing PLANEA testing rounds from 2017 to 2025. After 2018, several of these rounds, like ELSEN 2021 for primary schools and ELSEN 2022 for secondary schools, were not carried out; this is likely to be related to the pandemic and school closures in Mexico; what is unusual, however, is the Secretary's silence on the matter. The second shift concerns the reporting of student outcomes. For instance, before INEE was dissolved, they managed to administer a PLANEA for preschool testing round during the 2017–2018 school year. Different from its predecessor EXCALE for preschool, not one single report has been published from this survey.

In earlier chapters of this book, I discussed that ERCE has a history of being neglected or disregarded by teachers and education authorities in Mexico. In 2022, UNESCO released the 2019 ERCE outcomes; not surprisingly, the Secretariat for Public Education and MEJOREDU have remained, for the most part, reserved about this.

In sum, shifts concerning the current large-scale assessment program landscape include: i) the redistribution of assessment activities, ii) modifications to the testing agenda, and iii) less attention to student outcomes. Notably, these have taken place with discretion from the secretariat, scarce transparency, and little to no consideration for the audiences that these tools serve. From a large-scale assessment point of view, these issues represent key pillars and attacking one or all three puts at high risk the survival of the assessment culture that INEE had foreseen one day.

4 Future Research

This book offers opportunities for future research which could include but are not limited to: (a) expanding research findings; (b) using the same methodological approach but in other contexts; and (c) exploring additional cases from distinct scales and regions across Mexico. In the following paragraphs, I will briefly refer to some potential research options. It is important to note that this should not be considered as an exhausted list.

At the broadest level, the approach that I have put forward through this book, which employs global, regional and local assessments, can be picked up by others. For instance, given its linkages to UNESCO, researchers interested in the Southern and Eastern Africa Consortium for Monitoring Educational Quality (SACMEQ) could emulate this approach in the southern African context. Research in this regard can offer valuable data for developing a comparative analysis between the governing trajectory and dynamics of SACMEQ and LLECE. This could challenge or reinforce the arguments that I have advanced in this book.

Researching other subnational cases in Mexico constitutes an unexplored field, and an attractive opportunity. This research was only able to study one policy from one of the 32 subnational states that comprise this country. In this respect, it would be interesting to gauge what it is that other subnational states are doing. At the local level of this research, findings indicated that educators were employing teaching to the test practices, which focused on applying test like items and answering test items from previous test rounds. Given the scarce knowledge of educators regarding LSAs, applying test like items raises many questions and concerns as to what is actually occurring in these contexts. This particular issue is an important matter to explore in more detail. In Chapter 8, I highlighted that this book identified which governing tools underpin which particular large-scale bits. However, further research and data are needed to explore their relational dynamics, and the extent to which these tools follow patterns, and are enabled or enhanced by others. These questions also constitute a relevant area for further studies. Another opportunity for further research lies in the advancement of a research culture which gauges the role of LSA in policy decisions. This would constitute a mechanism for overviewing these instruments, which remain largely unaccountable.

In addition to the above, after 30 years of neoliberalism in Mexico, in the 2018 presidential elections the Mexican people voted-in a leftist anti-neoliberal federal government. Interestingly, this government also made use of LSAs data to justify many of the shifts that are currently underway. Thus, a fascinating opportunity of comparative education research would be the discourses, uses, dynamics and outcomes of LSA data between left-wing and right-wing administrations.

References

Ababneh, E., Al-Tweissi, A., & Abulibdeh, K. (2016). TIMSS and PISA impact – The case of Jordan. *Research Papers in Education, 31*(5), 542–555. http://doi.org/10.1080/02671522.2016.1225350

Adamson, F., Astrand, B., & Darling-Hammond, L. (Eds.). (2016). *Global educational reform: How privatization and public investment influence education eutcomes.* Routledge.

Addey, C. (2017). Golden relics & historical standards: How the OECD is expanding global education governance through PISA for development. *Critical Studies in Education, 58*(3), 311–325. http://doi.org/10.1080/17508487.2017.1352006

Adorno, T., Leppert, R., & Gillespie, S. (2002). *Essays on music: Theodor W. Adorno – Selected, with introduction, commentary, and notes by Richard Leppert* (S. H. Gillespie, Trans.). University of California Press.

Aghion, P., Boustan, L., Hoxby, C., & Vandenbussche, J. (2009). The causal impact of education on economic growth: Evidence from US. *Brookings Papers on Economic Activity, 1*, 1–73.

Aleman, V., & Rosas, T. (2018, August 8). 46% de los nuevos diputados; LXIV legislature. *Excelsior.* https://www.excelsior.com.mx/nacional/sin-titulo-46-de-los-nuevos-diputados-lxiv-legislatura/1259410

Anderson, J. A. (2005). *Accountability in education.* International Institute for Educational Planning.

Apple, M. W. (2000) *Official knowledge* (2nd ed.). Routledge.

Apple, M. W. (2016). *Ideologia y Currículo.* Artmed Editora.

Apple, M. W., Au, W., & Gandin, L. A. (Eds.). (2009). *The Routledge international handbook of critical education.* Routledge.

Auld, E., Rappleye, J., & Morris, P. (2019). PISA for development: How the OECD and World Bank shaped education governance post-2015. *Comparative Education, 55*(2), 197–219.

Aydın, A., Uysal, Ş., & Sarıer, Y. (2010). Analysing the results of PISA maths literacy in terms of social justice and equality in educational opportunities. *Procedia – Social and Behavioural Sciences, 2*(2), 3537–3544. http://doi.org/10.1016/j.sbspro.2010.03.548

Backhoff, E., & Contreras-Roldán, S. (2014). "Corrupción de la medida" e inflación de los resultados de ENLACE. *Revista Mexicana de Investigación Educativa, 19*(63), 1267–1283.

Baker, E. L., & O'Neill, H. F. (2016). The United States: The intersection of international achievement testing and educational policy. In L. Volante (Ed.), *The intersection of international achievement testing and education policy* (pp. 122–136). Routledge.

Barber, M., & Mourshed, M. (2007). *How the world's best-performing schools systems come out on top.* McKinsey & Company.

Bartlett, M., & Benavides, L. G. (2016). *El Fraude de la Reforma Educativa. Reflexión Crítica.* Obra Independiente.

Baumeister, R. F., Bratslavsky, E., Finkenauer, C., & Vohs, K. D. (2001). Bad is stronger than good. *Review of General Psychology, 5*(4), 323–370.

Bazán, A., Backhoff, E., & Turullols, R. (2016). Participación escolar, apoyo familiar y desempeño en Matemáticas: El caso de México en PISA (2012). *RELIEVE-Revista Electrónica de Investigación y Evaluación Educativa, 22*(1), 1–17.

Beese, J., & Liang, X. (2010). Do resources matter? PISA science achievement comparisons between students in the United States, Canada and Finland. *Improving Schools, 13*(3), 266–279. http://doi.org/10.1177/1365480210390554

Bennett, R. E. (1998). *Reinventing assessment: Speculations on the future of large-scale education testing. A policy information perspective.* ETS.

Berliner, D. (2011). Rational responses to high stakes testing: The case of curriculum narrowing and the harm that follows. *Cambridge Journal of Education, 41*(3), 287–302.

Bieber, T. (2016). *Soft governance, international organizations and education policy: Comparing PISA and the Bologna and Copenhagen processes.* Palgrave Macmillan.

Breakspear, S. (2012). *The policy impact of PISA: An exploration of the normative effects of international benchmarking in school system performance.* OECD Education Working Papers, No. 71. OECD Publishing (NJ1).

Breakspear, S. (2014). *How does PISA shape education policy making? Why how we measure learning determines what counts in education.* Centre for Strategic Education Seminar Series Paper (Vol. 40). Centre for Strategic Education.

Bronner, S. (2011). *Critical theory: A very short introduction.* Oxford University Press.

Buck-Morss, S. (1977). *The origin of negative dialectics: Theodor W. Adorno, Walter Benjamin and the Frankfurt Institute.* Free Press.

Budds, J. (2013). Water, power, and the production of neoliberalism in Chile, 1973–2005: Environment and planning. *Society and Space, 31*(2), 301–318.

Bürgi, R., & Tröhler, D. (2018). Producing the 'right kind of people': The OECD education indicators in the 1960s. In S. Lindblad, D. Pettersson, & T. S. Popkewitz (Eds.), *Education by the numbers and the making of society* (pp. 85–101). Routledge.

Camacho, J. L. (2013). *El Congreso Mexicano* (5th ed.). Cámara de Diputados, Mesa Directiva.

Carnoy, M. (2016). Four keys to Cuba's provision of high quality public education. In F. Adamson, B. Astrand, & L. Darling-Hammond (Eds.), *Global education reform: How privatization and public investment influence education outcomes* (pp. 50–72). Routledge.

Carr, W. (1987). What is an educational practice? *Journal of Philosophy of Education, 21*(2), 163–175.

Castro Cornejo, R. (2022). The AMLO voter: Affective polarization and the rise of the left in Mexico. *Journal of Politics in Latin America.* https://doi.org/10.1177/1866802X221147067

Centro Regional para el Fomento del Libro en America Latina y el Carbe [CERLALC-UNESCO]. (2012). *Comportamiento Lector y Hábitos de Lectura.* CERLALC.

Chambers M. J., Johnson, A., Jones-Rincon, A., Tsatenawa, V., & Howard, K. (2019). Why do teachers leave? A comprehensive occupational health study evaluating intent-to-quit in public school teachers. *Journal of Applied Biobehavioral Research, 24*(1), 1–13.

Chang, H. J. (2012). *23 things they don't tell you about capitalism.* Bloomsbury Publishing.

Choi, A., & Jerrim, J. (2016). The use (and misuse) of PISA in guiding policy reform: The case of Spain. *Comparative Education, 52*(2), 230–245. http://doi.org/10.1080/03050068.2016.1142739

Clarke, V., & Braun, V. (2013). Teaching thematic analysis. *Psychologist, 26*(2), 120–123.

Cohen, L., Manion, L., & Morrison, K. (2011). *Research methods in education* (7th ed.). Routledge.

Comber, B. (2012). Mandated literacy assessment and the reorganization of teachers' work: Federal policy, local effects. *Critical Studies in Education, 53*(2), 119–136.

Cox, C., & Meckes, L. (2016). International large-scale assessment studies and educational policy-making in Chile: Contexts and dimensions of influence. *Research Papers in Education, 31*(5), 502–515.

Cox, R. W. (1981). Social forces, states and world orders: Beyond international relations theory. *Journal of International Studies, 10*(2), 126–155. https://doi.org/10.1177/03058298810100020501

Creswell, J. W. (2012). *Educational research: Planning, conducting, and evaluating quantitative and qualitative research* (4th ed.). Prentice Hall.

Cresswell, J. W., Schwantner, U., & Waters, C. (2015). *A review of international large-scale assessments in education: Assessing component skills and collecting contextual data.* The World Bank/OECD Publishing.

Crotty, M. (1998). *The foundations of social research.* Sage.

Cuevas, Y., & Moreno, T. (2016). Políticas de evaluación docente de la OCDE: Un acercamiento a la experiencia en la educación básica mexicana. *Archivos Analíticos De Políticas Educativas Education Policy Analysis Archives, 24*(1), 1–20.

Cusso, R., & D'Amico, S. (2005). From development comparatism to globalization comparativism: Towards more normative international education statistics. *Comparative Education, 41*(2), 199–216.

Dale, R. (1997). The state and the governance of education. In A. H. Halsey, H. Lauder, P. Brown, & A. S. Wells (Eds.), *Education, culture, economy and society* (pp. 273–282). Oxford University Press.

Dale, R. (2003, March). *The Lisbon Declaration: The reconceptualisation of governance and the reconfiguration of European educational space.* RAPPE Seminar on Governance, Regulation, and Equity in European Education Systems, Institute of Education, London.

Darling-Hammond, L., & Lieberman, A. (Eds.). (2012). *Teacher education around the world: Changing policies and practices.* Routledge.

Darling-Hammond, L., & Rothman, R. (2011). *Teacher and leader effectiveness in high-performing education systems.* Alliance for Excellent Education and Stanford Center for opportunity Policy in Education.

Debeer, D., Buchholz, J., Hartig, J., & Janssen, R. (2014). Student, school, and country differences in sustained test-taking effort in the 2009 PISA reading assessment. *Journal of Educational and Behavioral Statistics, 39*(6), 502–523.

De Landsheere, G. (1997). *IEA and UNESCO: A history of working co-operation.* Paper on the accompanying CD to the UNESCO, Publication 50. http://www.unesco.org/education/pdf/LANDSHEE.PDF

Deng, Z., & Gopinathan, S. (2016). PISA and high-performing education systems: Explaining Singapore's education success. *Comparative Education, 52*(4), 449–472. http://doi.org/10.1080/03050068.2016.1219535

Dente, B. (2014). *Understanding policy decisions.* Springer.

Diario Oficial de la Federación [DOF]. (2016). *Decreto por el que se reforman, adicionan y derogan diversas disposiciones del Reglamento Interior de la Secretaría de Educación Pública.* Diario Oficial de la Federación.

Diario Oficial de la Federación [DOF]. (2017). *Estatuto Orgánico del Instituto Nacional para la Evaluación de la Educación.* Diario Oficial de la Federación.

Eisner, E. W. (1985). *The art of educational evaluation: A personal view.* Falmer Press.

Facultad Latinoamericana de Ciencias Sociales [FLACSO]. (2009). *Factores asociados al logro educativo. Un enfoque centrado en el estudiante.* FLACSO.

Fischman, G. E., Marcetti-Topper, A., Silova, I., Goebel, J., & Holloway, J. L. (2019). Examining the influence of international large-scale assessments on national education policies. *Journal of Education Policy, 34*(4), 470–499. http://doi.org/10.1080/02680939.2018.1460493

Fourcade, M. (2016). Ordinalization: Lewis A. Coser Memorial award for theoretical agenda setting 2014. *Sociological Theory, 34*(3), 175–195.

Franke, T. M., Ho, T., & Christie, C. A. (2011). The chi-square test: Often used and more often misinterpreted. *American Journal of Evaluation, 33*(3), 448–458.

Fraser, N. (2008). *Scales of justice: Reimagining political space in a globalizing world.* Polity Press.

Friedman, M. (1990, June). *A welfare state syllogism* [Speech]. Commonwealth Club, San Francisco, USA. https://www.commonwealthclub.org/blog/2010-11-29/milton-friedman-commonwealth-club-reader-part-ii

Fullan, M. (2011). *Choosing the wrong drivers for whole system reform.* Centre for Strategic Education. https://michaelfullan.ca/wp-content/uploads/2016/06/13396088160.pdf

Gamboa, L. F., & Waltenberg, F. D. (2012). Inequality of opportunity for educational achievement in Latin America: Evidence from PISA 2006–2009. *Economics of Education Review, 31*(5), 694–708.

Giroux, H. (1983). *Theory and resistance in education: A pedagogy for the opposition.* Bergin & Garvey.

Goldstein, H. (2004). International comparisons of student attainment: Some issues arising from the PISA study. *Assessment in Education: Principles, Policy & Practice, 11*(3), 319–330. http://doi.org/10.1080/0969594042000304618

Goldstein, H. (2017). Measurement and evaluation issues with PISA. In L. Volante (Ed.), *The PISA effect on global educational governance* (pp. 49–58). Routledge.

Goldstein, H., & Thomas, S. (2008). Reflections on the international comparative surveys debate. *Assessment in Education: Principles, Policy & Practice, 15*(3), 215–222. http://doi.org/10.1080/09695940802417368

Gorur, R. (2016). Seeing like PISA: A cautionary tale about the performativity of international assessments. *European Educational Research Journal, 15*(5), 598–616.

Green, N. (2015). *The politics of international large-scale assessment: The Program for International Student Assessment (PISA) and American education discourse, 2000–2012.* https://academiccommons.columbia.edu/doi/10.7916/D8DB80WW

Green, N. (2019). PISA rhetoric and the "crisis" of American education. In F. Waldow & G. Steiner-Khamsi (Eds.), *Understandings PISA's attractiveness: Critical analysis in comparative policy studies* (pp. 109–134). Bloomsbury Academic.

Grek, S. (2009). Governing by numbers: The PISA "effect" in Europe. *Journal of Education Policy, 24*(1), 23–37.

Grek, S. (2012). What PISA knows and can do: Studying the role of national actors in the making of PISA. *European Educational Research Journal, 11*(2), 243–254.

Grek, S., Lawn, M., Lingard, B., Ozga, J., Rinne, R., Segerholm, C., & Simola, H. (2009). National policy brokering and the construction of the European education space in England, Sweden, Finland and Scotland. *Comparative Education, 45*(1), 5–21.

Grek, S., & Ydesen, C. (2021). Where science met policy: Governing by indicators and the OECD's INES programme. *Globalisation, Societies and Education, 19*(2), 122–137. https://doi.org/10.1080/14767724.2021.1892477

Gronmo, L., & Olsen, R. (2008). *TIMSS versus PISA: The case of pure and applied mathematics.* http://www.timss.no/publications/IRC2006_Gronmo&Olsen.pdf

Guba, E. G. (1990). *The paradigm dialog.* Sage.

Harvey, D. (2005). *A brief history of neoliberalism.* University Press.

Horkheimer, M. (1972). *Critical theory, selected essays.* Continuum.

Husén, T., & Postlethwaite, T. (1996). A brief history of the International Association for the Evaluation of educational achievement (IEA). *Assessment in Education: Principles, Policy & Practice, 3*(2), 129–141.

IMCO. (2021, May 1). *México dejará de ser parte de la edición 2021 de PISA*. https://imco.org.mx/mexico-dejara-de-ser-parte-de-la-edicion-2021-de-pisa/

Instituto Nacional para la Evaluación de la Educación [INEE]. (2008a). *El Aprendizaje En Tercero De Preescolar En México*. INEE.

Instituto Nacional para la Evaluación de la Educación [INEE]. (2008b). *PISA en el Aula: Ciencias*. INEE.

Instituto Nacional para la Evaluación de la Educación [INEE]. (2012). *Los Textos Mixtos: ¿Cómo se leen? La competencia lectora desde PISA*. INEE.

Instituto Nacional para la Evaluación de la Educación [INEE]. (2014a). *El Aprendizaje En Preescolar En México. Informe De Resultados Excale 00 Aplicación 2011 Lenguaje Y Comunicación Y Pensamiento Matemático*. INEE.

Instituto Nacional para la Evaluación de la Educación [INEE]. (2014b). *Las Tareas de Matemáticas en PISA 2012*. INEE.

Instituto Nacional para la Evaluación de la Educación [INEE]. (2015a). *Plan Nacional para la Evaluación de los Aprendizajes (PLANEA)*. Documentos Rectores. INEE.

Instituto Nacional para la Evaluación de la Educación [INEE]. (2015b). *Los docentes en México. Informe 2015*. INEE.

Instituto Nacional para la Evaluación de la Educación [INEE]. (2016). *PLANEA: una nueva generación de pruebas*. INEE.

Instituto Nacional para la Evaluación de la Educación [INEE]. (2018). *La educación obligatoria en México. Informe 2018*. INEE.

International Labour Organization [ILO]. (1991). *Teachers in developing countries: A survey of employment conditions*. International Labour Office.

International Monetary Fund [IMF]. (1992). *Mexico: The strategy to achieve sustained economic growth*. IMF.

Jehangir, K., Glas, C. A., & Berg, S. V. (2015). Exploring the relation between socio-economic status and reading achievement in PISA 2009 through an intercepts-and-slopes-as-outcomes paradigm. *International Journal of Educational Research, 71*, 1–15. http://doi.org/10.1016/j.ijer.2015.02.002

Jennings, J. L., & Bearak, J. M. (2014). "Teaching to the test" in the NCLB era: How test predictability affects our understanding of student performance. *Educational Researcher, 43*(8), 381–389.

Jerrim, J. (2014). *Why do East Asian children perform so well in PISA? An investigation of Western-born children of East Asian descent*. https://johnjerrim.com/papers/

Jessop, B. (2005). Critical realism and the strategic-relational approach. *New Formations: A Journal of Culture, Theory and Politics, 56*, 40–53.

Jiménez-Moreno, J. A. (2016). El papel de la evaluación a gran escala como política de rendición de cuentas en el sistema educativo mexicano. *RIEE Revista Iberoamericana de Evaluación Educativa, 9*(1), 109–126.

Jiménez-Moreno, J. A. (2017). La calidad de la educación básica mexicana bajo la perspectiva nacional e internacional: el caso de lectura en tercero de primaria. *Perfiles Educativos, 39*(157), 162–180.

Johansson, S. (2016). International large-scale assessments: What uses, what consequences? *Educational Research, 58*(2), 139–148. http://doi.org/10.1080/00131881.2016.1165559

Kauchak, D. P., & Eggen, P. D. (2012). *Learning and teaching: Research based methods.* Pearson.

Keeley, B. (2007). *Human capital: How what you know shapes your life.* OECD Publishing.

Keohane, R. (2003). Global governance and democratic accountability. In D. Held & M. Koenig-Archibugi (Eds.), *Taming globalization: Frontiers of governance* (pp. 130–156). Polity Press.

Kincheloe, J. L., & McLaren, P. (2002). Rethinking critical theory and qualitative research. In P. Carspecken, P. Gilmore, & D. Foley (Eds.), *Ethnography and schools: Qualitative approaches to the study of education* (pp. 87–138). Rowman & Littlefield Publishers, Inc.

Knodel, P., Martens, K., & Niemann, D., (2013). PISA as an ideational roadmap for policy change: Exploring Germany and England in a comparative perspective. *Globalisation, Societies and Education, 11*(3), 421–441. http://doi.org/10.1080/14767724.2012.761811

Kohn, A. (2000). *The case against standardized testing: Raising the scores, ruining the schools.* Heinemann.

Komatsu, H., & Rappleye, J. (2021). Rearticulating PISA. *Globalisation, Societies and Education, 19*(2). https://doi.org/10.1080/14767724.2021.1878014

Kuramoto, N., & Koizumi, R. (2018). Current issues in large-scale educational assessment in Japan: Focus on national assessment of academic ability and university entrance examinations. *Assessment in Education: Principles, Policy & Practice, 25*(4), 415–433. http://doi.org/10.1080/0969594X.2016.1225667

Lascoumes, L., & Le Galès, P. (2007). Understanding public policy through its instruments – From the nature of instruments to the sociology of public policy instrumentation. *Governance, 20*(1), 1–21.

Leithwood, K., Harris, A., & Hopkins, D. (2019). Seven strong claims about successful school leadership revisited. *School Leadership & Management, 40*(1), 5–22. https://doi.org/10.1080/13632434.2019.1596077

Lewis, S. (2017). Governing schooling through 'what works': The OECD's PISA for schools. *Journal of Education Policy, 32*(3), 281–302. http://doi.org/10.1080/02680939.2016.1252855

Lewis, S., & Holloway, J. (2019). Datafying the teaching 'profession': Remaking the professional teacher in the image of data. *Cambridge Journal of Education, 49*(1), 35–51. http://doi.org/10.1080/0305764X.2018.1441373

Lewis, S., & Lingard, B. (2015). The multiple effects of international large-scale assessment on education policy and research. *Discourse: Studies in the Cultural Politics of Education, 36*(5), 621–637. http://doi.org/10.1080/01596306.2015.1039765

Lietz, P., & Tobin, M. (2016). The impact of large-scale assessments in education on education policy: Evidence from around the world. *Research Papers in Education, 31*(5), 499–501. http://doi.org/10.1080/02671522.2016.1225918

Lingard, B. (2013). Policy as numbers: Ac/counting for educational research. In B. Lingard (Ed.), *Politics, policies and pedagogies in education* (pp. 27–50). Routledge.

Lingard, B., & Lewis, S. (2017). Placing PISA and PISA for schools in two federalisms, Australia and the USA. *Critical Studies in Education, 58*(3), 266–279. http://doi.org/10.1080/17508487.2017.1316295

Lingard, B., Martino, W., & Rezai-Rashti, G. (2013). Testing regimes, accountabilities and education policy: Commensurate global and national developments. *Journal of Education Policy, 28*(5), 539–556. http://doi.org/10.1080/02680939.2013.820042

Lingard, B., & Rawolle, S. (2011). New scalar politics: Implications for education policy. *Comparative Education, 47*(4), 489–502. http://doi.org/10.1080/03050068.2011.555941

Liu, O. L., & Wilson, M. (2009). Gender differences in large-scale math assessments: PISA trend 2000 and 2003. *Applied Measurement in Education, 22*(2), 164–184.

López, F. (2011). The Cuban revolution: Historical roots, current situation, scenarios, and alternatives. *Latin American Perspectives, 38*(2), 3–30.

Low, E. L., Goodwin, A. L., & Snyder, J. (2017). *Focused on learning: Student and teacher time in a Singapore school.* Stanford Centre for Opportunity Policy in Education.

Loyo, E., & Staples, A. (2010). Fin del siglo y de un regimen. In D. T. De Estrada (Ed.), *La Historia Minima de la Educación en México* (pp. 127–154). El Colegio de México.

Ma, X., Jong, C., & Yuan, J. (2013). Exploring reasons for the East Asian success in PISA. In H. D Meyer & A. Benavot (Eds.), *PISA, power, and policy: The emergence of global educational governance* (pp. 225–246). Symposium Books.

Martens, K. (2007). How to become an influential actor – the 'comparative turn' in OECD education policy. In K. Martens, A. Rusconi, & K. Leuze (Eds.), *New arenas in education governance* (pp. 40–56). Palgrave Macmillan.

Martens, K., Niemann, D., & Teltemann, J. (2016). Effects of international assessments in education – A multidisciplinary review. *European Educational Research Journal, 15*(5), 516–522.

Martinez-Rizo, F. (2006). PISA en América Latina: lecciones a partir de la experiencia de México de 2000 a 2006. *No Extraordinario Marzo, 2006,* 153–167.

Martinez-Rizo, F. (2009). Formative classroom assessment and large-scale assessment: Toward a more balanced system. *Revista Electrónica de Investigación Educativa, 11*(2), 1–10.

Martinez-Rizo, F. (Ed.). (2015a). *Las pruebas ENLACE y EXCALE. Un estudio de validación.* INEE.

Martinez-Rizo, F. (Ed.). (2015b). *Las pruebas EXCALE para educación básica. Una evalu-ación para el Instituto Nacional para la Evaluación de la Educación.* INEE.

Martinez-Rizo, F. (Ed.). (2015c). *Las pruebas ENLACE para educación básica. Una evalu-ación para el Instituto Nacional para la Evaluación de la Educación.* INEE.

Martinez-Rizo, F., & Guerrero, J. (2016). Impact of large-scale assessment on Mexico's education policies. *Research Papers in Education, 31*(5), 556–566, http://doi.org/10.1080/02671522.2016.1225352

Masters, G. N. (2017). Using PISA to monitor trends and evaluate reforms in Australia. In L. Volante (Ed.), *The PISA effects on global educational governance* (pp. 175–188). Routledge.

McLaren, P. (2016). *Life in schools: An introduction to critical pedagogy in the founda-tions of education.* Routledge.

McLaren, P., & Giarelli, J. (Eds.). (1995). *Critical theory and educational research.* SUNY Press.

Meadows, D. (1988, May 5). *Singapore leads the good life under a benevolent dictator.* http://donellameadows.org/archives/singapore-leads-the-good-life-under-a-benevolent-dictator/

Mendoza, J. (2018) Políticas y reformas educativas en México, 1959–2016. In P. Ducoing (Ed.), *Educación Básica y Reforma Educativa* (pp. 51–77). IISUE-UNAM.

Meyer, H., & Benavot, A. (Eds.). (2013). *PISA, power, and policy: The emergence of global educational governance.* Symposium Books.

Morgan, C., & Volante, L. (2016). A review of the Organisation for Economic Cooperation and Development's international education surveys: Governance, human capital discourses, and policy debates. *Policy Futures in Education, 14*(6), 775–792.

Mortimore, P. (Ed.). (1999). *Understanding pedagogy: And its impact on learning.* Sage.

Navarro, C., Cordero, G., & Torres, R. M. (2011). Trayecto laboral en el magisterio: Los caminos para llegar a ser director escolar. *Revista Intercontinental de Psicología y Educación, 13*(12), 147–175.

Nichols, S. L., & Berliner, D. C. (2007). *Collateral damage: How high-stakes testing cor-rupts America's schools.* Harvard Education Press.

Niemann, D., Hartong, S., & Martens, K. (2018). Observing local dynamics of ILSA pro-jections in federal systems: A comparison between Germany and the United States. *Globalisation, Societies and Education, 16*(5), 596–608. http://doi.org/10.1080/14767724.2018.1531237

Organization for Economic Co-operation and Development [OECD]. (1999). *Measuring student knowledge and skills: A new framework for assessment.* OECD Publishing.

Organization for Economic Co-operation and Development [OECD]. (2001a). *Knowledge and skills for life: First results from PISA 2000.* OECD Publishing.

Organization for Economic Co-operation and Development [OECD]. (2001b). *The well-being of nations: The role of human and social capital.* OECD Publishing.

Organization for Economic Co-operation and Development [OECD]. (2001c). *Starting strong: Early childhood education and care.* OECD Publishing.

Organization for Economic Co-operation and Development [OECD]. (2002). *Reading for change: Performance and engagement across countries.* OECD Publishing.

Organization for Economic Co-operation and Development [OECD]. (2003a). *Learner for life, student approaches to learning, results from PISA 2000.* OECD Publishing.

Organization for Economic Co-operation and Development [OECD]. (2003b). *Literacy skills for the world of tomorrow: Further results from PISA 2000.* OECD Publishing.

Organization for Economic Co-operation and Development [OECD]. (2004). *Learning for tomorrow's world: First results from PISA 2003.* OECD Publishing.

Organization for Economic Co-operation and Development [OECD]. (2006). *Assessing scientific, reading and mathematical literacy: A framework for PISA 2006.* OECD Publishing.

Organization for Economic Co-operation and Development [OECD]. (2007). *PISA 2006: Science competencies for tomorrow's world, Vol. 1.* OECD Publishing.

Organization for Economic Co-operation and Development [OECD]. (2008). *The Marshall plan: Lessons learned for the 21st century.* OECD Publishing.

Organization for Economic Co-operation and Development [OECD]. (2009). *PISA 2009 assessment framework: Key competencies in reading, mathematics and science.* OECD Publishing.

Organization for Economic Co-operation and Development [OECD]. (2010a). *PISA 2009 results: What students know and can do – Volume I.* OECD Publishing.

Organization for Economic Co-operation and Development [OECD]. (2010b). *Mejorar las escuelas. Estrategias para la acción en México.* Editions OCDE.

Organization for Economic Co-operation and Development [OECD]. (2011a). *Lessons from PISA for Mexico, strong performers and successful reformers in education.* OECD Publishing.

Organization for Economic Co-operation and Development [OECD]. (2011b). *Establecimiento de un marco para la evaluación e incentivos docentes: Consideraciones para México.* Ediciones OCDE.

Organization for Economic Co-operation and Development [OECD]. (2014). *What students know and can do: Student performance in mathematics, reading and science – Volume I.* OECD Publishing.

Organization for Economic Co-operation and Development [OECD]. (2016a). *PISA 2015 results (Volume I): Excellence and equity in education.* OECD Publishing. http://dx.doi.org/10.1787/9789264266490-en

Organization for Economic Co-operation and Development [OECD]. (2016b). *Ten questions for mathematics teachers (...) and how PISA can help answer them.* OECD Publishing. http://dx.doi.org/10.1787/9789264265387-en

Organization for Economic Co-operation and Development [OECD]. (2016c). Understanding student performance beyond traditional factors: Evidence from PISA 2012. *OECD Development Centre Working Papers, 331*, 1–50.

Organization for Economic Co-operation and Development [OECD]. (2016d). *Low-performing students: Why they fall behind and how to help them succeed.* OECD Publishing. http://dx.doi.org/10.1787/9789264250246-en

Organization for Economic Co-operation and Development [OECD]. (2017a). *Starting strong 2017: Key OECD indicators on early childhood education and care.* OECD Publishing. http://dx.doi.org/10.1787/9789264276116-en

Organization for Economic Co-operation and Development [OECD]. (2017b). *Starting strong v: Transitions from early childhood education and care to primary education.* OECD Publishing. http://dx.doi.org/10.1787/9789264276253-en

Organization for Economic Co-operation and Development [OECD]. (2018a). *PISA 2015 results in focus.* OECD Publishing.

Organization for Economic Co-operation and Development [OECD]. (2018b). *Strong foundation for quality and equity in Mexican schools.* OECD Publishing.

Organization for Economic Co-operation and Development [OECD]. (2019a). *PISA 2018 assessment and analytical framework.* OECD Publishing. https://doi.org/10.1787/b25efab8-en

Organization for Economic Co-operation and Development [OECD]. (2019b). *PISA 2018 results (Volume I): What students know and can do.* OECD Publishing. https://doi.org/10.1787/5f07c754-en

Ornelas, C. (2006). El dominio del SNTE. In S. Cherem (Ed.), *Centro de Cooperación Regional para la Educación de Adultos en América Latina y el Caribe* (pp. 227–246). CREFAL.

Ornelas, C. (2018). *La Contienda por la Educacion. Globalizacion, Neocoporativismo y Democracia.* FCE.

Papadopoulos, G. S. (1994). *Education 1960–1990: The OECD perspective.* OECD Publishing.

Pawson, R. (2002). Evidence-based policy: The promise of 'realist synbook'. *Evaluation, 8*(3), 340–358.

Pawson, R. (2008). Causality for beginners. In *NCRM research methods festival 2008.*

Pawson, R., & Tilley, N. (1997). *Realistic evaluation.* Sage.

Pearson (2011). *A study of the Stanford achievement test series, tenth edition (Stanford 10) alignment to the common core state standards.* PEARSON Assessments.

Penk, C., Pöhlmann, C., & Roppelt, A. (2014). The role of test-taking motivation for students' performance in low-stakes assessments: An investigation of school-track-specific differences. *Large-scale Assessments in Education, 2*(1), 5.

Pidgeon, D. (1969). Current research of the International Association for the Evaluation of Educational Achievement (IEA). *Comparative Education Review, 13*(2), 213–216.

Pinar, W. (2011). *Curriculum studies in Mexico: Intellectual histories, present circumstances.* Springer.

Pizmony-Levy, O. (2017). Big comparisons, little knowledge: Public engagement with PISA in the United States and Israel. In W. Wiseman & C. Stevens (Eds.), *The impact of the OECD on education worldwide* (pp. 125–156). Emerald Publishing Limited.

Pizmony-Levy, O., & Bjorklund, P. (2018). International assessments of student achievement and public confidence in education: Evidence from a cross-national study. *Oxford Review of Education, 44*(2), 239–257. http://doi.org/10.1080/03054985.2017.1389714

Plá, S. (2018). La despolitización del ciudadano. Crítica al Modelo Educativo 2016 desde la pedagogía por la justicia social. In P. Ducoing (Ed.), *Educación Básica y Reforma Educativa* (pp. 243–267). IISUE-UNAM.

Pons, X. (2016). Tracing the French policy PISA debate: A policy configuration approach. *European Educational Research Journal, 15*(5), 580–597.

Popham, W. J. (1999). Why standardized tests don't measure educational quality. *Educational leadership, 56*, 8–16.

Popham, W. J. (2001a). *The truth about testing: An educator's call to action.* ASCD.

Popham, W. J. (2001b). Teaching to the test. *Educational Leadership, 58*(6), 16–20.

Prais, S. J. (2004). Cautions on OECD's recent educational survey (PISA): Rejoinder to OECD's response. *Oxford Review of Education, 30*(4), 569–573. http://doi.org/10.1080/0305498042000303017

Prunty, J. (1984). *A critical reformulation of educational policy analysis.* Deakin University.

Ramirez, F., Schofer, E., & Meyer, J. (2018). International tests, national assessments, and educational development (1970–2012). *Comparative Education Review, 62*(3), 344–364.

Ramirez, R. (2016). *Reforma en Materia Educativa. Un análisis de su diseño y aplicación, 2012–2016.* Dirección General de Investigación Estratégica del Senado de la Republica de Mexico.

Ranson, S. (1986). Towards a political theory of public accountability in education. *Local Government Studies, 12*(4), 77–98. http://doi.org/10.1080/03003938608433288

Ranson, S. (2003). Public accountability in the age of neo-liberal governance. *Journal of Education Policy, 18*(5), 459–480.

Rautalin, M., & Alasuutari, P. (2009). The uses of the national PISA results by Finnish officials in central government. *Journal of Education Policy, 24*(5), 539–556. http://doi.org/10.1080/02680930903131267

Rautalin, M., Alasuutari, P., & Vento, E., (2018). Globalisation of education policies: Does PISA have an effect? *Journal of Education Policy, 34*(4), 500–522.

Regional Bureau for Education in Latin America and the Caribbean-United Nations Educational, Scientific and Cultural Organization [OREALC-UNESCO]. (1998). *First report of the first international comparative study on language and mathematics, and associated factors, among third and fourth grade student.* LLECE.

Regional Bureau for Education in Latin America and the Caribbean-United Nations Educational, Scientific and Cultural Organization [OREALC-UNESCO]. (2008a). *Student achievement in Latin America and the Caribbean results of the second regional comparative and explanatory study.* LLECE.

Regional Bureau for Education in Latin America and the Caribbean-United Nations Educational, Scientific and Cultural Organization [OREALC-UNESCO]. (2008b). *Los aprendizajes de los estudiantes de América Latina y el Caribe.* LLECE.

Regional Bureau for Education in Latin America and the Caribbean-United Nations Educational, Scientific and Cultural Organization [OREALC-UNESCO]. (2016a). *Results report of the Third Regional Comparative and Explanatory Study (TERCE).* LLECE.

Regional Bureau for Education in Latin America and the Caribbean-United Nations Educational, Scientific and Cultural Organization [OREALC-UNESCO]. (2016b). *Recomendaciones de Políticas Educativas En América Latina en base al TERCE.* LLECE.

Regional Bureau for Education in Latin America and the Caribbean-United Nations Educational, Scientific and Cultural Organization [OREALC-UNESCO]. (2016c). *Aportes Para la Enseñanza de la Lectura.* LLECE.

Regional Bureau for Education in Latin America and the Caribbean-United Nations Educational, Scientific and Cultural Organization [OREALC-UNESCO]. (2016d). *Informe de resultados TERCE: factores asociados.* LLECE.

Regional Bureau for Education in Latin America and the Caribbean-United Nations Educational, Scientific and Cultural Organization [OREALC-UNESCO]. (2021). *Los aprendizajes fundamentales en América Latina y el Caribe. Evaluación de logros de los estudiantes. Estudio Regional Comparativo y Explicativo (ERCE 2019).* LLECE.

Rhodes, R. A. W. (1996). The new governance: Governing without government. *Political Studies, 44*(4), 652–667.

Robertson, S. L. (2012a). Placing teachers in global governance agendas. *Comparative Education Review, 56*(4), 584–607.

Robertson, S. L. (2012b). *Researching global education policy: Angles in/on/out (...).* Centre for Globalization, Education and Societies.

Robertson, S. L. (2018, September 5). *Governing through quantification: On the contradictory dynamics of 'flat earth', 'ordinalisation' and 'coldspot' education policies* [Keynote address]. ECER, Bolzano, Italy.

Robertson, S. L. (2022). V-charged: Powering up the world-class university as a global actor. *Globalisation, Societies and Education, 20*(4), 423–434. http://doi.org/10.1080/14767724.2022.2065970

Robertson, S. L., & Dale, R. (2008). Researching education in a globalising era: Beyond methodological nationalism, methodological statism, methodological education-ism and spatial fetishism. In J. Resnik (Ed.), *The production of educational knowledge in the global era* (pp. 19–32). Sense Publishers.

Robertson, S. L., & Dale, R. (2009). The World Bank, the IMF and the possibilities of critical education. In M. Apple, W. Au, & L. Gandin (Eds.), *The Routledge international handbook of critical education* (pp. 23–35). Routledge.

Robertson, S. L., & Dale, R. (2013). The social justice implications of privatisation in education governance frameworks: A relational account. *Oxford Review of Education, 39*(4), 226–445.

Robertson, S. L., & Dale, R. (2015a). Toward a 'critical cultural political economy' account of the globalising of education. *Globalisation, Societies and Education, 13*(1), 149–170.

Robertson, S. L., & Dale, R. (2015b). *Analyzing education policies: Theories, concepts and methodologies … A beginner's guide.* University of Bristol.

Robertson, S. L., Novelli, M., Dale, R., Tikly, L., Dachi, H. A., & Alphonse, N. (2007). *Globalisation, education and development: Ideas, actors and dynamics.* DFID.

Robinson, W. (2010). Documentary research. In D. Hartas (Ed.), *Educational research and inquiry* (pp. 186–198). Bloomsbury Publishing.

Rose, K. (1994). Unstructured and semi-structured interviewing. *Nurse Researcher, 1*(3), 23–30.

Ruiz, M. A., Jornet, J. M., & Backhoff, E. (2006). *Acerca de la Validez de los Examenes de Calidad y el Logro Educativos (EXCALE).* Coleccion Cuaderno de Investigacion. INEE.

Rutkowski, D. (2007). Converging us softly: How intergovernmental organizations promote neoliberal educational policy. *Critical Studies in Education, 48*(2), 229–247. http://doi.org/10.1080/17508480701494259

Rutkowski, D., & Prusinski, E. L. (2011). The limits and possibilities of international large-scale assessments. *Center for Evaluation & Education Policy, 9*(2), 1–4.

Rutkowski, L., & Rutkowski, D. (2016). A call for a more measured approach to reporting and interpreting PISA results. *Educational Researcher, 45*(4), 252–257.

Sahlberg, P. (2007). Education policies for raising student learning: The Finnish approach. *Journal of Education Policy, 22*(2), 147–171.

Sahlberg, P. (2012). The most wanted: Teachers and teacher education in Finland. In L. Darling-Hammond & A. Lieberman (Eds.), *Teacher education around the world* (pp. 15–35). Routledge.

Sahlberg, P. (2012b). A model lesson. Finland shows us how equal opportunity looks like. *American Educator, 36*(2), 20–27.

Sahlberg, P. (2014). *Finnish lessons 2.0: What can the world learn from educational change in Finland?* Teachers College Press.

Salas-Porras, A. (2014). Las élites neoliberales en México: ¿cómo se construye un campo de poder que transforma las prácticas sociales de las élites políticas? *Revista Mexicana de Ciencias Políticas y Sociales, 59*(222), 279–312.

Santiago, P., McGregor, I., Nusche, D., Ravela, P., & Toledo, D. (2012). *OECD reviews of evaluation and assessment in education.* OECD Publishing.

Schmidt, W., & Burroughs, N. (2016). Influencing public school policy in the United States: The role of large-scale assessments. *Research Papers in Education, 31*(5), 567–577. http://doi.org/10.1080/02671522.2016.1225355

Schultz, T. W. (1961). Investment in human capital. *The American Economic Review,* 1–17.

Scott, J. C. (1998). *Seeing like a state: How certain schemes to improve the human condition have failed.* Yale University Press.

Scott, T. (2011). A nation at risk to win the future: The state of public education in the US. *Journal for Critical Education Policy Studies, 9*(1), 267–316.

Secretaria de Educacion Publica [SEP]. (1979). *Programa de Educación Preescolar 1979.* SEP.

Secretaria de Educacion Publica [SEP]. (1981). *Programa de Educación Preescolar 1981.* SEP.

Secretaria de Educacion Publica [SEP]. (1992). *Programa de Educación Preescolar 1992.* SEP.

Secretaria de Educacion Publica [SEP]. (2004). *Programa de Educación Preescolar 2004.* SEP.

Secretaria de Educacion Publica [SEP]. (2011). *Programa de Educación Preescolar 2011.* SEP.

Secretaria de Educacion Publica [SEP]. (2014). *Perfiles, Parametros e Indicadores.* SEP.

Secretaria de Educacion Publica [SEP]. (2017) *Aprendizajes Clave para una Educación Integral.* SEP.

Sellar, S., & Lingard, B. (2013a). The OECD and global governance in education. *Journal of Education Policy, 28*(5), 710–725. http://doi.org/10.1080/02680939.2013.779791

Sellar, S., & Lingard, B. (2013b). Looking east: Shanghai, PISA 2009 and the reconstitution of reference societies in the global education policy field. *Comparative Education, 49*(4), 464–485. http://doi.org/10.1080/03050068.2013.770943

Sellar, S., & Lingard, B. (2014). The OECD and the expansion of PISA: New global modes of governance in education. *British Educational Research Journal, 40*(6), 917–936.

Sellar, S., & Lingard, B. (2018). International large-scale assessments, affective worlds and policy impacts in education. *International Journal of Qualitative Studies in Education, 31*(5), 367–381.

Sellar, S., Lingard, B., Rutkowski, D., & Takayama, K. (2018). Student preparation for large-scale assessments: A comparative analysis. In B. Maddox (Ed.), *International large-scale assessments in education: Insider research perspectives* (pp. 137–155). Bloomsbury Academic.

Senado de la Republica. (2012). *Dictamen De La Comisiones Unidas De Puntos Constitucionales, Educación Y Estudios Legislativos Segunda Con Respecto De La Minuta Con Proyecto De Decreto Por El Que Se Reforman Los Artículos 30 Fracciones Iii, Vii Y Viii, Y 73, Fracción Xxv; Y Se Adiciona La Fracción Ix Al Artículo 30, De La Constitución Política De Los Estados Unidos Mexicanos.* http://www.senado.gob.mx/comisiones/puntos_constitucionales/dictamenes.php

Sharpe, D. (2015). Your chi-square test is statistically significant: Now what? *Practical Assessment, Research & Evaluation, 20*(8), 1–10.

Sim, J. B. Y. (2011). 'Simple ideological "dupes" of national governments'? Teacher agency and citizenship education in Singapore. In K. J. Kennedy, W. O. Lee, & D. L. Grossman (Eds.), *Citizenship pedagogies in Asia and the Pacific* (pp. 221–242). Springer.

Simon, M., Ercikan, K., & Rousseau, M. (2013). *Improving large-scale assessments in education.* Routledge.

Sistema Educativo Estatal [SEE]. (2017). Principales Cifras Estadísticas. http://www.educacionbc.edu.mx/publicaciones/estadisticas/

Slobodian, Q. (2018). *Globalists: The end of empire and the birth of neoliberalism.* Harvard University Press.

Sorensen, T. (2017). *The political construction of the OECD program teaching and learning international survey.* University of Bristol.

Sorensen, T., & Robertson, S. L. (2020). Ordinalization and OECD governance on teachers. *Comparative Education Review.* https://doi.org/10.17863/CAM.42349

Sorensen, T., Ydesen, C., & Robertson, S. L. (2021). Re-reading the OECD and education: The emergence of a global governing complex – an introduction. *Globalisation, Societies and Education, 19*(2), 99–107. https://doi.org/10.1080/14767724.2021.1897946

Spaull, N. (2018). Who makes it into PISA? Understanding the impact of PISA sample eligibility using Turkey as a case study (PISA 2003–PISA 2012). *Assessment in Education: Principles, Policy & Practice, 26*(4), 397–421. http://doi.org/10.1080/0969594X.2018.1504742

Spring, J. (2015). *Economization of education: Human capital, global corporations, skills-based schooling.* Routledge.

Starr, P. (1992). Social categories and claims in the liberal state. *Social Research, 59*(2), 263–295.

Steiner-Khamsi, G., & Waldow, F. (2018). PISA for scandalisation, PISA for projection: The use of international large-scale assessments in education policy making – an introduction. *Globalisation, Societies and Education, 16*(5), 557–565. http://doi.org/10.1080/14767724.2018.1531234

Stuckey, H. L. (2013). Three types of interviews: Qualitative research methods in social health. *Journal of Social Health and Diabetes, 1*(2), 56–59.

Taber, K. S. (2017). *Principles of research design* [Presentation outline]. Lecture at Cambridge University.

Takayama, K. (2008). The politics of international league tables: PISA in Japan's achievement crisis debate. *Comparative Education, 44*(4), 387–407.

Takayama, K., & Lingard, B. (2019). Datafication of schooling in Japan: An epistemic critique through the 'problem of Japanese education'. *Journal of Education Policy, 34*(4), 449–469. http://doi.org/10.1080/02680939.2018.1518542

Tan, C. (2018). *Comparing high-performing education systems: Understanding Singapore, Shanghai, and Hong Kong.* Routledge.

Thomas, S., Gana, Y., & Muñoz-Chereau, B. (2016). The intersection of international achievement testing and educational policy development in England. In L. Volante (Ed.), *The intersection of international achievement testing and educational policy: Global perspectives on large-scale reform* (pp. 37–57). Routledge.

Thompson, S. J., Johnstone, C. J., & Thurlow, M. L. (2002). *Universal design applied to large scale assessments* (Synbook Report 44). University of Minnesota, National Centre on Educational Outcomes.

Tienken, C. (2014). Poverty and test performance. *Kappa Delta Pi Record, 50*(3), 106–108.

Tikly, L., & Barrett, A. M. (2011). Social justice, capabilities and the quality of education in low income countries. *International Journal of Educational Development, 31*(1), 3–14.

Tobin, M., Nugroho, D., & Lietz, P. (2016). Large-scale assessments of students' learning and education policy: Synbooking evidence across world regions. *Research Papers in Education, 31*(5), 578–594. http://doi.org/10.1080/02671522.2016.1225353

Tripp, D. (1992). Critical theory and educational research. *Issues in Educational Research, 2*(1), 13–23.

UN General Assembly. (1948). *Universal Declaration of Human Rights* (217[III]A). https://www.un.org/en/universal-declaration-human-rights/

Volante, L. (Ed.). (2016). *The intersection of international achievement testing and educational policy.* Routledge.

Volante, L. (Ed.). (2017). *The PISA effect on global educational governance.* Routledge.

Wagemaker, H. (2014). International large-scale assessments: From research to policy. In L. Rutkowski, M. von Davier, & D. Rutkowski (Eds.), *Handbook of international large-scale assessment: Background, technical issues, and methods of data analysis* (pp. 11–36). Taylor & Francis.

Waldow, F., Takayama, K., & Sung, Y. K. (2014). Rethinking the pattern of external policy referencing: media discourses over the 'Asian Tigers'' PISA success in Australia, Germany and South Korea. *Comparative Education, 50*(3), 302–321. http://doi.org/10.1080/03050068.2013.860704

Weis, C. C., & Garcia, E. (2014). Student engagement and academic performance in Mexico: evidence and puzzles from PISA. *Comparative Education Review, 59*(2), 305–331.

Wendt, H., Bos, W., & Goy, M. (2011). On applications of Rasch models in international comparative large-scale assessments: A historical review. *Educational Research and Evaluation, 17*(6), 419–446. http://doi.org/10.1080/13803611.2011.634582

Winner, E., Goldstein, T. R., & Vincent-Lancrin, S. (2013). *Art for art's sake? The impact of arts education.* OECD publishing.

Woodward, R. (2009). *The Organisation for Economic Co-operation and Development (OECD).* Routledge.

Wu, M. (2009). A comparison of PISA and TIMSS 2003 achievement results in mathematics. *Prospects, 39*(1), 33–46.

Index

Printed in the United States
by Baker & Taylor Publisher Services